Sport and the Female Disabled Body

This path-breaking book analyses the experiences of young sporting women with physical impairments. Taking phenomenology as a point of departure, Elisabet Apelmo explores how the young women handle living with a body which, on the one hand, is viewed as deviant – the disabled body – and, on the other, is viewed as accomplished – the sporting body. A polarization is apparent between the weak, which is manifested through the expression of belonging as 'we', and the strong individual. The subject position as strong, positive and capable – as a reaction towards the weak, the negative – is one of the few positions that are available to them. Furthermore, the book demonstrates the strategies of resistance the young women develop against the marginalization, stereotyping and othering they experience in their everyday lives.

Finally, the author discusses the paradox of gender. Disabled bodies are often seen as non-gendered; however, these young women's experiences are structured by both the gender regimes within sports and the larger gender order of the society.

Elisabet Apelmo is Lecturer in the Department of Social Work at Malmö University, Sweden. She is a visual artist with a PhD in Sociology.

Interdisciplinary Disability Studies

Series editor: Mark Sherry
The University of Toledo, USA

Disability studies has made great strides in exploring power and the body. This series extends the interdisciplinary dialogue between disability studies and other fields by asking how disability studies can influence a particular field. It will show how a deep engagement with disability studies changes our understanding of the following fields: sociology, literary studies, gender studies, bioethics, social work, law, education, or history. This ground-breaking series identifies both the practical and theoretical implications of such an interdisciplinary dialogue and challenges people in disability studies as well as other disciplinary fields to critically reflect on their professional praxis in terms of theory, practice, and methods.

For a full list of titles in this series, please visit www.routledge.com/series/ ASHSER1401

Sport and the Female Disabled Body

Elisabet Apelmo

Routledge
Taylor & Francis Group
LONDON AND NEW YORK

First published 2017
by Routledge
2 Park Square, Milton Park, Abingdon, Oxon OX14 4RN

and by Routledge
711 Third Avenue, New York, NY 10017

Routledge is an imprint of the Taylor & Francis Group, an informa business

British Library Cataloguing in Publication Data
A catalogue record for this book is available from the British Library

Library of Congress Cataloging in Publication Data
Names: Apelmo, Elisabet, author.
Title: Sport and the female disabled body / Elisabet Apelmo.
Description: London ; New York : Routledge, [2016] | Includes
bibliographical references and index.
Identifiers: LCCN 2016017950 | ISBN 9781472455147 (hbk) |
ISBN 9781315610412 (ebk)
Subjects: LCSH: Women athletes with disabilities--Psychology. | Body image
in women.
Classification: LCC GV709.3 .A74 2016 | DDC 796.087--dc23
LC record available at https://lccn.loc.gov/2016017950

ISBN: 978-1-4724-5514-7 (hbk)
ISBN: 978-1-315-61041-2 (ebk)

Typeset in Times New Roman
by Taylor & Francis Books

Contents

Preface

This book is a revised version of my doctoral thesis, and the result of several years of work, others' and mine. First and foremost I want to thank the ten young women who so generously shared their experiences with me.

Thereafter I would like to thank my two supervisors. Ann-Mari Sellerberg enthusiastically helped with great and small, not least with a careful analysis of the empirical data. Diana Mulinari: every time I have left our meetings I was exhilarated because completely new perspectives – which I did not know existed – were opened.

Many readers have commented on my text during those years. Two seminar groups at Lund University have been of great importance to me: Critical Studies in Sociology at the Department of Sociology, and the Crip Seminar at the Department of Gender Studies. The opponent Tomas Peterson and the evaluation committee Maud Eduards, Johanna Esseveld, Håkan Larsson, Kerstin Sandell and Mårten Söder gave me insightful comments on the dissertation.

Many thanks to the Swedish National Centre for Research in Sports, Sparbanksstiftelsen Skåne, Stiftelsen Sunnerdahls handikappfond and Norrbacka-Eugeniastiftelsen who provided financial support for the pilot studies and for my employment as a doctoral candidate. STINT made it possible for me to spend autumn 2009 at the Department of Women's Studies at Syracuse University. I want to thank Professor Chandra Talpade Mohanty who held the class 'The Practice of Transnational Feminism', as well as the graduate students in The Beyond Compliance Coordinating Committee (BCCC) at Disability Studies, who generously invited me to their discussions.

Finally, I thank my partner, Per, and our two daughters, Sally and Marie, for all their love, support and encouragement.

Elisabet Apelmo, Malmö, October 2015

Acknowledgement

The section 'Disability sports in Sweden' in Chapter 1 was first published as '(Dis)abled bodies, gender, and citizenship in the Swedish sports movement' in *Disability & Society* (2012), vol 27(4). Parts of Chapters 3 and 4 originally appeared as 'Crip heroes and social change' in *Lambda Nordica*, vol 17(1–2). A version of Chapter 5 was published as 'Falling in love with a wheelchair: Enabling/disabling technologies' in *Sport in Society* (2012), vol 15(3). All three pieces have been thoroughly rewritten and developed.

1 Introduction

After having worked as a visual artist for many years, I began to study sociology in the autumn of 2003. As an artist I had been interested in ideas about body, gender, inequality and difference. At this time my family moved to a housing area close to Malmö's main sports stadium, and suddenly my daughters and I could watch athletics and figure-skating competitions on weekends. Marit, my performance colleague in the art world, had a daughter who played football and talked about life as a football mum: biting wind at the side of the pitch early Sunday mornings and lumpy inflatable mattresses in the gym; but also about girls who elbowed their way along in the school corridor when the boys were fooling around. My newly awakened interest led to a master's thesis about the construction of femininity among football girls, going for the top level in a masculine context. Some time after taking that degree I was asked if I wanted to carry out a pilot study about disabled children and youth and their experience of disability sports. I accepted and began the work that led to a doctoral thesis and eventually this book.

How, then, has my understanding of the body changed during this time, through the sociological gaze? A more societal perspective on the body is, of course, inevitable: the increasingly important questions of what influence globalization, governmental policy and social movements have on different bodies. From chiefly having focused as an artist on questions about gender, the interest has widened to include more power and status structures. When the study on the football girls was finished I regarded them as subordinate to the players in the boys' and men's teams. Certainly they challenged the feminine norm by their way of acting physically and mentally; but at the same time change was hindered by other people's conservative approach to girls who play football, by the sports movement's sticking to the view of women and men as two separate, homogeneous groups and by the sluggishness of the media. However, it was not until after a year or more of work with the thesis that I realized how close to the norm those young players' bodies were.

A shift has taken place in my artistic activity from a psychological focus to a more society-oriented one. But the difference between the artistic and the sociological practice has also become more evident. In social science the ethical framework, which I sometimes have missed in the field of art, is to be found, while art has a playfulness that is not easily perceived in the field of science. An interest in methodology and theory unite the two.[1]

The study's aim and research questions

The aim of this research project is to explore young Swedish women's lived experience of the body, which, on the one hand, is viewed as deviant – the disabled body – and, on the other, is viewed as accomplished – the sporting body. The research questions posed are: how do the young women handle the two subject positions that emerge as a result of the perception of them as deviant and as accomplished? What forms of femininity are available to them? What are the strategies of resistance they develop against the marginalization, stereotyping and othering (i.e. being regarded as entirely different from an imagined 'us') they experience in their everyday life?

The four research fields in which this research project is situated are the sociology of the body, feminist research, the sociology of sports, and disability studies. With my study I want to contribute to a growing consciousness of the disabled body but also the idealized able body in social science research. By exploring the margin, knowledge about the centre can be obtained; by studying the Other, deviant body, the normal body can be made visible. It is a matter of an approach that is slightly different from the current, a rereading from a new perspective.

Methodologically I have tried to develop a way to catch experiences of disability and sports that takes my informants' standpoint as its point of departure. My background as an artist, with photo, video and performance as the main means of expression, has influenced the choice of method. In the study qualitative interviews are combined with participant observations and video diaries made by the participants in the study.

Disposition

Chapter 1 presents the Swedish context in which the young women who participate in the study are situated: the part of the disability movement that organizes people with physical impairments, the disability sports movement, disability policy and media representations of disabled people. Swedish disability research, with its connections to social policy, is discussed on a more general level and compared to disability studies as well as critical disability studies. Previous research from the four research fields is presented in dialogue with the empirical material in the analysis chapters.

Chapter 2 introduces the theoretical field that I have found most suitable for analysing my empirical material: phenomenology. I set out from philosophers Maurice Merleau-Ponty's (1945/2012) and Simone de Beauvoir's (1949/2011) phenomenologies and the philosopher Toril Moi's (1999; 2008) interpretation of de Beauvoir. Methodological considerations are discussed. I take standpoint theory as my starting point, describe how I proceeded when approaching the research field, collecting research data and deciding on which methods to apply. The final section deals with the process of interpretation and how the concepts that are central to the analysis have been chosen.

The four chapters that follow analyse the empirical material. The questions about the tension between the subject positions as disabled and as a sportswoman, about available femininities and about strategies of resistance in use are explored from different aspects. Chapter 3 begins with a discussion of dependence versus independence, and how capacity and autonomy are linked to normality. Moreover, the young women's striving for a normative femininity is examined. The concluding section deals with the importance of being together with equals – that is, being with other disabled people.

Chapter 4 considers experiences that are more explicitly associated with the body: experiences of the surgically operated body and the ambivalence about the interventions and about being extra tested. Furthermore, this chapter deals with experiences of the uncontrollable body and emotions that have to be managed, of bodily pleasure and strength, and finally of the beautiful body and the teenager's dissatisfaction.

The body is the subject of Chapter 5, too, but here it is linked to the use of technology. Merleau-Ponty's account of how new instruments, through habit, can become extensions of the body is combined with the metaphor of the cyborg. The chapter explores the role of technology in othering, when the participants present themselves as active young women and in experiences of – once again – pleasure and strength.

Chapter 6 is devoted to the young women's experiences of the disability sports movement. The potential of disability sports for change is considered in relation to experiences of infantilizing training and of being a young woman in a male context. The kinds of language used in sports are discussed too.

Chapter 7, lastly, contains a summary of the research project's results. Different forms of oppression and resistance to it are brought up, as well as the young women's emphasis on strength and capacity, their endeavour for normality and their experiences of pleasure. Finally, the research project's contributions to the four research fields are discussed.

The Swedish disability movement and disability policy

From philanthropy and charity to collective organization

The Swedish disability movement originates from institutions for crippled children that were established at the end of the nineteenth century.[2] The institutions were founded by philanthropists and initially financed by charity. Not until the twentieth century did the government begin to give financial support, and, as time went on, assumed the responsibility. The institutions' primary aim was the gains for the public economy. By education in handicraft and orthopaedic treatment crippled people would get the opportunity to support themselves and the public expenses for poor relief would be reduced (Holme 1995: 232–3, 236; Förhammar 2004: 47, 51–2).

At the beginning of the 1920s the matron of the institution for the crippled in Gothenburg founded the association The Well-being of Crippled.[3] This inspired the establishment of associations at other institutions, and a few years later the local associations joined on a national level in the forerunner of today's Association for a Society without Mobility Obstacles (DHR), an organization for people with impaired mobility.[4] The purpose of the organization was to give individual support, improve the treatment and finance better mobility assistive devices – with the overall aim of increasing the opportunities to earn one's living (Berg 2007: 9, 13). During the first years of the 1930s voices were heard urging for the liberation of both the organization and its members from the institutions for the crippled, and the first disabled president took up his duties. Criticism of the dependence upon charity did not arise until the 1970s, when the subject of human dignity was brought up for discussion within DHR. At that time 45 per cent of DHR's budget came from charity collection boxes, lotteries and sales. Raised governmental subsidies made it possible to bring the charitable activities to an end in 1977 (Berg 2007: 96). DHR's youth association was founded in 1987. Parents of disabled children and youths had run the traditional disability movements. However, DHR's youth association is run by the young people themselves, and can be seen as a joint effort to get self-determination and emancipation from grown-ups (Barron 1997: 35).

The historian Staffan Förhammar (2004) notes that the Swedish disability movement, in contrast to, say, women's lib, had very little influence on disability policy during the first half of the twentieth century. Instead it was politicians, philanthropists, and pedagogical and medical experts who elaborated this policy. Not until the 1960s, when disability organizations began to unite in the newly founded national cooperative organization The Swedish Disability Federation (HSO) did the movement become a powerful force with the potential to exert influence on policy (Förhammar 2004: 63–4).[5] A contributory cause was the radicalization of the public debate at that time. The insistence on equality came to include disabled people too.

Politicizing and individualization

The radical organization Anti-handicap was founded in Lund during the 1960s (Holme 2000; Bengtsson 2004: 39).[6] According to the spokesman Vilhelm Ekensteen it was the capitalist society's focus on the market and competition that hindered reforms. The freedom of the individual was emphasized, and disabled people were regarded as the most suitable to formulate their own needs and, thus, should be the ones who organized and decided how social care was designed. Anti-handicap criticized all forms of charity. The organization was also critical of the rest of the disability movement that defined themselves as a 'needy social group' (Holme 2000: 68, author's translation).

Anti-handicap was the first to formulate the relative or environmental definition of disability, according to which a disability appears in the meeting between an individual with an impairment and an inaccessible society. However, the idea was soon acknowledged by the rest of the disability movement as well as in the first official disability report of the Swedish government in 1976 (Bengtsson 2004: 39–40). The disability is looked upon as relative to time and space – a person with a specific impairment can be disabled in some contexts and regarding some functions, while the same person is not disabled in other situations. The society has to change in order to include all citizens (Tøssebro 2004: 4; Grönvik 2007: 14–15). Since then Swedish disability policy has officially been based on the relative definition of disability, and a similar understanding of the notion of disability is to be found in the other Scandinavian countries as well. Two goals of Swedish disability policy were brought up in the Swedish government's *Official Report* from 1976. On the one hand, normalization, which meant that disabled people should have the same rights, duties and opportunities as other people. On the other, integration – disabled people should no longer live segregated at institutions, but integrated within society.

During the 1980s participation and equality became the new catchwords in Swedish disability policy. A new agent entered the arena: Independent Living (IL). This movement started in Berkeley, California, during the 1960s and 1970s, inspired by the civil rights movement, women's lib and the protests against the Vietnam War (Berg 2008: 12; see also Morris 1995: 73–4). The Stockholm Cooperative for Independent Living (STIL) was founded and worked for publicly financed personal assistance, organized by the user. Instead of rigid bureaucracy and a focus on the interests of the employee, the users' interest should be central (Lindqvist 2000: 403). Like Anti-handicap, STIL emphasized the freedom and self-determination of the individual. Their work should be based on self-respect, peer support, self-fulfilment, pride in one's own identity and the right to expose oneself to risks (Berg 2008: 84–5). STIL's ideas were met with resistance. They were seen as a threat to the Swedish general welfare system, and unions for municipal employees stressed the risk of employees being exploited. The established disability movement, which had striven for general solutions, was against the idea of personal assistance too. Furthermore, many found the municipal responsibility secure (Berg 2008: 40–3, 48). It was argued that STIL's model only would function for those with plentiful resources, and those who did not find it as easy to express their needs would be excluded (Berg 2008: 53; see also Barron 1995: 68). However, as time went on DHR began to work actively for the personal assistance reform. In 1993 the Act Concerning Support and Service for Persons with Certain Functional Impairments (LSS) and the Act Concerning Compensation for Assistance (LASS) were adopted by the Swedish Parliament. During the rest of the 1990s STIL and DHR made united efforts to defend the personal assistance reform against recurrent demands for retrenchment (Berg 2007: 130–1).

The disability movement and gender

Previous studies have shown that disabled people's financial situation is worse, they have more health problems and are unemployed to a greater extent than the rest of the Swedish population. But there are big differences within the group: disabled women are worst off in income, health and on the labour market (Sjöberg 1998: 9, 17; Arnhof 2008: 18–19; Statistiska centralbyrån, 2014; Folkhälsomyndigheten 2015). However, this is not brought up in any of the accounts of the development of the disability movement referred to above. As a result of the unequal conditions together with a non-existent discussion regarding those inequalities, Forum – Women and Handicap (now Forum – Women and Disability in Sweden) was founded in 1997 as a further development of a project beginning in 1986. The association works for an increase in women's influence and against all forms of discrimination and threats and violence directed against those women (Forum Women and Disability in Sweden, 2015).

In a study on the struggle for social justice within the Swedish disability movement, representatives of six disability organizations were interviewed (Hugemark and Roman 2007). The results showed that they were well aware of the inequalities between disabled men and women, but the priority given to the work for equality varied. One representative maintains that these questions are important; nevertheless, she admits that this perspective is missing in her organization. Several interviewees go on to say that the gender order in society is obvious in their own organizations too, manifested in women having difficulties in making their voices heard (Hugemark and Roman 2007: 39–40).

To sum up, there have been several shifts within the disability movement. Firstly, disabled people replaced the benevolent philanthropists that initially ran the organizations. However, DHR was dependent on charity until the end of the 1970s. From the 1960s Anti-handicap called for increased individual freedom and self-determination. During the 1980s those demands were taken up by STIL and, as time went on, by the broader disability movement. The picture of disabled people as grateful recipients of charity or subsidies was criticized by both Anti-handicap and STIL, who demanded equality. STIL emphasized the importance of self-respect and pride. Lack of influence for groups within the movement resulted in new organizations for young people and women during the latter half of the 1980s.

Later social policy and its criticism

All evaluations of the personal assistance reform show that it has led to increased quality of life for persons who receive the benefit (Gynnerstedt 2004: 15). But what about those with less extensive disabilities? The overall retrenchments that have been made since the 1990s have been criticized. The Swedish welfare system's idea of universality is still prevailing, but cuts have been made. Benefits have been reduced and entitlement criteria for sickness benefits, early retirement and workers' compensation have been sharpened. Activation measures have been introduced and participation in these is often a condition to get benefits (Lindqvist 2000: 412). Thus what the sociologist Rafael Lindqvist calls a 'deservingness ethic' has grown strong within Swedish disability policy (2000: 412). The selective social and civil rights that were introduced during the 1990s in the shape of, for example, the Swedish Disability Reform of 1994 (of which the personal assistance reform is part), the establishment of the Disability Ombudsman (since 2009 Equality Ombudsman, DO) and an act from 1 May 1999 banning discrimination against disabled persons in working life imply a reorientation in Swedish disability policy. The selectivity, together with decentralization – social policy is now implemented on a municipal or regional level – has led to increased differences depending on place of living and socio-economic status (Lindqvist 2000: 413). This means a shift from a disability policy characterized by an 'emphasis on politics, collective organization and equality to an emphasis on market, individualism and freedom' (Barron et al 2000: 138, author's translation). This also implies a shift from a universal to a more liberal-conservative welfare state (Lindqvist 2000: 413), inspired by the market-oriented welfare state of the United States (Hvinden 2004: 185).

The shift to decreased general benefit levels, sharpened benefits criteria and new selective social and civil rights are problematic, as several researchers argue (Barron et al 2000; Lindqvist 2000; Riksförsäkringsverket 2002). Those who are entitled to the selective benefits certainly have gained increased freedom of choice, influence and self-determination. Large groups of disabled people who previously received the general benefits but are not entitled to the new selective support systems, risk being rendered invisible. The competition to obtain special support becomes tougher too (Barron et al 2000: 143). Lindqvist claims that the division of the welfare policy into separate sectors with sharpened criteria makes it extra troublesome for disabled persons: 'While most citizens with well-defined temporary problems in terms of either sickness, unemployment or economic difficulties, benefit from the universal, albeit sectoral welfare model, clients having numerous problems are disadvantaged because they do not fit into the "boxes" of welfare bureaucracies' (Lindqvist 2000: 414). For those people it can be difficult to depict a complex everyday life so that it suits the support systems of different sectors (Riksförsäkringsverket 2002: 20–2).

'Exposed groups' and the normal worker

It is thus more difficult for disabled persons to get into the labour market, which leads to greater needs of different kinds of support. What consequences have the Swedish labour market policy had for this group? The building and expansion of the Swedish welfare state required economic growth. Productivity and profitability had to be improved. Rationalizations and wage increases were negotiated centrally between employers and labour unions. The state remained in the background, encouraged the negotiations, ready to intervene when needed. The sociologist Bjørn Hvinden, who has a Nordic perspective, points out the difficulties of making demands on the employers that resulted from the spirit of agreement: '[The Nordic] Social Democratic governments … were more effective in developing public income maintenance and vocational rehabilitation services than in obligating employers and business interests to take on responsibility for providing work for people with impairment' (Hvinden 2004: 179). The early Swedish welfare state as well as the labour unions strove for improvements for workers as a collective, not for disabled workers *per se*. If they paid attention to disabled people it was to improve the working conditions for already employed, not for people outside the labour market (Lindqvist 2000: 403; Hvinden 2004: 179–80).

Rather than forcing employers to remove obstacles and make workplaces accessible for disabled persons by legislation, changes were based on voluntariness and information from the State. Social Democratic governments gave economic support to employers and offered service such as income maintenance and vocational rehabilitation for disabled persons (Hvinden 2004: 179). The focus was not on inaccessible workplaces, but on disabled people. In this way the latter were constructed as in need of support and measures and as an exception from the normal productive worker.

This is even more evident in how disabled people are named. The economic historian Paulina de los Reyes (2000) notes that those people, together with immigrants and elderly, are often included in the expression 'weak groups' or 'exposed groups'. De los Reyes continues: 'The label "weak groups" is in contrast to both research results and political guidelines that emphasize, on the one hand, situational factors regarding the disabilities, and on the other hand, the integrity of the individual and the obligation of society to provide necessary resources' (2000: 25, author's translation). Instead of accentuating obstacles that hinder participation in working life, the responsibility of the individual is stressed. Deficiencies, limitations and deviations are contrasted against the norm: the strong, able-bodied worker (de los Reyes 2000: 25).

Disability sports in Sweden

Swedish sports are both a product and an effect of the social democratic hegemony that considered it a vehicle for social inclusion and equality. It is organized as a *folkrörelse*, or popular movement, supported by volunteer work and public financing, and includes children's, recreational and professional sports (RF 2002: 6–7). The sports sociologist Tomas Peterson (2000; 2008) claims that the Swedish sports movement (as in all Scandinavian countries) balances two tasks: cultivating democracy and encouraging competition. Democratic forms of social intercourse are grounded in respect and equal rights for all, regardless of gender, class, religion, or 'race'/ethnicity. For society, the most important role of sport is training good citizens and providing meaningful activities for children and youth. Competition is also inherent in the logic of sport, involving individual performance, selection, ranking and elitism (Peterson 2000: 148–50; 2008: 5–6; see also Trondman 2005: 225–6).

Swedish disability sports are organized within the larger Swedish sports movement, but differ from the rest of the sports movement regarding this dual focus. Nor did international competitive disability sports originally aim at democratic or competitive training. The physician Ludwig Guttmann of the Spinal Injuries Centre at Stoke Mandeville Hospital in Aylesbury, England, is a central figure in the history of competitive disability sports, although there have been other agents and earlier competitions (Hargreaves 2000: 181; Östnäs 2003: 2; Bolling 2008: 31; Peers 2009: 656). In 1944 Guttmann introduced a programme of sports as rehabilitation and recreation for soldiers and civilians who had been injured in the war – most of them in wheelchairs as a result of amputations or spinal cord injuries. The first Stoke Mandeville Games took place in 1948 and became an annual event. The first international competition was held in 1952, a forerunner to the Paralympics. Guttmann regarded them as therapeutic, providing physical as well as psychological and social rehabilitation. The identity of participants as disabled people was underlined: 'It was their *disabilities* that created a sports world specifically for them – separate, spatially and symbolically, from the "real" world of sport outside' (Hargreaves 2000: 181, italics in original). Thus, a medicalized view characterized the emergence of disability sports. This was supported by a classification system based on impairment or diagnosis that was intended to ensure fair competition. Nowadays the system of classification has changed and is based on functionality instead. However, previous research shows that this medicalized view of disability sports still exists (Brittain 2004).

The development of the Swedish disability sports movement can be seen as part of the building of *folkhemmet*, the people's home. The preparatory work during the 1950s and 1960s was clearly inspired by the ideas of Guttmann (Östnäs 2003: 7). It is remarkable that initially the Swedish Sports Confederation (RF) did not want to organize disability sports, but rather thought that it should be part of the disability movement (Fellers 2010: 9–10).[7] From 1962 disability sports were organized within DHR. The Swedish government's Sports Commission's final report *Sports for All* came out in 1969, and in this disability sports were pointed out as especially important, 'not only as a recreational activity, but also as rehabilitation and social adjustment' (Fellers 2010: 14, author's translation). In that same year the Swedish Sports Organization for the Disabled – now Parasport – was founded and became part of RF. Parasport is today one of 71 specialized sports federations within RF, and administers 18 sports: alpine skiing, bench press, boccia, carpet curling, cross-country skiing and biathlon, electric wheelchair hockey, floorball, football, goalball, judo, shooting, showdown, sledge hockey, swimming, table tennis, track and field sports, wheelchair dance and wheelchair rugby. All sports are open for persons with mobility impairments, except for goalball and showdown which only address those who are visually impaired. Besides sports such as bowling, archery, cycling, golf, orienteering, riding, rowing, wheelchair basketball, wheelchair curling, wheelchair tennis, sailing and water skiing are integrated in the specialized sports federations (Svenska Parasportförbundet 2015).

That the contemporary Swedish disability sports movement differs considerably from the rest of the Swedish sports movement is also shown in an analysis of two policy documents, *Disability Sports Policy Programme* (SHIF 2006) and *Sports Objectives – A Summary of Aims and Guidelines for the Sports Movement* (RF 2009), which compares how the effects of sports upon bodies and society are portrayed (Apelmo 2012c).[8] In the RF programme, physical, psychological, social and cultural development on all levels is described as the main goal, alongside of promoting democracy and striving for gender equality:

> On all levels we want to carry on our sport in order to positively develop people both physically and mentally, as well as socially and culturally … An important part of the sports movement's democratic fostering is that every member, given their age and other qualifications, can have an influence through being responsible for themselves and their group, through meetings that are democratically structured, as well as through everyday training and competition. This is especially true of children and young people, who in this manner receive early training in the basic rules of democracy through sports clubs … All planning of sports activities should be carried out with a conscious gender equality perspective.
>
> (RF 2009: 11, author's translation)

However, these somewhat contradictory aims do not characterize all parts of the Swedish sports movement. The original aim of disability sport was, as cited earlier, neither democracy nor competition. The SHIF *Disability Sports Policy Programme* does not mention competition or democracy at all (SHIF 2006). Instead, rehabilitation and social integration are presented as its main goals, together with an eye toward lowered public expenditures. As the introduction to the programme states: 'There is hardly any other activity operating so effectively for the rehabilitation and social integration of disabled people as disability sports. It has added benefits for society in the form of reduced costs for care and social welfare' (SHIF 2006: 3, author's translation). Furthermore, the programme characterizes disabled people as weak:

> It is no overstatement to say that disabled people have a pressing need to improve their physical status, in order to master assistive technologies that are necessary for mobility. Wheelchairs, crutches, etc., require strength that must be acquired. Training solely for the movement of one's own body is the first prerequisite for having a tolerable existence.
>
> (SHIF 2006: 8, author's translation)

This alleged inherent weakness should be valid for all the different groups of disabled people that SHIF organizes: those with physical, visual and intellectual impairments. Similarly, the assumption seems to be that such individuals only have a 'tolerable existence' if they receive training. It appears that by not teaching children and adolescents about the democratic process and the possibility that they may someday make positive contributions to society, SHIF constructs disabled people as passive clients of the Swedish welfare state, instead of capable, active citizens. In describing such individuals as weak, in need of social integration, and a burden on public finances, SHIF contributes to a negative view of disabled people as pitiful, needy unfortunates. By not mentioning gender in the document, SHIF also contributes to a discourse that regards disabled people as ungendered (Apelmo 2012c). As in the Stoke Mandeville Games, the impaired body – the one that deviates from the norm – is the central focus. A medicalized view of disability sports is also to be found in media, both in Sweden and internationally, and that will be discussed in the following section.

Media portrayals: Victims and heroes

Two studies of Swedish Television

> Extreme Home Makeover, that's a programme I dislike ever so much! [It is usually about] a family with a miserable house, it's cold, it's overcrowded and they can't cook, and, moreover, one member of the family is injured or disabled. ... It's sentimental, the family members cry and they cheer when the house is torn down and the disabled person gets help and assistive devices and becomes so happy because 'now I become a little bit more independent!' Ahh! It gives me the creeps and I get sores in my ears, ohh! ... I immediately show my claws when it's about disabled persons and what a pity it is and how good they are and how important it is that they can live a satisfactory life. ... I don't like it when you pity people.
>
> (Maria, 19, video diary)

> In most cases it's pity-documentaries. It is like ... when you have been interviewed for a newspaper. ... Before you have revised it, it's always written like: 'Sara suffers from XX.' I don't suffer! Sure, some days are like hell, but I don't suffer. I have a rich life. ... That's why I think the Paralympics is so good! It's not shown so often, but there's more bloody fighting spirit all the way.
>
> (Sara, 23, video diary)

The media are not a central theme in this research project, but they are relevant partly because they influence the agenda for the public debate – what we consider important to have an opinion on – by what they choose to pay attention to (Ghersetti 2007: 4–5), partly because in many cases disabled people are only present in everyday life through media representations (Briant et al 2013: 887). Those representations were also brought up spontaneously during one interview and in two out of three video diaries. In the quotations Maria and Sara object to reality shows and documentaries that are shown on television. They claim that those portray disabled people as suffering and tragic victims, who thankfully receive help to attain a luckier and more independent life. However, Sara points out that there are rare but more positive examples, such as when the Paralympics are broadcast on television.

I will now discuss two studies of Swedish public-service television: the media researcher Karin Ljuslinder's (2002) study of disability discourses in Swedish Television (SVT) between 1956 and 2000, and the media researcher Marina Ghersetti's (2007) examination of how disabled people were represented in SVT's news programmes during 2005 and 2006. The two studies show that disabled persons do not participate in the capacity of ordinary citizens, but as (often anonymous) representatives of the category of disabled and in questions regarding precisely this part of their life and identity. In Ljuslinder's material impairments and disabilities as a subject or disabled persons are chiefly to be found in news and fact programmes. Since 1975 the share of programmes and features of this kind has been around just 1.8 per mille, compared with 0.7 per mille in Ghersetti's study. The great majority of programmes have a medical, individualizing perspective on impairments and disabilities. In those cases where a social perspective is highlighted, it is about society's responsibility for physical and technical accessibility in public settings (Ljuslinder 2002: 144; Ghersetti 2007: 19).

Ljuslinder observes that it is often experts without impairments of their own who comment, whereas disabled persons remain as anonymous illustrations (2002: 71). If the latter get a chance to speak they answer the interviewer's questions. Disabled persons are given the opportunity to speak for themselves or tell about their experiences only in a minority of cases during the entire investigation period (Ljuslinder 2002: 95).

The body is central in the reports and is given a symbolic meaning, according to Ljuslinder: 'The physical body tends to serve as an index for the entire person. The entire human being with his or her personality, characteristics, mental abilities and physical appearance is considered in the same way as the impaired body; as incomplete, imperfect, abnormal' (2002: 117, author's translation). Men generally participate more often than women and in activities that are directed towards society, whereas women are portrayed in their home. This could be interpreted as an attempt to preserve a traditional femininity, but since disabled women often have been denied the opportunity to become wife or mother, it may seem good that they are depicted in these situations (Ljuslinder 2002: 74–5). Women's sexuality is rendered invisible to a higher degree then men's, and during the entire period there is no programme that deals specifically with the situation of women (Ljuslinder 2002: 132–4). Displays of normality, Ljuslinder argues, are central in the narratives. The normal is indicated by the biological, whole body and through the ability to support oneself, to have a job. Through a focus on their struggles to achieve the normal, and on what they do not manage to do in relation to a hegemonic discourse of normality, disabled persons paradoxically are constructed as deviant, as the Other (Ljuslinder 2002: 100).

Both studies show that the pictures of disabled people are stereotypical: some characteristics are stressed at the expense of others. Ghersetti (2007) emphasizes that the news features often have a negative point of departure, characterized by hopelessness, poor health, problems or alienation. Disabled persons are depicted as weak, passive and helpless victims. In those rare cases when they get to speak for themselves, they participate as private persons – only in exceptional cases do they express their opinions as representatives of public life (Ghersetti 2007: 38). However, as Ghersetti points out, in sports news the picture is partially different. The features are more positive and about named individuals or teams (2007: 24). The stereotype of the victim is most common in Ghersetti's material, next comes the hero, which is most frequent in sports features. Those stereotypes are also stressed in the quotations from the interviewees in my research project that introduced this section. When the media report from the Paralympics we see 'more bloody fighting spirit', as Sara puts it, complicating the picture by pointing out that the media tend to describe her as a victim when they write about her own successes. The fighter is the third most common stereotype, and is to be found in features about leisure, culture, amusements or media (Ghersetti 2007: 32–3).

Ljuslinder, on the other hand, takes the stereotypes of the hero, the victim, the villain and the infantile as her starting point. An interesting observation made by Ljuslinder is the frequent use of the word 'despite' in the narratives of the hero. Despite his/her impairment, the hero manages to attain something that would not attract attention if the person in question did not have an impairment, or, in some cases, something that is rare and difficult but is seen as an even greater achievement if it is performed by a person with an impairment (Ljuslinder 2002: 119).

Robert McRuer (2006), professor of English, claims that a new, changed and more flexible discrimination against disabled people (and homophobia, which is not dealt with here) has developed. Difference and tolerance are two celebrated notions within neo-liberalism. When homosexuals and disabled persons demonstrated for their rights in the US during the 1960s and 1970s the previously naturalized, able-bodied, heterosexual subject was made visible. Hence this subject ended up in a crisis that, according to McRuer, was handled by showing a flexible tolerance. Heterosexual, able-bodied people now cooperate with disabled people in a 'discursive climate of tolerance', in which the latter, however, have to adapt (McRuer 2006: 18). In contemporary cultural representations disabled people are no longer openly objectified freaks and, as a result, the situation may seem to have improved. But, McRuer points out, they are still visually and narratively subordinated or completely erased (2006: 18, 28–9). This is confirmed by Ghersetti's and Ljuslinder's studies.

In recent years Swedish public service television has broadcast three series, all of them about disabled people: the documentary series *Köping Hillbillies* (2010) and *A Second Chance* (*En andra chans*, 2011), and the reality series *Against All Odds* (*Mot alla odds*, 2012, 2013). To perform a media analysis of these is beyond the scope of this book, but one can easily see that much of what Ljuslinder and Ghersetti expose is prevalent in these series too. The reason why they participate in these series is that they are disabled and, consequently, it is this part of their identity that is stressed – irrespective of their gender, class, 'race'/ethnicity or sexuality. They are private persons who are filmed and interviewed by able-bodied persons. They are depicted as heroes, but the dramaturgy and displays of normality are built up around the word 'despite' – despite injuries and impairments they play wheelchair basketball (*Köping Hillbillies*), get a job, a partner and children (*A Second Chance*) or walk 1020 miles from the Victoria Falls in Zambia to Namibia's Skeleton Coast (*Against All Odds*, 2012). However, a completely new phenomenon is Lovisa Söderberg, since 2011 working as a presenter of the children's programme *Bolibompa*. Söderberg is the first presenter ever in the history of SVT with a visible impairment.

Disability sports in media

In international research about how disability sports are represented in the media, the narrative of the hero in the form of the 'the supercrip' has been widely debated (Berger 2004; Hardin and Hardin 2004; Swartz and Watermeyer 2008; Peers 2009). The psychologists Leslie Swartz and Brian Watermeyer (2008) talk about a binary stereotype: on the one hand, the dependent, injured and incapable invalid – the victim – and, on the other, the supercrip. They continue:

> The latter is that much celebrated media persona of the disabled person who has 'overcome adversity' in a heartwarming manner and not been restricted by his or her 'flaws', but believes that 'everything is possible' for those who work hard. Naturally these ideas of fairness and reward for hard work are cornerstones of the neo-liberal just world tradition. Both poles of the stereotype of course fail to make it possible to see individual lives, much less conceptualize such issues as disablist oppression and exclusion. Further, all disabled people are oppressed by the imperative to 'overcome' in some superhuman fashion in order to be afforded basic acknowledgement.
>
> (Swartz and Watermeyer 2008: 189–90)

Wendell (1997) claims that the supercrips (or 'disabled heroes' in Wendell's words) make the able-bodied feel safe and secure, since they show that it is possible after all to take control over the body. The only thing that seems to be required is individual efforts. However, for many disabled people the impairment itself takes so much energy and power that there is no room for this kind of grand achievement. Thus the supercrip creates an ideal for disabled people that is unattainable for most, and for the vast majority the position as the Other is strengthened (Wendell 1997: 271). Several authors have also pointed out that these supercrips often have social, economic and physical resources or support that other disabled persons may not have (Wendell 1997: 271; Berger 2004: 801).

In a discourse analysis of Swedish news stories about the Paralympics in Sydney 2000 by the researcher in physical education and sport Kim Wickman (2007a), the supercrip is present too. According to Wickman the focus of the texts is on how the athletes overcome their disabilities rather than their athletic performances, and doing sport is described as a victory over tragedy. On the whole, to be able to do sport is constructed as larger than winning or losing in the Paralympics. The diagnosis (in the case of a congenital impairment) or the accident (in instances of acquired impairment), as well as the subsequent rehabilitation, is the concern, rather than sporting achievements. A hierarchy is prevalent in the texts, according to which able-bodied athletes are superior to impaired, and those with acquired impairments are superior to those who are born with theirs. Moreover, since the norm, the able-bodied athlete, is ubiquitous, the participants in Paralympics appear as second-rate athletes (Wickman 2007a: 6–8, 10; see also Hargreaves 2000: 203; Brittain 2004: 445, 447)

Yet, there are exceptions to these medicalizing media representations. For instance, a combining of the Olympic Games and the Paralympics is suggested and that able-bodied athletes too should be allowed to compete in wheelchair sports. In this way prevailing social and cultural norms could be challenged. This can also happen in interviews with the athletes: 'when the athletes have the opportunity to speak, the media texts seem to be more focused on sports specific aspects than on impairment and disability' (Wickman 2007a: 6).

Wickman also establishes that sports can be normalizing for disabled men, as a strong and muscular body brings them closer to the hegemonic masculinity:

> As the image of the able-bodied sportswoman's body and appearance is given attention as long as it can still be referred to certain notions and expectations of femininity, this might not be the case for the disabled sportswoman's image, as it may be experienced to get even further away from the ideal image of femininity through sports-related activities.
>
> (Wickman 2007a: 9)

This is confirmed by the sports sociologist Jennifer Hargreaves who argues that 'the sporting body represents a pivotal form of "physical capital" for disabled men, more so than for disabled women' (2000: 186).

To summarize, when disabled people appear in the media, the impairment or disability is in focus, no matter whether it is in sports features or not. The picture of them is stereotyped – most frequent are the stereotypes of the victim and the hero. The sports features differs in that disabled people more often appear as individuals instead of as anonymous representatives of the group. Ljuslinder's study shows that the word 'despite' is recurrent in the narrative of the hero – the supercrip succeeds despite his or her disability. The synonyms 'in spite of' as well as 'against all odds' are also to be found in Wickman's (2007a) quotations from Swedish press.

The field of research

Swedish disability research and disability studies

The building of the Swedish welfare state was based on social engineering: scientific methods were used to analyse social problems and find solutions to be implemented. In Sweden, as in other Nordic countries, disability research was developed as part of the disability policy during the 1970s. The aim of the research was to evaluate social reforms and ascertain whether the goals of the disability policy – normalization and integration – were being attained. Groups of people with different impairments did not take part in the welfare development. They were defined as problematic and in need of special support (Söder 2005: 96; 2013: 91–2). As the sociologist Mårten Söder (2005) argues, this discourse about disability as problematic is still prevalent within much Swedish disability research. Researchers therefore run the risk of reproducing prevailing understandings of disability and of missing inherent complexities and ambiguities. On the one hand, research findings of a high level of subjectively experienced life quality amongst disabled people are explained away as a lowered level of expectation. On the other hand demands from disabled people and their parents are explained as unrealistic expectations and as evidence that they have not accepted the disability (Söder 2005: 97–8).

Internationally, researchers in disability studies, an emancipatory field that emerged in the Western world during the 1970s, have levelled similar critique (Meekosha and Shuttleworth 2009: 48). While in the UK disability studies mostly have been developed in sociology, in the US this research is more established in the humanities. The debate is summarized by theatre scholar Carrie Sandahl: 'Disability scholars critiqued the fact that disability had long been relegated to academic disciplines (primarily medicine, social sciences, and social services) that considered disabilities "problems" to be cured and the disabled "defectives" to be normalized, not a minority group with its own politics, culture, and history' (2003: 26). However, in a report on Swedish disability research 2002–2010 it is noted that disability studies have not yet been established in Sweden (Rönnberg et al 2012).

It has been claimed that the close connection between Swedish disability research and social policy is problematic. The sociologist Dimitris Michailakis maintains that the research risks 'losing its critical distance' (2005: 126, author's translation). Söder (2005) claims that even when researchers do not perform evaluations on commission from public authorities, they nevertheless tend to use the notions that are politically correct for the time being. The research then risks falling either into what Söder calls the evaluation trap – the reformer's point of view, goals and aims are taken over by the researcher and the results will only legitimize the politics – or into the normative trap – the researcher has an opinion beforehand of what is right and desirable or wrong and not desirable (2005; see also Söder 2009: 70).

This coupling between research and the welfare state in Sweden as well as in other Scandinavian countries has also mattered for who carries out the research. While researchers in the UK and the US often have impairments of their own and are closely linked to the disability movement, this is uncommon in Sweden. This, according to Söder (2009), has its explanation in the origin of Swedish research in evaluations of reforms about, above all, the situation for people with intellectual impairments, concerning, for example, de-institutionalization. Since these individuals could not speak for themselves it was able-bodied researchers who performed the evaluations (Söder 2009: 70).

In the UK an animated discussion has been going on in disability studies regarding which function the impaired body has in the policy pursued by the disability movement and, in recent years, how it should be theorized (Thomas 2007: 120). The background to this debate is to be found in the social model, which was developed in the UK during the 1980s, and in the standpoints its proponents took. The sociologist Jan Tøssebro (2004) claims that both the social model and the relative definition of disability are parts of an 'environmental turn', which also is manifest in international documents such as the *United Nations Standard Rules on the Equalization of Opportunities for Persons with Disabilities* (1993), and the World Health Organization's (WHO) *International Classification of Functioning, Disabilities and Health* (2001). The Scandinavian version belongs to the weaker examples and the social model to the stronger in this environmental turn (Tøssebro 2004: 3–4). The social model has its conceptual origin in the British disability movement and its foremost spokesman in the disability researcher Michael Oliver (Oliver 1996, 2004; Thomas 2007: 54, 57–8). British activists and researchers criticized what is often called the medical or individual model, which they thought had been dominating in disability policy and in care and social welfare. According to this model the 'problem' lies in the functional or psychological restrictions of the individual, and the solution is rehabilitation and care offered by the medicine and the State. As Oliver argues, one of the foundations of the model is 'the personal tragic theory of disability': the impairment is regarded as a tragic event that has randomly struck some individuals, and hence they should be treated with tolerance and acceptance (1996: 89). Another main component, Oliver continues, is medicalization (1996: 31). Oliver took his point of departure in Marxist theory when he developed the social model, and argues, like *Anti-handicap*, that disabilities stem from the capitalist mode of production (Thomas 2007: 53–4). The proponents of the social model admit that problems exist, but do not attribute them to the limitations of the individual, but rather to:

> … society's failure to provide appropriate services and adequately ensure the needs of disabled people are fully taken into account in its social organisation. Hence disability, according to the social model, is all the things that impose restrictions on disabled people; ranging from

individual prejudice to institutional discrimination, from inaccessible public buildings to unusable transport systems, from segregated education to excluding work arrangements, and so on.

(Oliver 1996: 32–3)

Oliver contends that there is no causal connection between the physical body and its injury or diagnosis, on the one hand, and the disability, on the other. He puts forward three arguments against a focus on the physical body. Firstly, he sees questions about the body as diverting attention from what must be central: social change. Secondly, he believes it is better to join forces against the discrimination that disabled persons experience, instead of stressing physical differences. Finally, the social limitations that come with a physical impairment, as well as the physical, psychological and emotional consequences that follow pain, belong to the private sphere, Oliver claims (1996: 35, 38–9; 2004; see also Thomas 2007: 122). Vic Finkelstein, another prominent figure in the British disability movement, maintains: 'disability is created by a world designed for able-bodied living rather than by the way our bodies are impaired' (1996: 1). Hence, activists as well as researchers should focus on removing societal obstacles instead of emphasizing subjective experiences of discrimination. Furthermore, Finkelstein is afraid that a focus on the personal could lead to a split within the disability movement and that the distinction between the physical injury and the disability created by society should be erased (1996: 2–3). Finally there is a risk, the sociologist Colin Barnes points out, that negative cultural stereotypes of disabled people are strengthened if experiences of pain, fatigue or depression are included (1998: 77).

However, several researchers have criticized the social model for leaving out the lived experiences of the body, such as experiences of physical limitations, pain or fear of death (Crow 1996; Hughes and Paterson 1997; Paterson and Hughes 1999; Hall 2000; Edwards and Imrie 2003). The sociologists Bill Hughes and Kevin Paterson (1997) emphasize that by completely avoiding the body within disability research, the body will be regarded as pre-social, a physical object separated from the self, as biology is separated from culture. Paradoxically, this results in 'the medicalisation of disabled people's bodies and the politicisation of their social lives' (Hughes and Paterson 1997: 331). In striving for politicizing disabled people's experiences, the body has become de-politicized. Feminist disability researchers have accentuated political reasons for including the physical body in the research, as subjective experiences tied to the physical body make visible differences in gender, class, 'race'/ethnicity, sexuality and age (Crow 1996: 221; Thomas 2007: 123). Liz Crow (1996), artist and activist, argues that if the impairment is disregarded, it can be harder for some social groups such as women, who more often have chronic pain as an effect of problems such as rheumatoid arthritis. What counts as impairment also changes over time, and is dependent upon social and cultural factors; homosexuality, for example, was previously regarded as an illness (Crow 1996: 221–2).

Disability research, gender and feminism

During the 1980s international research about gender and disability began to appear. Sweden was a bit later; the first studies about the intersection came during the 1990s (Söder 2013: 98). However, mainstream disability studies and Swedish disability research seldom have had a gender perspective (Barron 1997: 27; Barron et al 2000: 161; Reinikainen 2004: 258; Bê 2012: 363). This research risks contributing to the representation of disabled people as genderless and asexual. It has been argued that while women to a larger extent are judged by the appearance of their bodies, they are at greater risk being defined by their impairments (Wendell 1997: 260) and thus being devalued (Sjöberg 1998: 41).

Previous research has also shown that feminist research and disability research/disability studies have many similarities, but have seldom been combined (Garland-Thomson 1997; Traustadottir and Kristiansen 2004). The disability researchers Rannveig Traustadottir and Kristjana Kristiansen (2004) note that women and disabled persons share the exclusion from working life, political participation and economic power. In feminism as well as in disability studies and the disability movement, demands for self-determination and equal rights have been put forward, as well as demands for the possibility to speak for oneself. The two fields of research have voiced similar critique against traditional research methods and theories and advocated non-hierarchic research relations. The discussions about sex/gender are similar to the debates about impairment/disability. Besides, both feminist researchers and those within disability studies have criticized the exclusion of their experiences and the negative representations of them as passive and weak (Traustadottir and Kristiansen 2004: 39–40). The literary scholar Rosemarie Garland-Thomson also emphasizes the body when she summarizes feminism and the disability studies tradition she works in:

> Both feminism and my analysis of disability challenge existing social relations; both resist interpretations of certain bodily configurations and functioning as deviant; both question the ways that differences are invested with meaning; both examine the enforcement of universalizing norms; both interrogate the politics of appearance; both explore the politics of naming; both forge positive identities.
>
> (Garland-Thomson 1997: 22)

However, Garland-Thomson points out that these subjects have been more explored within feminism. But in spite of the interest in the body within feminism surprisingly few have paid attention to the impaired or disabled body. Neither disability as an axis of power, nor the results of research that has been done, have been incorporated in mainstream feminisms (Bê 2012: 263, 273). The remaining question is what effects this has had and still has for feminist theory.

Critical disability studies

Since the mid 2000s several researchers have employed the term 'critical disability studies' (CDS) (Campbell 2008; Meekosha and Shuttleworth 2009; Goodley et al 2012; Shildrick 2012; Slater 2012; Goodley 2013). One of the factors behind the emergence of CDS was the critique of the impairment/disability distinction and the underlying binary way of thinking, referred to above (Meekosha and Shuttleworth 2009: 50). CDS is characterized by its trans-disciplinarity, breaking the boundaries between feminist, postcolonial, queer, poststructuralist, psychoanalytical and phenomenological theory (Goodley et al 2012: 3; Shildrick 2012: 32, 37). Disability theories from the Global South are acknowledged, and, furthermore, this field of research has an intersectional perspective, exploring how (dis)ability relate to and intersect with other axes of power such as gender, class, 'race'/ethnicity and sexuality.

In CDS there is also a shift of attention from the disabled, problematized body, to able-bodied normativity and how it is produced and maintained (Campbell 2008, 2012; Ghai 2012). This is quite unusual in empirical disability research, in contrast to research about gender, class, 'race'/ethnicity and sexuality, which studies not only subordinate but also dominant groups, as, for example, in masculinity studies and whiteness studies. To be able-bodied is often regarded as a non-identity, even more naturalized than for example heterosexuality (McRuer 2006: 1) or whiteness. One attempt to change this is made by Fiona Kumari Campbell (2012), who advocates a new field of research: studies in ableism. She argues that when focusing on how to get rid of disablism, disabled people are often made the Other. The implicit 'us' is supposed to be able-bodied, asking 'what can "we" do for them?' (Campbell 2012: 213). In contrast, studies in ableism concentrate on how ableist normativity is created and reproduced. Campbell identifies two main components in ableism. Firstly, the notion of the normal human being or, in other words, of normativity. Secondly, the idea that it is possible to draw a clear dividing line between the normal and the deviant. This division is upheld through purification; everything that blurs the line is ignored (Campbell 2012: 215–16). The notion of the Other in studying the workings of ableism is elaborated by the psychologist Anita Ghai (2012). Drawing on postcolonial theory, Ghai contends that the Other is constitutive of the rational, able-bodied subject. The Other is characterized by lack, and by the negation of every valued quality that is ascribed to the able-bodied actor. The group of Others is dehumanized and seen as homogeneous (Ghai 2012: 273–4).[9]

What then characterizes the able-bodied 'us'? Garland-Thomson (1997) has coined the term 'normate', which refers not only to the body and its functions but also to the societal position as a whole:

> The term *normate* usefully designates the social figure through which people can represent themselves as definitive human beings. Normate, then, is the constructed identity of those who, by way of the bodily

configurations and cultural capital they assume, can step into a position of authority and wield the power it grants them.

(Garland-Thomson 1997: 8, italics in original)

The normate signifies an ideal that only a small number of people achieve (Garland-Thomson 1997: 8), and includes several axes of power.

A further example of this is to be found in McRuer's (2006) crip theory, a coupling of disability studies and queer theory. McRuer introduces the idea of a system of compulsory able-bodiedness, by analogy with Adrienne Rich's (1980) notion of compulsory heterosexuality. He explores how it produces disability and is interwoven with compulsory heterosexuality, drawing parallels between able-bodiedness and heterosexuality. Both are defined by their opposites, and both are connected to an idea of normality. It is considered self-evident that having a body and living a life without a disability are preferable to being a disabled person. Thus the disabled body is subordinated, and able-bodiedness becomes compulsory (McRuer 2006: 2, 8–9). Old ideas about homosexuality as a mental or physical illness or as a deviation from a hetero-sexual, healthy, true identity linger on and show how compulsory heterosexuality is associated with being able-bodied. The disabled body, on the other hand, is often constructed as asexual and non-gendered, or – when it comes to intel-lectual disabilities – as overly sexual (Malmberg 1996, 2002; Marston and Atkins 1999: 89; Reinikainen 2004; Grönvik 2008: 53). However, McRuer does not discuss how these ideas about the disabled body are connected to compulsory heterosexuality.[10]

To sum up, within CDS the able-bodied position is coupled with normality. Normality is defined by, and thus dependent on, its opposite, what is considered deviant. They are hierarchically ordered: normality is superior.

Not much has been written about the able-bodied norm in Swedish disability research. One of a few examples is a special issue of *Lambda Nordica*, a Nordic scholarly journal for LGBT (lesbian, gay, bisexual and transgender) and queer studies, which was dedicated to crip theory (Rydström 2012). Several of the Nordic contributors discussed the workings of the able-bodied norm. The lack of theorizing about this norm is apparent in the language too. There is no Swedish translation of the term able-bodied, except for the negation non-disabled people. While the notions of sexism and racism (*sexism* and *rasism* in Swedish) are well established, there was no equivalent Swedish notion for disablism or ableism until 2015, when the term *funkofobi*, a fusion of the two words *funktionsnedsättning* (impairment) and *fobi* (phobia), was incorporated in *The Swedish Academy Glossary*.[11]

How, then, is this research project positioned within the field of disability research? Bringing with me insights from disability studies and the social model, I also draw from critical disability studies and feminist theory to analyse the research participants' experiences of the disabled body as young women. The shift of focus that 'the environmental turn' involved, from the individual's impairment to societal obstacles, is of course historical. However, I adopt the critique against the social model regarding the exclusion of lived experiences of the body. The splitting of the movement that Oliver and Finkelstein predict if physical differences are taken into account can be overcome by means of coalitions between different groups – I will come back to this in the next chapter when discussing methodological considerations. Swedish HSO is one example of precisely such a coalition between different disability associations.

Notes

1 More about my artistic practice can be found in, for instance, Hindsbo, K. and Kroneberg, E.-B. (eds) (2013) *The Beginning Is Always Today: Contemporary Feminist Art in Scandinavia*, Kristiansand, Norway: SKMU Sørlandets Kunstmuseum; Nyström, A. (ed.) (2005) *Konstfeminism/Art Feminism: Strategies and Consequences in Sweden from the 1970s to the Present*, Stockholm, Sweden: Atlas; Nacking, A. (2004) 'Killing the Bogy Man', in *Elisabet Apelmo*, Växjö, Sweden: Växjö Konsthall; Olsen, S. K (2001) 'Identification of a Given Situation', *Make*, December–January; Kölle, B. (2000) 'From Anxiety to Horror: A Conversation with Elisabet Apelmo', in Folie, S. (ed.) (2000). *North: contemporary art from Northern Europe*. Austria: Kunsthalle Wien.
2 I use 'disabled people' to capture how a disability is 'done' and embodied in the social interaction of the everyday life. However, in the following historical review I use the expressions of that time, well aware that, for example, 'crippled' and 'handicapped' are considered deeply offensive nowadays. For more about terminology see, for instance, Shildrick (2012: 40).
3 *De Vanföras Väl.*
4 *Förbundet för ett samhälle utan rörelsehinder.*
5 *Handikappförbundens samarbetsorgan.*
6 *Anti-handikapp.*
7 *Riksidrottsförbundet.*
8 *Handikappidrottpolitiskt program* and *Idrotten vill – en sammanfattning av idrottsrörelsens idéprogram*, respectively.
9 In *The Second Sex*, de Beauvoir argues that while men are regarded as subjects, women are socially constructed as the Other: 'she is determined and differentiated in relation to man, while he is not in relation to her ... the Other is posited as Other by the One positing itself as One' (de Beauvoir 1949/2011: 6–7).
10 For a further criticism of McRuer's crip theory, see Apelmo (2012a).
11 *Svenska Akademiens ordbok.* This glossary constitutes the unofficial norm of the Swedish language.

2 Theoretical framework and methodological considerations

The troublesome body

The body seems to be a constant bother. It leads the philosopher's thoughts astray and tempts the religious to sin. It is irrelevant in the social science research field that the early sociologist claimed. Feminists have shunned it to avoid biological determinism, and the disability movement has shunned it to avoid medicalization. In this book, the body is central. It is a source of pleasure and annoyance: it is fast and flexible, it causes pain and leakage.

In this chapter I concur with researchers who argue for the necessity of including the body within sociology, disability research/disability studies as well as feminist theory.[1] When the sociologist Bryan S. Turner (2008: 40–1) draws up guidelines for a sociology of the body he claims it has to relate to:

1 the body as part of both nature and culture;
2 the sharp dividing line that often are drawn between self and body in sociological theory;
3 the body as central in political struggle; and
4 the distinction between the individual's and the population's body.

My argumentation proceeds from Turner's first three arguments.[2] Firstly, *the body is created in the intersection between the biological and the cultural* (Hughes and Paterson 1997: 336; Bordo 2004: 35–6; Turner 2008: 40). Spina bifida can cause several physiological complications such as different degrees of paralysis, weakened muscles and loss of feeling in the lower part of the body, difficulties in relieving oneself and also risk of cerebrospinal fluid accumulation in the head. But these physiological complications can only be understood by means of culturally created ideas such as ideas about bodies that need assistive technology to move or to empty the urinary bladder. It can be ideas about the age at which these conditions occur, how the consequences of the conditions ought to be handled or where those who have these conditions tend or ought to be. Perhaps these ideas are coupled with aged or sick bodies that are in nursing homes or hospitals. Whereas strong and productive bodies are associated with the public sphere, as the philosopher Susan

Wendell points out, impaired, weak, sick, old and dying bodies are associated with the private, hidden sphere (1997: 266). What is more, there are concrete elements of culture more or less interconnected with the body, such as a wheelchair, catheter or shunt, which is inserted in the body to drain excess fluid from the brain to the abdomen. They become part of the body, or what the philosopher Merleau-Ponty calls 'an extension of the bodily synthesis' (1945/2012: 154). The dichotomy between, on the one hand, biology, the (female) body, desire and the uncivilized, and, on the other, culture, (male) reason and the civilized is in this way transgressed in the body.

Secondly, it is *impossible to separate body from self or consciousness*. In early sociology the central question at issue was the relation of the self to society. The social actor's body was regarded as of no interest (Turner 2008: 34–5). Turner notes that a sharp distinction has often been made between self and body, something that has been strengthened in symbolic interactionism (2008: 35, 41). The sociologist Erving Goffman, for instance, describes how the body disturbs the interaction between individuals on a micro level – by bodily secretions, stumbling or different kinds of impairments – and how the self through discipline, control and cautiousness can handle and prevent disturbances (1959/1990; 1963/1990). But Turner points out that the representation of the self is always done through the body and that this representation is socially interpreted. Goffman's sociology could be seen as 'not the study of the representation of the self in social gatherings but the performance of the self through the medium of the socially interpreted body' (Turner 2008: 41). Researchers in disability research/disability studies have also made the distinction between body and self, where the distinction between impairment and disability has led to 'a disembodied subject, or more precisely a body devoid of history, affect, meaning and agency' (Hughes and Paterson 1997: 329). The division between self and body can be reconciled through the idea of embodiment.

The third argument is about *the body's central position in political struggle*. There are physiological differences between women and men, or physiological conditions such as spina bifida; but the notions of gender identity and impairment and their meaning are culturally created, historically changeable and the object of political struggle (Turner 2008: 40). This became evident when the second wave of feminism at the end of the 1960s politicized women's bodies and made visible how they were socially and culturally constructed (Bordo 2004: 16–9) and subsequent discussions in the disability movement and disability studies regarding the importance of the body. The second wave of feminism paid attention to the meaning that reproduction, sexuality, socialization of children and ideals of beauty have for women's subordination, and the feminist slogan of that time was coined: 'the personal is political' (Hanisch 1969; Redstockings 1969; Mitchell 1971). During the 1970s the philosopher and historian of ideas Michel Foucault demonstrated the body's historicity (Foucault 1976/1990; Bordo 2004: 17; Turner 2008: 37), which was of great importance for feminist theory formation. Feminism's accentuation of the personal as political, according to activist and disability researcher Jenny Morris, has formed the basis for the disability movement too. The latter has shown that personal experiences of exclusion are due to societal barriers rather than physical impairments (Morris 1996: 5).

How, then, is it possible to create a sociological theoretic framework that does not ignore the biological body or separate it from culture, consciousness and politics? Below I present the field I have found most suitable for the analysis of my empirical material: the phenomenological. This framework consists of two perspectives on acting that complement each other. Through the phenomenologies of the philosophers Maurice Merleau-Ponty (1945/2012) and Simone de Beauvoir (1949/2011) and the philosopher Toril Moi's (1999, 2008) interpretation of de Beauvoir the acting is linked to the body. With help of the political philosopher Lois McNay's (2004) reading of Pierre Bourdieu's (1987/1990) 'phenomenology of social space' the dynamic between structural limitations and the individual's space for acting can be understood.

The field of phenomenology

According to a number of researchers, phenomenology's strength lies in its ability to overcome the body–mind dualism (Hughes and Paterson 1997; Paterson and Hughes 1999; Turner 2001; Fagrell 2005). Merleau-Ponty maintains that it is impossible to separate the two: 'The union of the soul and the body is not established through an arbitrary decree that unites two mutually exclusive terms, one a subject and the other an object. It is accomplished at each moment in the movement of existence' (1945/2012: 91). The body is not an object that I have, but I am my body and the world is experienced through the body. 'Consciousness is originally not an "I think that," but rather an "I can"', Merleau-Ponty (1945/2012: 139) writes, directed or oriented towards the surrounding world, and thus embodied (Ahmed 2006: 27). The embodiment is an ongoing social process and practice in which bodily techniques are learned (Turner 2001: 259).

In *The Second Sex*, de Beauvoir describes the body as a situation, 'If the body is not a *thing*, it is a situation: it is our grasp on the world and the outline for our projects' (1949/2011: 46, italics in original). In other words, it is through the body that we are in, perceive and interact with the world. This situation should not be understood as external in relation to the subject, Moi indicates, 'but rather [as] an irreducible amalgam of the freedom (projects) of that subject and the conditions in which that freedom finds itself' (1999: 74). Accordingly, the embodied consciousness is situated in time and place. Moi describes how the historical situatedness of the body is created in an ongoing process:

> The way we experience – live – our bodies is shaped by this interaction. The body is a historical sedimentation of our way of living in the world, and of the world's way of living with us. ... If I have to negotiate the world in a crippled body or sick body I am not going to have the same

experience of the world or of myself as if I had a healthy or particularly athletic body. Nor will the world react to me in the way it would if I had a different body.

(Moi 1999: 68)

Thus, how I am situated in the world is influenced by how I have lived and now live in the world, and how those around interact with me. Which body I have and my physiological prerequisites are central, as the way in which people I meet react to this body. Those experiences create my situatedness (see also Ahmed 2006: 56).

It is the role de Beauvoir gives the body and biology that makes her theory so fruitful in this research project. In contrast to the poststructuralist feminist theory tradition that separates sex from gender, and leaves biology to focus on women's socially constructed subordination, de Beauvoir does not make this distinction. De Beauvoir emphasizes that biology does not define the woman (1949/2011: 47, 283; see also Moi 1999: 69–71), but, as we saw above, the body is one of several components in our situatedness. 'Her relation to her body, to the male body, and to the child will never be the same as those man has with his body, with the female body, and with the child', de Beauvoir states (1949/2011: 765). In a similar way a young woman with an impaired body does not have the same relation to her body and to able-bodied men and women as those who are able-bodied have to their bodies and to hers. Biology is important but not determining (Moi 1999: 62–3). One is not born, but rather becomes, disabled.

In the interaction with the surroundings, with things as well as other people, the individual goes from immanence to transcendence. What meaning do these two notions have? Merleau-Ponty describes transcendence as 'this movement by which existence takes up for itself and transforms a *de facto* situation' (1945/2012: 173, italics in original), while de Beauvoir speaks in terms of freedom: 'Every subject posits itself as a transcendence concretely, through projects; it accomplishes its freedom only by perpetual surpassing toward other freedoms; there is no other justification for present existence than its expansion toward an indefinitely open future' (1949/2011: 16). Immanence is characterized by passivity and alienation (de Beauvoir 1949/2011: 10). In those cases when the subject does not pursue its projects the subject relapses into immanence, into 'in-itself' instead of 'for-itself'. If it is the individual itself who has fallen for the temptation to flee freedom or failed to act, de Beauvoir regards it as a 'moral fault' (1949/2011: 16). Thus, it is to some extent an individual's responsibility to act.[3] But the meeting with other individuals is ambiguous: these meetings bring the individual out of his or her passivity; on the other hand, conflicts can arise between different individuals' acting. If the agency is hindered or limited by other subjects, it is a manifestation of oppression that can give rise to feelings of frustration (1949/2011: 10, 16). One example of this oppression is if the subject is posited as object, and hence is made the Other (de Beauvoir 1949/2011: 161). The oppression does not only exist on an individual level but can also be structural – de Beauvoir analyses women's subordination. But the individual almost always has a possibility to act, no matter how oppressed he or she is (Moi 1999: 83).

The conflicts that arise between different subjects' actions can be surmounted, de Beauvoir argues, 'by the free recognition of each individual in the other, each one positing both itself and the other as object and as subject in a reciprocal movement. But friendship and generosity, which accomplish this recognition of freedoms concretely, are not easy virtues' (1949/2011: 159). Through recognizing each other as acting subjects and taking over the other's perspective for a while (and thus seeing oneself as an object), conflicts can be settled.

It should be added that I here have followed de Beauvoir's official, conscious attitude (Arnfred 2002: 6). Her text is highly contradictory. Moi (2008) notes that the metaphors de Beauvoir uses to describe the transcendence are male, phallic – and full of admiration. It is a movement forward and upward that is described: 'the basic image of the project remains male erection and ejaculation', establishes Moi (2008: 172). Thus, the projects are coupled to a linear development, whilst non-linear projects are not included in the transcendence. While a male physiological function is praised like this, de Beauvoir regards the female functions, including pregnancy, childbirth and the female orgasm, as immanent and describes them in strongly negative terms (Arnfred 2002: 6; Moi 2008: 174). Moi claims that this is an expression of the time and place that de Beauvoir lived in, and stresses that de Beauvoir constantly comes back to how the meanings that are ascribed to the male, the female and the biological are socially constructed (2008: 182).

However, the cultural sociologist Signe Arnfred (2002) contends that de Beauvoir's approach is even more problematic. The thought that the woman is the second sex, that is to say, subordinate to the man, is strong in Western feminisms. But how can feminism imagine another future if the starting point is that the man is the model, and that equality is defined in male terms (Arnfred 2002: 6)? 'With woman-as-other being embedded in the very concept of "woman" – as is the case in most feminist thinking – imagining futures with woman *not* as *the other* becomes an impossible task', argues Arnfred (2002: 18, italics in original). This view is closely connected to the female body: 'the idea conveyed here is "woman against her body"' (Arnfred 2002: 7).

Embodied limitations and gender

The embodiment also implies that a lived experience is produced. The lived experience orients us towards some objects while other are relegated to the background, Sara Ahmed (2006), professor of race and cultural studies, points out. This is of vital importance for the individual's self understanding:

> The term [lived experience] describes the way an individual makes sense of her situation and actions. Because the concept also comprises my freedom, my lived experience is not wholly determined by the various

situations I may be a part of. Rather lived experience is, as it were, sedimented over time through my interactions with the world, and thus itself
becomes part of my situatedness.

(Moi 1999: 63)

Taking the impaired body as an example, Hughes and Paterson (1997) argue
that the embodiment makes it clear that body and consciousness as well as
nature and culture are impossible to separate. The oppression and prejudices
that an individual with a physical impairment encounters are embodied
as pain. The chronic impairment structures the experience of the world, but is at
the same time an object whose meaning arises both from personal, embodied
knowledge about pain, and from abstract, cultural assumptions about pain.
Thus, the social obstacles that an individual with an impairment confronts
are embodied, and the impairment is both physical and social (Hughes and
Paterson 1997: 335–6).

Another example of how this embodiment can appear is given by the political
philosopher Iris Marion Young (1980) in the essay 'Throwing Like a Girl'.
Young claims that in a specific sociocultural situation – in this case urban,
Western society – women are defined, in addition to individual variations, by
historical, social, cultural and economic limitations. The 'female' is constituted
by precisely these structures and conditions that create demarcations for what
it is to be a woman in a specific situation. The embodied limitations lead to a
bodily style that is typical for women. 'What we "do do" affects what we "can
do",' as Ahmed writes (2006: 59). Repeated interactions shape the body, its
abilities and way of moving. Young maintains that the female goal-oriented
movement manifests in three ways. Women have a tendency not to stretch out,
lean or turn completely or follow through the movement in the direction of the
intended goal. The transcendence is ambivalent, in other words. They also tend
to use less space than is available to them. Next, doubt often arises regarding
whether the body is capable of doing what is required, and fear of hurting
oneself when performing physically demanding tasks. The movement towards
the goal is carried out with hesitation. Power, weight, technique and skill are
not fully utilized and the prediction is confirmed. Finally, the whole body is
not used, but only the part of the body that is most connected to the task. It
is possible to go beyond this typically female bodily style, yet it is still determining in a negative sense: something has been avoided or overcome (Young
1980: 152). One of the factors behind this embodiment is that the woman
when moving simultaneously sees herself as both subject and object, which
hinders her action (Young 1980: 148).

There are individual variations in women's living conditions, Young contends.
Despite this, her typically 'female' style can be understood as generalizing –
factors such as class, 'race'/ethnicity, sexuality, functionality and age influence
the embodiment too. I rather interpret the bodily style that Young describes
as an expression of a normative femininity (Ambjörnsson 2004: 57, 61), or
what the sociologist Raewyn Connell (2014) calls emphasized femininity, that

is to say, one of several bodily styles that correspond to several different femininities. I will come back to this below. Young also uses physical impairments as a metaphor for women's limitations – or a metaphor for 'innocent suffering' in the words of the disability researchers David Mitchell and Sharon Snyder (1998) – when she asserts that 'women in a sexist society are physically handicapped' if they do not escape from their determination (Young 1980: 152). Would Young's analysis have come to the same results if she had taken women with physical impairments as her point of departure?

Moi (1999) emphasizes that it is impossible to apply the distinction between sex (connected to biology) and gender (connected to social norms) to de Beauvoir's categories. Biology cannot be separated from social norms in the lived experience of gender differences. 'To consider the body as a situation ... is to consider both the fact of having a specific kind of body and the meaning that concrete body has for the situated individual. This is not the equivalent of either sex or gender' (Moi 1999: 80–1). Consequently, when I discuss gender in the following I do not make this distinction. Connell regards gender as a multidimensional social structure that shapes and is reshaped in social relations. A gender regime is a pattern in an organization's or an institution's gender arrangement. The gender regime is often in accordance with the larger pattern in society, the gender order, but it can also differ. It is possible to change a gender regime but changes often meet resistance (Connell 2002). The gender regime and the gender order are composed of many direct or indirect (through a market or the Internet) gender relations. Gender relations are continuously created, and only exist if individuals create them through gender practices in everyday life. These gender practices are governed by social structures. However, the structures of gender relations have no existence outside the practices, but must be maintained through social action (Connell 2002). Gender is, in sociologists Candace West and Don Zimmerman's words, something we do, and have to do, in the interaction with others in everyday life – 'doing gender is unavoidable' (1987: 137), no matter whether we comply or resist.

De Beauvoir analyses gender, but class, 'race'/ethnicity, sexuality and so on are also inscribed in our bodies. Thus, there are many different types of masculinities and femininities. But on a simplified, global level, Connell (2014) argues, men dominate women. Hegemonic masculinity is made up of those gender practices that are currently dominating, in relation to other men and women. The most subordinate masculinity is the homosexual one. Furthermore, there is the masculinity that benefits from the dominant position as men, and thus is complicit in the hegemonic project. As women in general are subordinate to men, this rules out a hegemonic femininity. Instead, the femininity that is normative at present is termed emphasized femininity. This femininity is characterized by compliance with the subordination of women by men, and adaptation to the requests of men. Other femininities are defined by non-compliance and resistance, or by different combinations of resistance, compliance and cooperation (Connell 2014: 295–7). Both hegemonic masculinity and emphasized femininity are historically changeable and can be challenged.

Four faces of oppression

The analysis of the oppression that an individual is exposed to when projects or the agency are hindered can be refined by the five faces of oppression that Young suggests (1990/2011): exploitation, powerlessness, marginalization, cultural imperialism and violence, of which the first three are effects of the social division of labour. Different oppressed groups are exposed to different combinations of these aspects. Young claims that disabled people are subject to marginalization and cultural imperialism; but it has been argued that even if those two are the most common, all five faces of oppression can be found in the lived experience of disabled people (Thomas 2007: 75–6). In my empirical material, I contend, examples of powerlessness, marginalization, cultural imperialism and violence are to be found.

Young defines *exploitation* as 'the transfer of the results of labor of one social group to benefit another' (1990/2011: 49). The transfer leads to the emergence of a structural power relation between the groups. One example is women's paid or unpaid care work, which transfers resources to men; another is menial work performed by racialized groups. Since most of my informants were still studying and their thoughts about future working life were not part of the research questions, I have chosen to not include exploitation in the analysis. *Powerlessness* is related to exploitation. Groups who lack authority in working life as well as in social settings are powerless. They have few choices and little control over their life. Moreover, they lack opportunities to develop their own capacities and have limited chances to get recognition. Because of their low status, they risk disrespectful treatment (Young 1990/2011: 56–8).

Marginalized are the groups that stand outside productive life, which affects young people and disabled people among others. The marginalization, according to Young, leads to material deprivation and dependence on allowances. Through this dependency on public institutions, people who cannot support themselves risk integrity-insulting fostering, depreciation and degradation. Social and medical professionals have the power to define their needs and what kind of life the applicant is to live, about which a great deal has been written in previous research (Barron 1995: 71–4; Thomas 2007: 96–7). They are deprived of the civic right to be met with respect, and of the freedom to decide over their own lives (Young 1990/2011: 53–5).

Cultural imperialism signifies being rendered invisible and simultaneously stereotyped and made the Other. Examples of this were given in Chapter 1, when media representations of disabled people were discussed, and the participants in my study are subject to this as women and as being disabled. The dominant group's perspective is made universal and the subordinated are characterized by deficiency or defect. The subordinated do not have any possibilities to influence the dominant culture either (Young 1990/2011: 58–61). The negative stereotypes are internalized, and the subordinated will regard themselves through the dominant group's perspective – Young refers to the sociologist W. E. B. Du Bois notion of 'double-consciousness' (1903/2007: 8).[4]

One form of othering consists of what Hughes calls 'the non-disabled gaze', a gaze that is 'disfiguring yet it assumes itself to be an act that identifies disfigurement' (1999: 165). According to Hughes the classification that is done by the non-disabled or able-bodied gaze, when the bad and ugly are sorted out, is not neutral but constitutes a moral and aesthetic discourse. Hughes associates the able-bodied gaze with medicalization, through which disabled people are reduced to a diagnosis. The diagnosis confirms the gaze and the subject is completely defeated (Hughes 1999: 165). In an early text by Garland-Thomson, she instead speaks about the stare, which she regards as an intensified gaze, 'the gesture that creates disability as an oppressive social relationship. And as every person with a visible disability knows intimately, managing, deflecting, resisting, or renouncing that stare is part of the daily business of life' (Garland-Thomson 1997: 26). In her book *Staring* Garland-Thomson (2009) opens up for more positive encounters that can result from the stare, which I will come back to later on.

Finally, *violence* is part of the structural oppression. The violent actions are systemic and routine and this makes them oppressive, together with 'the social context surrounding them, which makes them possible and even acceptable' (Young 1990/2011: 61). Furthermore, bullying, threat and scorn fit in here, as well as the awareness that one risks being hit by violence because one belongs to a certain social group. The psychoanalytical explanation for the violence is, according to Young, fear of identity loss. The subordinated challenge or disturb the dominating culture by their mere presence. The violence is institutionalized and legitimized in the sense that it is tolerated (Young 1990/2011: 61–3). Young does not include violence among the faces of oppression that affects disabled people, but I argue that violence in the form of bullying constitutes real oppression at least for younger individuals in this category.

Structure, experience and acting

Previous researchers have criticized phenomenology for its one-sided focus on the individual, and its lack of historical and social context (Young 2002: 427; Turner 2008: 55). This makes it impossible to analyse on a structural level how different bodies to different degrees are controlled and regulated. Moreover, it has been criticized for its belief in the individuals' possibilities to govern their own bodies. 'To talk about our phenomenological rulership of our bodies is to miss the crucial sociological point, namely the regulation of the body in the interests of public health, economy and political order' argues Turner (2008: 55). However, as we have seen in *The Second Sex,* de Beauvoir offers a way of theorizing about the body that includes a power analysis. To elucidate the relation between structural obstacles and the individual's agency I now turn to McNay (2004) and Bourdieu (1984/1993; 1987/1990; 1994/1998).

It is only in lived social relations that abstract social structures and their effects are visible, McNay points out (2004: 177). McNay uses Bourdieu's phenomenological analysis of the social space to understand the relation between material and symbolic power relations. Bourdieu's (1994/1998) concept of habitus explains the 'choices' the social actors make. Habitus is created by the social conditions that are associated with the position the actor has in the social space and is defined as 'this kind of practical sense for what is to be done in a given situation – what is called in sport a "feel" for the game' (Bourdieu 1994/1998: 25). Habitus also constitutes the basis for classificatory schemes according to which, for instance, the good is separated from the bad, and right is separated from wrong (Bourdieu 1994/1998: 8). Actors occupy positions in several mutually demarcated social fields, Bourdieu goes on to say, and one's habitus facilitates entrance to the different fields or renders it more difficult. The positions are determined by access to economic and symbolic capital in each field, but also by the structural relations between different fields (Bourdieu 1984/1993; 1994/1998). The social positions and the distance between them are inscribed in the actors' bodies – just like the individual's experiences, they are embodied and become a part of habitus. Bourdieu has been criticized for his notions of habitus and field being determined by material structures, which hence should be given priority over cultural representations. However, in *In Other Words* (1987/1990) Bourdieu asserts that his intention has always been to overcome the contradiction between the two viewpoints that according to him have dominated social science: objectivism, represented by for example Émile Durkheim and Karl Marx, and subjectivism, for instance phenomenology. The objectivism is inclined to deduce action from social structures, while subjectivism reduces structures to interaction, since only the reality that can be apprehended directly is acknowledged (Bourdieu 1987/1990: 129). But Bourdieu claims that the opposition between, on the one hand, structure and, on the other, the individual's representation of reality is artificial and that the relation rather is dialectic. Social structures constitute a starting-point for the individual's interpretations of his or her experiences and to some extent set limits to the individual's actions, but at the same time the individual's interpretations form the basis of individual and collective efforts to change or maintain structural conditions (Bourdieu 1987/1990: 125–6). The embodiment of the social positions implies a dynamic process, influenced by the material as well as the symbolic (the value that is ascribed to the individual in a certain field). In this process the actors negotiate their identities. According to Bourdieu the objects of the social world include a certain vagueness and indefiniteness. This makes possible a variety of ways of seeing the world, and constitutes 'a base for symbolic struggles for the power to produce and to impose a vision of the legitimate world' (1987/1990: 134). This struggle of the legitimate vision and classification of the world is crucial to bring about change (Bourdieu 1987/1990: 137).

McNay (2004) argues that in order to examine how this symbolic struggle against, for example, structural oppression is carried on, an abstract power analysis is not enough, but action as well as experience must be included in the analysis. Immediate experiences have to be analysed in a social and historical context, and in this way the experiences become coupled with abstract structural power relations (McNay 2004: 184). For instance the history of the disability movement can be seen as a struggle within the field that the movement constitutes, a struggle between different actors – philanthropists, relatives, individuals and groups of disabled persons of different age and gender – regarding the definition of the aim of the movement as well as the actors and their positions. The individual experiences of subordination have been a strong driving force in the changes that have been made.

Identity, experience and difference

Thus, the experience does not mirror the reality, as McNay stresses, but constitutes a culturally constructed and disputed understanding of reality. In and through the experience the subject is formed: the subject is ascribed meaning, at the same time as it ascribes meaning in a dynamic process between structural relations and the individual (Brah 2001: 467). The subject is neither completely determined, nor free to choose between different subject positions. The subject is not unified and unchangeable, but constituted by a number of different subject positions in an ongoing process.

The sociologist Avtar Brah (2001) points out that identity is intimately coupled together with experience, social relations and subjectivity. Identity is formed through the experiences that are gained in social relations:

> Identity may be understood *as that very process by which the multiplicity, contradiction, and instability of subjectivity is signified as having coherence, continuity, stability; as having a core – a continually changing core but the sense of a core nonetheless – that at any given moment is enunciated as the 'I'.*
>
> (Brah 2001: 473, italics in original)

Hence, identity appears to be solid. Personal identity corresponds to some degree to collective identity, but differs from it too. Whereas a person's specific experience of life has its ground in the lived everyday social relations, the collective identity implies a process in which the collective accentuates some common experiences and gives them a specific significance – such as the lived experience of a disabled body – at the expense of other experiences, such as those of a gendered body. The collective's previous heterogeneity is to some extent erased, even if different identities can co-exist and internal power relations remain (Brah 2001: 473). The collective identity that is being constructed is historically specific and contextual. The announcement is a political process in which the collective identity is created. A collective history (economic, political and cultural) is interpreted and emphasized. However, for disabled persons a collective identity is not self-evident. Due to this, the disability sports movement can, as we will see, have great significance in the creation of a collective identity.

The collective identity can only be created through negation and exclusion: we define ourselves by saying that we are *not* homosexual, Muslims or disabled (Pratt 1991; Fundberg 2003: 186–8). Brah (2001) uses the notion of 'difference as social relation'. This notion 'refers to the ways in which difference is constituted and organized into *systematic* relations through economic, cultural and political discourses and institutional practices' (Brah 2001: 467, italics in original). The notion concerns relations on both a macro level (economic, cultural and political relations on a global or national level) and on a micro level (in a household, at a place of work or in a sports club) (2001: 468). Brah continues:

> Some constructions of difference, such as racism, posit fixed and immutable boundaries between groups signified as inherently different. Other constructions may present difference as relational, contingent and variable. In other words, difference is not always a marker of hierarchy and oppression. Therefore, it is a contextually contingent question whether difference pans out as inequity, exploitation and oppression *or as* egalitarianism, diversity and democratic forms of political agency.
>
> (Brah 2001: 475, italics in original)

Thus, constructions of difference are not negative per se. Questions have to be asked regarding how the Other is constructed: Is disability constructed as lack and inability or as one difference among many others (Ghai 2012: 273)? Who defines the difference? What underlying norms are necessary in order to construct the difference? And what social practices and which policy are legitimized by the created difference (Brah 2001: 465–7)?

To sum up, I have shown by means of the concept of embodiment how nature/culture and body/self are linked together, that is the first two arguments in this chapter. The various situatedness of bodies results in various practices and bodily styles. In the interaction with the surroundings the individual becomes an active and acting subject. However, the agency is not free from conflict. It can be hindered or limited by other actors or structural power relations (such as the gender order in a society or a gender regime in an organization), and this in its turn leads to oppression. I use of four of Young's five faces of oppression to refine the analysis: powerlessness, marginalization, cultural imperialism and violence. The individual also has a responsibility to act, instead of accepting the subordinate position. The ability to act must be regarded in the light of how major the limitations and great the hindrances are. Through the embodiment of social obstacles and through the acting, which is done through the body as a situation, the central position of the body in political struggle is shown. The collective identity that often forms the basis in the striving for social change is created through negation and exclusion.

Methodological considerations

In this second part of the chapter I present the notions and discussions in standpoint theory that I have found most relevant to my study. I will explain how I went about approaching the field of research, collected data and which methods were used. To capture bodily experiences and give the participants control over which experiences to convey and in what way, I chose to combine participant observation and semi-structured interviews with video diaries. Finally the process of interpretation is described. To elucidate the conditions of understanding I make use of hermeneutics.

Feminist standpoint theory

The aim of the study is to explore young women's lived experiences of a body that on the one hand is regarded as deviant, and on the other hand is seen as accomplished. Early on questions were raised about the possibility to understand the experiences of subordinated groups and about the specific character of these experiences, which led me to feminist standpoint theory. This theory was developed during the 1970s and 1980s, and had its origin partly in the political methodology of women's lib, partly in Marxism. Its proponents criticized the view of science as abstract, rationalistic and universal, pointed out the connection between knowledge production and power, and argued that all theory of science, epistemology and methodology are pursued from specific standpoints, and hence are normative (Harding 1997: 382; 2004: 1–2; Hill Collins 1997: 375). The historian of science Donna Haraway (1988) uses the notion 'situated knowledge production'. She writes:

> I am arguing for politics and epistemologies of location, positioning, and situating, where partiality and not universality is the condition of being heard to make rational knowledge claims. ... I am arguing for the view from a body, always a complex, contradictory, structuring, and structured body, versus the view from above, from nowhere, from simplicity.
>
> (Haraway 1988: 589)

By accentuating the physical body – with or without impairment – as the starting point for knowledge production, the social, cultural and political situatedness of knowledge becomes evident. Feminist standpoint theory has an explicit emancipatory aim – knowledge and politics, which often have been kept separate to guarantee the neutrality of the researcher, are here linked together.

Is knowledge, then, produced by the situated bodies of a subordinated group different from the one that is produced by dominant groups? The

sociologist Dorothy Smith indicates that another sort of knowledge, not previously formulated, can be manifested: 'a knowledge of what is tacit, known
in the doing, and often not yet discursively appropriated (and often seen as
uninteresting, unimportant, and routine)' (1997: 395). Subordinated groups
generally have another access to knowledge about one's own position and an
interest in using the knowledge (New 1998: 368). It is also pointed out that
dominant groups have a greater interest in withholding their group affiliation
and the effect it has on social relations (Harding 1997: 384; Hill Collins 1997:
380). By for example maintaining the idea about able bodies as completely
different from disabled bodies, the frightening thought of the vulnerability of
one's own body can be kept at a distance.

As an able-bodied researcher studying the experiences of disabled young
women, an important question for this project is the possibility to understand
other people. Several feminist researchers reject the thought that dominant
groups or other subordinated groups could never understand experiences that
they have not had themselves (Trinh 1989; Narayan 2004). The filmmaker and
postcolonial theorist Trinh T. Minh-ha claims that many dominant people have
now understood that they cannot speak 'for the other', and that has become 'an
excuse for their complacent ignorance and their reluctance to involve themselves in the issue' (1989: 80). However, it is the responsibility of dominant
groups to try to understand: 'The understanding of difference is a shared
responsibility, which requires a minimum of willingness to reach out to the
unknown' (Trinh 1989: 85). The philosopher Uma Narayan (2004) stresses
the importance of emotions in the knowledge process. Feminists have claimed
that subordinated groups often have a more critical perspective on their
situation, stemming from 'critical emotional responses that subjects experience
vis-à-vis their life situation' (Narayan 2004: 218). Taken together, this type of
emotions, the critical insights generated from the subordinated position and
the contextual nature of knowledge lead to a specific epistemological position.
Narayan goes on to say that the idea that researchers only can study and
understand their own position results in relativism. However, the understanding of others can run into obstacles: 'Those who display sympathy as
outsiders often fail both to understand fully the emotional complexities of
living as a member of an oppressed group and to carry what they have
learned and understood about one situation to the way they perceive another'
(Narayan 2004: 220). Thus, the understanding is always partial.

During the 1970s and 1980s ideas similar to feminist standpoint theory
were developed in other social justice movements based on, for instance,
'race'/ethnicity or sexuality (Harding 2004: 3). As a consequence of the critique
from lesbian, black and postcolonial feminists, the discussion within standpoint
theory has in some cases been widened to deal with subordinated groups in
general. But if the supposedly homogeneous group of women is abandoned,
does this lead to an infinite amount of standpoints? Is it at all possible to
pursue a policy with social change as a goal? From black and postcolonial
feminists came also the idea of coalitions between different subordinated

groups (Combahee River Collective 1977; Mohanty 1984). The sociologist Patricia Hill Collins points out that groups that occupy different subordinated positions in power hierarchies can have similar experiences: 'Groups who share common placement in hierarchical power relations also share common experiences in such power relations. Such shared angles of vision lead those in similar social locations to be predisposed to interpret these experiences in a comparable fashion' (Hill Collins 1997: 377). These can form a basis for coalitions, and social change becomes possible.

In an effort to reconcile the dichotomy between bodies seen as fully functional and those that are seen as damaged and tragic, I identify with feministic standpoint theory's emancipatory ambition. I also argue, following Trinh (2002: 219), that it is my responsibility, belonging to a dominant group, to try to understand subordinate's position and to try to communicate experiences and knowledge that previously have been silenced or regarded as unimportant. The core of standpoint theory as well as that of this research project is that knowledge emanates from the situated body. I am a woman, just like the participants in my study. But I was older than the participants, which gave me a verbal, experiential and educational advantage. The participants have physical impairments, while I do not. On the contrary, I belong to the naturalized and invisible group with 'normal' bodies. What epistemological consequences does this have? Since I lack the emotional experiences that the participants have, extra carefulness is required during the analysis (Narayan 2004: 218, 220). I will come back to an empirical example of this below, when I discuss the conditions of understanding.

The fieldwork: Material and selection

I began this research project with a pilot study. I spent four days and nights at a disability sports camp for young people with physical or intellectual impairments (or both), doing participant observations and semi-structured interviews. After the camp I contacted disability sports clubs and conducted additional interviews with young sporting women. Participant observations were also made at four disability sports contests – one national and three international.

In total, ten semi-structured interviews were conducted with young women aged 15 to 28, three of them at the camp. They lasted 30–80 minutes, the greater part of them about one hour. At the camp interviews were also conducted with three boys, aged 10–15, and (more or less informally) with five leaders, coaches and volunteers. A small camcorder and a lightweight tripod were lent for roughly two months to three of the participants, who made one video diary each. The diaries were approximately 85–110 minutes in length. That three out of ten interviewees made video diaries means that they are more frequently quoted.

The participants' parents were white and were of working- or middle-class background. When questioned whether they had a girl or boyfriend, the young women either said no or answered that they had a boyfriend. They played sledge hockey, wheelchair basketball, table tennis, and rode on horseback. In Sweden, team sports for disabled people differ from team sports for able-bodied people. Since female teams are rare, women must play in mixed teams, where they are in the minority. To capture this particular situation in disability sports, both team and individual sports were included in the study. Two participants were competing on an international level, and the rest of them at national level. When I made the selection for the video diaries the aim was to get a spread as regards class, congenital or acquired impairment, degree of impairment and strategies that came up during the interviews.

Methods

The reason I chose a camp for the pilot study was to get an initial understanding of the field: the language, routines and power structures (Kvale 2007: 40). In this study the observations have chiefly come to function as a means to make myself acquainted with the field. However, the concluding analysis chapter, which deals with the young women's experiences of the disability sports movement, begins with a long excerpt from my field notes.

Instead the interviews and video diaries constitute the basis for the analysis. To attain a relaxed atmosphere I let the interviewees decide by themselves where the interviews would take place. Three chose to meet at their disability sports club, two in their homes and two at a sports centre during a tournament. The rest of them were interviewed at the camp. To begin with, I presented the project, its design and purpose. I explained that the material would be anonymized, their participation was voluntary, they could choose not to answer questions and they could withdraw their participation at any time, all in accordance with the requirement of informed consent in social science research (Bryman 2012: 138–42). In addition, since some of the interviewees at the sport camp were minors, their parents gave written consent before the camp. I used a thematically ordered interview guide, but the interviewees were encouraged to speak freely. After each interview I made field notes about where we met and my impressions of the meeting. All interviews were taped, transcribed and then analysed. Repetitions and some colloquial speech have been removed from the quotations to facilitate the reading (Kvale 2007: 132–3).

Feminist methodological discussions have challenged traditional ideas within qualitative method and emphasized the hierarchic relation between the researcher and the researched (see Skeggs 1997: 18–9; Harding 2004: 3; Narayan 2004: 217–8). Given that, the participants in this study are treated as knowledgeable subjects/actors rather than passive knowledge objects. I tried to avoid being yet another adult making decisions for them, and instead give them autonomy and an adult's subject position. Moreover, I tried to develop a way to catch the experiences from my participant's standpoint. My background as an artist, with photography, video and performance as the main means of expression, contributed to the choice of visual method. Although there is a growing interest in visual methods in social research – the sociologist Catherine Kohler Riessman speaks of a 'visual turn' (2007: 142) – these methods have not yet spread to mainstream social science (Pauwels 2010: 546), and is an unexploited resource in research on disability and sport (Smith and Sparkes 2013: 344). One purpose of using video diaries as a method for data collection was to increase the participants' autonomy in relation to me, the researcher. Besides, the video diaries made it possible to catch bodily language and facial expressions. Kohler Riessman stresses the potential of visual methods: 'Visual representations of experience – in photographs, performance art, and other media – can enable others to see as a participant sees, and to feel' (2007: 142). Gazes, a forehead with a frown, a gesticulating hand or a changed distance to the camera can convey a changed emotional state and strengthen or contradict an interpretation.

While the interviews dealt with the informants' relation to physical activity, their body, and their physical capacity, the scope of the video diaries was broader. The informants were asked to videotape their daily lives, as though they were going to show them to a stranger. As they had the opportunity in this way to decide for themselves which experiences they wanted to communicate and how, subjects that I had not broached or had dealt with only briefly during the interviews were brought up in the diaries. For example, I saved the question about what diagnosis or injury they had until the end of the interview, to show them that I saw them as complex individuals whose identity was composed of several different aspects, of which the diagnosis only was one part. But in the video diaries all three of them talk about surgical operations, about how the impairment affects their everyday life and appearance, about pain and how walking or using a wheelchair are a strain on the body, and about complications such as frequent urinary infections. Furthermore, media representations of disabled people were also discussed in two of the diaries, as we saw in Chapter 1. My interpretation was that these subjects played an important role in the participants' everyday life, and resulted in a couple of new questions during the last interviews and a slightly new direction of the analysis. The video diaries were transcribed too.

In order to anonymize the material, all proper names have been changed, names of places have been removed and in some cases additional details have been changed. As there are only a few female sledge hockey players in Sweden, the participating sledge hockey players are treated as basketball players in the analysis. Since both sports are fast and tough and the sledge as well as the wheelchair can be overturned when tackling, my opinion is that this will have no effect on the analysis. With these anonymizations done, I do not think that information which may be experienced as ethically sensitive will cause the participants any harm either in the long term or in the short term (Bryman 2012: 135–8).

Interpretation of data: Pre-understanding and the Hermeneutic Circle

> I sit at the side of the gymnasium during the training session in the morning. It's quite boring and a bit absurd to just sit and watch, so after the table tennis warm-up I change to training clothes. I play floorball since there is no place for me at the table tennis. … Our team (which consists of one player with an intellectual impairment and me and one more without any impairment) are leading against the other team; all of them have intellectual impairments. I realize that I think that we must help the other team, as if I was playing against small kids. But after the break the other team wins with a big goal difference.
>
> (Field notes at sports camp, day 2)

All actors have individual prerequisites and limitations due to their situatedness. For the researcher this leads to specific research interests that give the research a direction and influence what the researcher can perceive (Ahmed 2006: 29). The philosopher and hermeneutic Hans-Georg Gadamer calls this phenomenon *prejudices* or *pre-understanding* of the world (1986/2006: 51). The pre-understanding has three constituent parts, according to the philosophers Nils Gilje and Harald Grimen (2007). Firstly, language and concepts bring out some phenomena and hide others, which leads different individuals to see different things. Before I began this research project, I was not aware that the notion 'able-bodied' was missing in the Swedish language, which made it difficult to see bodies that were characterized by 'ablebodiedness'. Secondly, belief systems and ideas have an effect on what we regard as evident or as a problem, and how we look at society, other people and nature. Insights such as the one in the excerpt above, in which my ideas about people with intellectual impairments become visible, are recurrent in my field notes from the participant observations. Finally, the way we act is influenced by previous personal experiences of how, for instance, other people act (Gilje and Grimen 2007: 180–3). The experiences are, as we have seen earlier, gained through the situated body.

The pre-understanding is not always conscious. The different components in the pre-understanding form a whole or a system that can be more or less coherent. The whole is changeable, but it is a slow process; the pre-understanding changes step by step as we get new experiences that not fit in the system (Gilje and Grimen 2007: 183–5), as when I realize that I do not need to pay extra attention to the opponents in the floorball match. This can happen, for example, in the meeting with another person or when reading a text: 'the interpreter and the text each possess his, her, or its own horizon and every moment of understanding represents a fusion of these horizons' (Gadamer 1986/2006: 45). In a meeting between two persons who both consciously aim at understanding, a shift of their pre-understanding takes place as their horizons fuse. Gadamer even contends that understanding is only possible if one's prejudices are at stake (1986/2006: 45).

Narayan's (2004) line of argument about the importance of emotions in the knowledge process can contribute to a deeper understanding of the notion of pre-understanding. One reason for its sluggish changeability could be the emotional aspects of personal experiences. In other words, if I do not have emotional experiences of being treated with prejudice, becoming aware of my prejudices on one single occasion is not enough to change my pre-understanding (see Narayan 2004: 220–1).

A phenomenon acquires its meaning in a specific context; hence it can only be understood in this setting (Gadamer 1986/2006: 46). The hermeneutic circle signifies the connection and movement between that which is to be interpreted, the context and the researcher's pre-understanding. Interpretations are motivated by reference to these three components. It is impossible to go beyond or outside the hermeneutic circle in the motivation, to make 'the god trick of seeing everything from nowhere' (Haraway 1988: 581). The interpretation implies a spiral movement between the three, and between whole and details (Gilje and Grimen 2007: 187–9).

The central concepts of this research project come from different parts of the hermeneutic circle. The use of the notions of normality and autonomy has grown out of the analysis of the material. In a previous study I explored how femininities were constructed among young football girls going for the top level (Apelmo 2005). This probably made me especially observant when the participants in this project talked about themselves as young women. Oliver's frequently cited theory about the personal tragedy could explain some of the emotions that my interviewees came back to, such as pity and benevolence (1996: 89). The choice of phenomenology as a theoretical framework rather results from my readings of the theoretical discussions in disability studies, and particularly in the British disability movement, about the body's role in research and politics. One of the questions that I included in the last interviews was about technology. It had its origin in the analysis of the interviews and the video diaries in which wheelchairs and sports equipment were recurrent themes, even though I did not specifically ask about it. For the discussion about technology I found Haraway's (1991) metaphor of the cyborg useful as a complement to phenomenology.

Notes

1 For the inclusion of the body in the above-mentioned fields and about philosophy and religion see Michel Foucault 1982/2000; Susan Bordo 2004: xxi; Bryan S. Turner 2008: 5–6, 18–19; on classical sociology see Turner 2008: 33–5; about postmodern feminism see Bordo 2004: 227–9; on classical sociology and the gendered dichotomy between body/consciousness and the effects it has had for feminist sociology see Lisa Adkins 2004: 142–3; on disability research see Liz Crow 1996; Bill Hughes and Kevin Paterson 1997; Edward Hall 2000; Claire Edwards and Rob Imrie 2003.

2 It is remarkable that in Turner's *The Body and Society*, a standard work in the sociology of the body, neither 'disability' nor 'impairment' is to be found in the book's index in the third revised edition from 2008. However, in *Handbook of Disability Studies* (2001) Turner contributes the chapter 'Disability and the Sociology of the Body'.

3 De Beauvoir's description of how women, out of convenience, can accept and thus participate in their own subordination has similarities to STIL's view of how

disabled people in some cases accept the medicalization: 'The clinical picture is easily turned into a part of one's own identity. As sick you do not have to work, nothing is expected of you and no demands are made on you. It can be comfortable to escape the demands from the majority groups of society and instead lower the expectations of your own life by disregarding the resources that you actually have (Berg 2008: 86, author's translation).

4 Du Bois writes about the situation of black people in the US at the beginning of the twentieth century and 'this sense of always looking at one's self through the eyes of others' (1903/2007: 8).

3 'I am just like everyone else'

Between dependence and autonomy

Previous youth research has examined how prevailing ideas of youthfulness influence young people. Youthfulness is often regarded as something positive and a desirable ideal, associated with health, beauty, vitality, strength, hope and happiness (Ganetz 1991: 8; Barron 1995: 24; Hughes et al 2005; Slater 2012). Young people are often compared with and compare themselves with this idealized view of youthfulness, yet it rarely corresponds to their own experiences of their everyday life. This concerns the body as well as the life situation taken as a whole. 'Although the ideal body is always young, the young body is not always ideal', as the disability researcher Jenny Slater puts it (2012: 201). Commercial interests, media, educational institutions and the labour market put pressure on young people (Ganetz 1991: 8; Sandvin 2008: 72). High unemployment rates and difficulties getting into the housing market have led to increased dependence on parents and the institutions of the welfare state. As unemployed they have to be constantly available for labour market measures, such as courses, occupational training and therapy (Sandvin 2008: 72).

This description of the situation for young people is valid for disabled youth too, but the discrepancy between desired youthfulness and everyday life experiences is even larger. The qualities associated with disability are contrary to the above-mentioned signifiers of youth: ugliness, tragedy, asexuality, invalidity and frailty, and, as the sociologists Bill Hughes, Rachel Russell and Kevin Paterson (2005: 12) maintain, all this makes the two of them incompatible. As a consequence of attitudinal and structural barriers, young disabled people run a higher risk of being permanently excluded and marginalized (Sandvin 2008: 72–3). They may also have continuous need of assistance and help, as Barron (1995) points out in an interview study with men and women with physical impairments aged 17 to 24. Hence they are marginalized both as young in relation to adults and as disabled young people in comparison to able-bodied youth. They may, for instance, be dependent on their parents to be able to get to certain leisure activities. Further to this, they have limited options because some activities are not accessible, and as a result they are reduced to organized special activities (Barron 1995: 35; see also Hughes et al

2005). The environments of these special activities are often characterized by high social control, in comparison to alternative places where subcultural identities can be developed (Sandvin 2008: 73). Due to inaccessible public transport and built environments, young disabled people may also be denied access to public spaces of consumption, and hence cannot choose among the same consumer lifestyles as their able-bodied peers (Hughes et al 2005). Thus, compared with the picture of youthfulness, disabled young people and their everyday life risk being interpreted stereotypically – both by themselves and by others – as characterized by isolation and loneliness (Barron 1995: 25).

Adolescence is also characterized by the search for one's own identity and detachment from the parents, which can cause emotional stress and anxiety (Ganetz 1991: 9–10; Barron 1995: 26). As the sociologist Gisela Helmius (2004) claims, disabled children often require more aid than other children and the parents are often regarded as the self-evident providers of help. The parents' protection can also aim at avoiding disappointments for the children. However, the parents' care risks resulting in the children being hindered from acting on their own initiative and taking care of everyday tasks. Their freedom is limited by what Barron (1995: 85–92) calls 'intrusive parental support'. When they become teenagers the separation from the parents is rendered more difficult, as is the creation of an identity and a life of their own (Helmius 2004: 104–6). Becoming an adult is often considered synonymous with being more independent, which is looked upon as normal. If a grown-up individual is not conceived as autonomous it often leads to an infantilization of the individual (Barron 1995: 57–8).

There is debate within the disability movement and disability studies regarding independence versus dependence. On the one hand, there is a strong critique of the presumption that a disability inevitably leads to dependence. It is argued that the degree of dependence is related to the context and in what way help, if any, is given (Morris 1995: 87; Thomas 2007: 96). This critique could possibly be true of the above children and youth research too and its assumption that young disabled people are dependent on their parents. How is this dependence measured and how is a dependence on practical help distinguished from, say, emotional dependence? Furthermore it is claimed that professionals in medical and social institutions strengthen the dependence, partly by preventing self-determination, partly by contributing to the medicalization of disabled people and the view of them as being in need of care and support (Thomas 2007: 97). Professionals can, for instance, make decisions without consulting with the person concerned, or, if it is a question of young people, only consult with their parents. Besides, independence is often defined as being capable of doing everything by oneself, while the disability movement defines it as being capable of choosing and controlling the assistance needed (Barron 1995: 61; Morris 1995: 74–5; Berg 2008: 19). According to STIL it is not what or how much assistance a disabled person needs that determines the degree of independence, but what quality of life he or she has with the assistance (Berg 2008: 19).

On the other hand, it is claimed that a complex reality of mutual relations is simplified when the caregiver is separated from the cared-about, and the latter is considered dependent on the former (Morris 1995). What is more, the social ideal of independence is questioned as a whole. Garland-Thomson criticizes the one-sided aim of feminism for independence: 'One of the most pervasive feminist assumptions that undermines some disabled women's struggle is the liberal ideology of autonomy and independence that fuels the broader impulse toward female empowerment' (1997: 26). A shift towards other social values, such as reciprocity, is considered necessary 'if *all* the disabled are to be fully integrated into society without symbolizing failure' (Wendell 1997: 273, italics in original). Otherwise, there is a risk that severely disabled people are ignored and depreciated. Endless time can also be spent on completing trivial tasks by oneself, time that could have been used for more meaningful activities (Wendell 1997: 273).

Thus, the question of dependence and independence is more complex than it may seem at first. Parents (and professionals) can limit young disabled people's freedom and their agency by making decisions for them (not with them) or by exaggerated care. But care and assistance can also enable the disabled youth to make their own decisions, to achieve a high quality of life, and time and energy to realize their projects. Associating dependence and independence with certain phases of life also involves a simplification of a complex reality.

'A completely ordinary childhood'

Hanna, 25 years old, plays table tennis and works for a disability sports club as leader of a girls' group. The first quotation is from the beginning of the interview. I have asked her to tell me about herself, her background and family:

> [I had] a completely ordinary childhood, like everyone else. I had no contact with the disability movement at all. ... Above all, I was lucky enough to grow up in a sports family, I suppose. Besides, my parents treated me just like they treated my siblings. I should help myself. Now it's fun when you look at pictures. I always had wounds here and here [points at her nose and chin]. I always fell, you know. The skin on my nose and chin was always scraped off.
>
> (Hanna, 25, interview)

The ordinariness is the background against which the interview and story about the rest of Hanna's life stands. One expression of her ordinariness was not being part of the disability movement. Hanna points out that her parents did not give her special treatment over her siblings and that she lived just like others of her age. Normality, being 'like everyone else', is coupled with capacity and independence, to 'help myself'. The wounds in her face could be interpreted as a result of an active life, but Hanna also connects it to her tendency to fall, to her impairment. Hanna emphasizes her background in sports too. Her dad was crazy about sport, played table tennis and was a football coach. Her elderly sister and brother also practised several sports. Hanna played tennis, table tennis and miniature golf and trained both football and ice hockey in boys' team. During the breaks in school she was always at the football or bandy field with the boys when the rest of 'the girls were dancing'. She continues:

> There were girls who went to [the neighbouring village] and trained [in the girls' team], you know. But I thought it was much more fun [to train with the boys], I was also a bit of a tomboy when I was small. I was together with the boys a lot. I don't know if that's the reason why I never got into trouble. I was never left outside. Because it was like, if you were great pals with the boys, you were sort of accepted, I'm afraid. I have never been exposed to any bullying. And I always took part in everything. I have been on the go and I have gone in for sports.
>
> (Hanna, 25, interview)

Hanna went through childhood and adolescence without being bullied, and she gives two explanations for this. Firstly, she says that it is positive for a girl to be associated with boys – girls who had boys as pals were accepted. Secondly, she states that extensive training and the fact that she took part in the same activities as others of the same age also gave her status. The implicit meaning in the quotation, as I interpret it, is that as disabled the norm would have been to *not* be accepted. Further on during the interview Hanna adds that everybody in the village where she lived knew her: 'The coaches were parents of my pals and friends of my parents ... everybody knew who I was and about my situation.' In the small place where she lived, she escaped the prejudices that could have caused unknown people not to accept her.

Two more interviewees tell about how their parents brought them up to be able to manage everyday tasks. Sara, who is 19 years old, grew up in a small place in the countryside too, and describes her childhood as physically active:

> On the other side we had a football field and there we hung out. And a field that dad cut with the lawnmower so we could be there and play. ... Everything, from running in the water sprinkler and everything that was fun. ... I always stood and played tennis against the carport.
>
> (Sara, 19, interview)

Sara went cycling and played football and rounders with the neighbour's children and her father facilitated the pleasure-filled play by cutting the grass on the field. But her father also made demands on her: 'I might also have been told to get up and fetch the vacuum cleaner from upstairs, and almost stumble over the hose when going downstairs ... He [dad] has never given special treatment to me over my siblings', Sara tells. However, just like

Hanna, Sara risked falling. Felicia, 28 years old and a wheelchair user, recalls what happened when she, as a small child, got her injury:

> Then they came to adjust our home. It was a lot of wall-to-wall carpet at that time. 'We will change to parquet flooring.' My father said, 'No, no, no, no! She must fight! She has to fight to make her way.' I got really strong arms. Until fifth or sixth grade I beat all the boys both in my class and in the class above at arm wrestling.
> *That was fun!*
> Wounded their male pride [laughs]; it was great fun! Then the boys caught up, but until then I had terrific arm muscles.
>
> (Felicia, 28, interview)

Felicia proudly tells me about the muscular strength that was the consequence of her parents' wish that she should be able to help herself in everyday life, and she enjoys recalling how she beat all the boys. In the interaction with the surroundings she has had to fight (against wall-to-wall carpets among other things), and these experiences have been sedimented in the body, and materialized as muscles as well, shaping how she experiences her body (Moi 1999: 68). On the occasion of the interviews Felicia was the only one of these three using a wheelchair – when Sara four years later made a video diary she had begun to use a wheelchair too. Hence, the parents' way of upbringing does not seem to have anything to do with the degree of impairment. This is confirmed by Barron's study, which shows that a 'normalized' childhood in which the child has been taught not to deviate or ask for help and to conceal the impairment, is not dependent on the type or extent of the impairment (1995: 121).

What these three young women's memories of their childhoods have in common is the joy experienced when doing physical activities as well as the desire for normality and the demonstration of strength. They train, play and compete with or against the boys, which further proves their physical compe- tence. Their parents' have forced them to fight, which is presented as positive. Pain is left out of their narratives; instead Hanna's and Sara's stories about how they fall and hurt themselves are examples of their struggle. Indirectly, they distance themselves from weakness and, in Hanna's case, distancing from other disabled people appears to be a condition of being normal. The consequence is an almost exaggerated accentuation of normality. Present in these descriptions of childhood plays is, as I interpret the empirical material, the word 'despite' that recurred in the narratives of the hero that Ljuslinder (2002: 119) found in her analysis of disability discourses on SVT. The interviewees did not need special treatment by their parents; the other children have accepted them and they are physically capable, all 'despite' their disabilities. They stand out as young disabled heroes of everyday life (Wendell 2007).

In her autobiography the disability activist and psychotherapist Harilyn Rousso (2013) describes how her upbringing affected her view of her own body and relations to others. Her mother wanted to normalize Rousso and the way she walked and talked, to avoid strangers' stares and questions. This well-meaning protection had as its consequence that Rousso saw herself as defective. Like my interviewees she tried to 'prove that I'm like everyone else – that is, "normal", human' (Rousso 2013: 79–82, 97). The mother's efforts to achieve her daughter's independence (for instance expressed in her insistence on Rousso going to college in another city) led to an exaggerated fear of dependency that Rousso still struggles with (2013: 54). When the parents of my interviewees treat them just like their non-disabled siblings and teach them to fight, this can be interpreted as their attempts to normalize their daughters.

'Who wants to bring mum on a night out?'

Several of the participants in the study who also work as sports coaches mention parents who give too much help to their children as a problem. One of them is Sara:

> I was four years old when I inserted a catheter by myself for the first time. My parents told me 'Now it's about time, you should be able to go to the lavatory by yourself. I can't help you all the time.' I always thought it was normal, something most [children] do. I have met young people who are 15 years old, who are not in need of assistance or help from their parents, but still get help with this. I really think that's a pity. Because there will be a time when they too are interested in having a night out. And then you have a problem. ... Who wants to bring mum on a night out [small laugh]?
>
> (Sara, 23, video diary)

Sara gesticulates repeatedly with her hand in the air, as if to stress her argumentation. With a concrete example, she illustrates how the transition from childhood, when most children get help with everyday tasks from their parents, to an independent teenage life can be rendered difficult for disabled young people. The example appears to be extra striking since it deals with the intimate sphere: being able to go to the lavatory by oneself. Having bodily integrity is one more aspect often associated with adulthood and independence. The autonomy and maintenance of her integrity were facilitated for Sara as her parents made it clear very early that they will not be constantly present, long before adolescence when autonomy is considered to express normality. Julia, who is 26 years old, speaks about her experiences as coach in a team sport:

> Basketball is tough. You butt each other and you fall. ... Maybe I'm a bit mean now, but I very seldom meet disabled people [with congenital impairments] who do what they are supposed to do on the court. It is difficult, you know. They become spoiled at home; they get everything handed to them on a silver platter. And then, suddenly, playing

basketball, you will go away by yourself, you have to help yourself, you will stay at non-accessible hotels, you will bath in a tub and there are many people who go 'oh!' ... Their parents are with them and that's great fun, sure enough, but there's a lot of, like: 'oh, will you jump over to the chair', and you know like that, and I really can't handle it. You should shoulder your own responsibility I think. ... I don't think it's their fault; it's the parents' fault. They help them far too much.

(Julia, 26, interview)

Wheelchair basketball is a tough team sport and during matches it requires that the players make their own decisions and are fearless when they go in for tackles. Julia thinks that those who get too much help from their parents have difficulties managing practical duties while travelling during competitions. Julia exemplifies with taking a bath, which makes one think of bodily integrity as well. But it is not only about tasks that they have not learnt to take care of by themselves; she also considers how they have troubles acting on the basketball court. Julia associates the 'spoiling' specifically with the parents of those who have a congenital impairment. If the parents in the three introductory quotations, who encouraged the children to fight, appeared as good examples, Julia thinks that these parents are doing wrong.

Both Sara and Julia dissociate themselves from those who are more dependent on their parents. By doing this, they also heighten their own self-esteem, and move closer to the subject position of the normal (Deal 2003: 904).

Mothers and their daughters

At my very first meeting with the field at the sports camp for children and adolescents, there was talk about the problem of overprotective parents. In a recorded conversation with David, one of the leaders, he saw the overprotection as one reason why it is so hard to recruit children to disability sports: 'Today, it all depends on the parents. I'm afraid that they overprotect their disabled children. ... They don't believe they can do as much as they ought to, and in fact can do. So, they keep them at home instead.' During breakfast David, Oskar (one of the coaches) and I continue the talk:

David: I think the girls are more overprotected than the boys. The moms hold on tight to their daughters. They are a bit tougher, the boys. ...

It's the first time; you almost have to pick them up by car. If they just have been there once, they will come back. ...

Oskar: You prefer to drive the daughters to the training more often than the boys. The boys, it feels more secure. ... And then, they may come more often to the training, more spontaneously, they pop off by themselves. The girls are more dependent on their parents to get to their training, just because of how society is. You don't let your daughters walk to training late in the night, for instance. The boys can get on in a completely different way.

(David, leader, and Oskar, coach, recorded conversation)

David and Oskar link the, in their opinion, exaggerated care to gender – they both state that girls are more overprotected than boys, and besides, David refers to mothers as being more inclined to protect their daughters. The association between mothers and care was also made by Sara, as she asked herself, 'Who wants to bring mum on a night out?' and is also confirmed by Rousso (2013), who has been working for many years with projects for disabled women and girls in the US. Through her work she has met several young disabled women whose mothers 'won't let go, believing that they are their daughter's best caregivers and their most reliable protectors' (2013: 54). David talks about boys as tough, as if it was a character trait. Oskar also points out an external factor: it is considered more dangerous for girls to be out at night. If girls are not allowed to move around by themselves, they become dependent on parents who must have the time and the will to drive them to different activities.

Malin and Natalie, both 15, have their mothers as personal assistants. Natalie's mother is always with her when Natalie goes riding. She helps her daughter to mount the horse and walks alongside during the riding. 'I have one of those belts, and she walks by my side, holding me by the belt', Natalie explains. Malin uses the 'we' form when she talks about her physical activities and decisions that have been taken regarding the activities. She began playing table tennis when she was 13 years old. When asked how she got information about the sport she answers, 'Ping-pong, I don't really know how we got into that either.' Malin still goes to her intermediate school once a week and has lessons in physical education (PE) by herself with her former PE teacher. I ask her how come, and she answers, 'We began with this, you know, when I was in [intermediate] school, just so that I would get some extra exercise. And then we thought it was so good so we continued even when I began senior level. And we have done it since then.' It is not completely clear who 'we' refers to, but it is obvious in these two quotations that adults – parents and/or teachers? – are involved in the decisions about Malin's physical activities. In her study, Barron (1995) gives examples of the use of 'we' too. A young woman tells Barron in an interview that she has entered a folk high school and 'we [the young woman and her mother] thought that this is a beginning' (1995: 111). Barron claims that the girl is so used to others making decisions for her so that she has become completely passive. She is one of the young women who, according to Barron, are characterized by resignation. When Barron poses questions about individual choices and their autonomy they react with confusion; they never seem to have thought about it. An alternative interpretation of the statement above is that the mother supports the girl in the decision to enter a new school. This is a first step, 'a beginning' in a separation where the next step, as the young women say later in the interview, is to move away from home (Barron 1995: 111; see also Sellerberg 1999: 66–7).[1] The 'we' who contributed when Malin began to play table tennis and got extra exercise can also be interpreted as support for her, so she can devote herself to what she really likes to do.

An ambiguous field

Ingela, 17 years old, has taken precisely this first step away from her parents. When I initially tried to get in contact with Ingela I got her mobile phone number from her father, and as I called, I found out that her father had recorded the message on the answering machine. When I came to the disability sports centre where we were going to see each other, I met a young woman in a wheelchair at the entrance. In my field notes after the interview I write:

> I see a girl in a wheelchair in the corridor. She looks at me with her head bowed down, I think that it may be my interviewee, but I hesitate. She doesn't take any initiative. I walk into the café where we have decided to meet. Some people are sitting there holding a meeting. I ask for Ingela and it turns out to be the girl in the corridor. She enters the café and asks them where we can sit. We end up in the corner of a huge empty gym.
>
> (Field notes after interview with Ingela, 17)

It was not until I had asked in the café that I understood that the girl in the entrance actually was Ingela. I turned around and introduced myself. Considering that I was the stranger who came to the club in which Ingela had been active since she was eight years old, I got the impression that she was a bit shy. During the interview the door suddenly opened and a man, who I soon understood was her father, came in. He said that he only wondered where we were sitting, and we said hello.

The family is very present in Ingela's leisure time. Her father is employed as leader and coach in the club. Ingela's elderly brother, who does not have any impairment, is also a member of the team. When Ingela was abroad in a competition 'my sister came with me as a sort of assistant. ... She helps a lot.' The mother too is involved in Ingela's training: 'sometimes my mum also comes along and helps out,' Ingela recounts. However, this is nothing unusual in organized sports, in which parents' non-profit work as leaders, functionaries or with practical duties such as driving and washing clothes often is essential for the activities to go on (Patriksson and Wagnsson 2004: 7). In the interview Ingela often gives curt answers such as 'I don't know' or 'It's fun.' However, on a few occasions she develops her answers a bit more as in the following quotation, in which she tells me about her move eight months earlier, when she entered the upper secondary school in a city just over an hour's trip from home:

> Now it's actually not so bad after all. But in the beginning it was like: 'Oh, I want to be at home!' ... But in a way it feels quite strange, 'I'm

going home to mum and dad', my classmates say, and I'm not going home until the weekend. ... I moved away from home when I was 16. It's not so common. You usually don't do that. I think you become more, you know, you can do more. ... You have already taken that step and moved away from home.

Yes, that's right...

So you know for certain how it feels. So it's, you know... No, it's... I think you become more grown-up when you move like that.

In what way?

You can clean up by yourself and such things. Now as a matter of fact I get help with that, but if you want to. ... Washing and such, you get help with that too, but you can do it by yourself. But 16 years old and doing the washing, that's maybe not so common. You have to learn to be more independent, I think. And most people maybe move away from home when they are 20.

(Ingela, 17, interview)

Already as a 16-year-old Ingela moved away from home. It becomes clear that indeed it was not easy, both from the opening negation: 'Now it's actually not so bad after all' and when she describes her initial homesickness and the weird feeling when she cannot meet her parents daily. She compares herself with classmates and repeatedly stresses the unusualness of her situation. As a consequence of the move she says she has grown up faster and become more independent. Ingela receives help with everyday tasks such as cleaning and washing, but she has the opportunity to do it by herself. It is, on the one hand, an opportunity to do things by herself that she couples with being adult and independent, and, on the other, the emotional maturity – she knows 'how it feels' to get on without her family. That Ingela suddenly becomes talkative strengthens the impression that this recently acquired independence is of considerable importance to her. She could have belonged to the group of young women that, according to Barron, is characterized by resignation (1995: 110–11). But in the interview, as in the quotation above, examples of agency and pride over the independence she has obtained are to be found.

Instead of speaking about overprotection or intrusive parental support, the physiotherapist Barbara Ellen Gibson (2005) uses the notion of 'shared family identity'. She uses video diaries in her research about identity and young men, who are 22–36 years old and have physical impairments. Gibson discusses how one of the participants in her study got help from his father to make the video diary:

How the video came about and the choices that participants made about who will help produce the video (especially since they were not explicitly given this choice) provided information about participants' identities and lifeworlds. This particular participant, for example, had a very strong connection with his parents, what I interpreted in light of all the data as a 'shared familial identity'.

(Gibson 2005: 4)

Gibson may seem to avoid the discussion about overprotection, but it is an unequal relation she describes. Three people are mentioned, two of them – the parents – are most likely conceived as having their own identities, while the third, the young man, has a shared familial identity.

To sum up, the problem with intrusive parental support exists and also manifests itself physically. The ways in which parents interact with their children are sedimented in the children's bodies (Moi 1999: 68) and give rise to an embodied experience. It may lead to a bodily style comparable with the one which, according to Young, characterizes the female goal-oriented movement: ambivalence and under-use of physical power, body weight, technique and skill (1980: 146–8). This makes it difficult to be physically active. But my empirical material also indicates that it can give rise to the opposite bodily style, irrespective of the degree of impairment, as when Hanna's and Sara's parents treated them just like their siblings and Felicia was taught to fight. Barron notes that parents' support and presence are regarded as most important when it concerns able-bodied children and adolescents, as a way for the parents to assume their responsibility (1995: 86). Just as the interviewees' lives are more open to different authorities to scrutinize compared to able-bodied young people, their parents' actions are more contested, and support and presence are problematized as overprotection. Hanna's, Sara's and Felicia's positive pictures of their parents, who want their children to fight to learn to help themselves, may be strengthened by the frequently recurrent discussion about overprotection – both Hanna and Sara work as coaches and leaders in their respective associations and are probably acquainted with the debate about disabled young people's dependence on their parents. Consequently, it is even more important to position themselves as autonomous individuals and, hence, to dissociate themselves from those who are considered overprotected. But as a result, the parents are burdened with guilt and the work they carry out in the form of help with personal care as well as driving and planning of training on schooldays and in leisure time is made invisible.

Reciprocity and (non-)acceptance

The participants also give other pictures of their parents. When I ask Sara about the relation to her family and if they see each other a lot, she soon gets on to the reciprocity that, according to Sara, characterizes the family:

> We have always been close and we help each other in every way. I mean, I help out as well as I can with driving my siblings to their training to make it easier for my parents. … They work, you know, and now I don't

work. Sure, I have my training. On the other hand I can borrow the car when I'm going to the training, we sort of give and take.

(Sara, 19, interview)

Although Sara adds 'as well as I can', which can be interpreted to show that she considers her capacity deficient, otherwise she describes the family situation as one of give-and-take. By describing herself as a big sister and a holder of a driver's licence, on a fairly equal level to her parents, and by emphasizing her own contributions at home, she once more portrays herself as grown-up and as autonomous.

In the video diary that Sara makes when she has reached the age of 23, she tells about her parents' open attitude concerning her wish to try new things:

In those days, Spice Girls shoes, the platform shoes, were enormously popular and that wasn't really my thing. But then my parents were quite good, because I got a pair of those. Of course they realized that this would never work. But they didn't say it to me; they let me understand that by myself. ... Of course it was a complete defeat. At that age it's so important to look like everybody else. ... Rollerblades were also immensely popular, and I got a pair of them. I think I got a fracture in the caudal vertebrae once [small laugh] and then I got a really big wound on my back that took two years to heal and then I realized, no rollerblades, I can't do that.

(Sara, 23, video diary)

Sara smiles when she talks about the platform shoes. She wanted to look and be like others of her age and is happy that her parents let her explore her limits by herself instead of trying to protect her from disappointments and risk underestimating her capacity. But her body put an end to her attempts. In the diary she keeps a distance from the injuries she received by laughing. However, in the quotation below the parents' attitude rather seems to be a matter of her father's reluctance to accept her disability:

He let me do things in the belief that I would cope with them anyhow. Just as an example, when I was at the Child Habilitation when I was 18–19 and was going to be registered at the Adult Habilitation, he asked the nurse and the doctor, absolutely seriously, if they thought I would ever learn to walk properly. And then you sit there and declare your father an idiot [looks up at the ceiling] in your thoughts, sort of, 'what kind of question are you asking?'

(Sara, 23, video diary)

Sara looks very serious when she speaks about the visit to the hospital's Child and Youth Habilitation. She had been walking without aids until the age of 20, but her dad, in the presence of the nursing staff, strongly disapproved of the *way* in which she walked. Besides, he showed a lack of understanding of the physical limits that his daughter's impairment imposed on her. By that time Sara had got to know her body's limits and in her thoughts she rejected – with emphasis – her father's lack of insight. When Sara was 20 years old she was given her first wheelchair, and it provided her with much needed relief: 'You're not so old when you are 20, but still I have worn out my body in the 19 years that I have been able to walk', she explains. Her father's reaction is vehement:

> When I came home with this wheelchair, my father almost died actually: 'But hey, you can walk, can't you? Why a wheelchair?' When you tried to explain to him that I have a wheelchair because then I'll be spared from walking unnecessary distances or if I'm in pain I'll be able to move. It hurt him *so* much. I think that has contributed a lot to the fact that it took such a long time for me to accept who I am. Accept that I *will* never be able to walk properly. I *will* never be able to pee by myself. Or *shit* by myself [little laugh]. Or go rollerblading.
>
> (Sara, 23, video diary)

This is as far away as you can come from intrusive parental support. It is not Sara who has been protected from disappointments and physical and mental pain, but her father. Sara is the one who has to explain to her father that she cannot manage to walk. The body makes itself felt here too and thus the specific feature of Sara's situation as a young disabled woman. The interview and video diary with Sara, like the interview with Ingela, shows the complexity: on the one hand, the fact that her parents, especially her father, have treated her as if she did not have an impairment has its disadvantages. When she was younger she had difficulty in accepting herself and her body was worn out by the walking. On the other hand, her parents' upbringing and her father's unwillingness to see her impairment has made her more independent.

Susanne, who is 22 years old, acquired her impairment when she was 15. She only has contact with her mother, but she describes their relation as good: 'We talk about everything. She is my best friend. We came closer to each other after the accident.' Later on Susanne tells about her approaching move to another city:

> On the first of August I'll move to the city. It'll be super. I was there this Friday and showed my mother around a bit. She has been a bit afraid [laugh]. Her youngest kid is going to move into the city, move from the village, move from her because she lives maybe 10 minutes away so she's used to having me nearby. But she became very relaxed when she got to see the district where I'm going to live. It's even a bit more quiet than here, because there's a lot of traffic here. ... So I got to show Ma that she needn't worry, I'll get on.
>
> (Susanne, 22, video diary)

Susanne records this late at night – in the daytime the traffic is constantly heard through the open balcony door and sun reflections from passing vehicles flash by on the wall behind her. If Susanne had a congenital impairment, this statement could have been interpreted as an example of intrusive parental support: her mother had 'been a bit afraid', her 22-year-old daughter will 'move from her' and finally she became 'very relaxed' and realized that 'she needn't worry' – all this indicates her anxiety. Like Ingela, Susanne moves to a new city at some distance from her parent, but while the five-year younger Ingela talks about her own uneasiness, Susanne speaks of her mother's anxiety and is looking forward to the change. As someone who has recently been injured, however, Susanne has not been socialized in the same way as those with congenital impairments.

Like 'Wow, what a girl'

To be just sexy enough

As we have seen there is a striving for normality, both among some of the young women and among their parents. This can also reveal itself in a wish to portray oneself as a 'normal' teenage girl or young woman, as when Sara in her video diary talks about her childhood and adolescence: 'I'm just like everyone else. I've also gone to the pub, I've also come home dead drunk and mum has mopped up my vomit, I've also scrumped apples in the neighbour's garden and I have driven too fast on the motorway and got a fine too.' In the interview a few years earlier Sara describes similar actions and how those have disturbed the expectations of people around her: 'It isn't as if I am the nicest child in the world. And sure, there are enormous reactions when you … I remember at the pub, sometimes when you were drunk. Then they think, "Shit, she's drunk! And she's disabled!"' As a teenager with a visible physical impairment she risks being infantilized, but she clearly makes resistance against this. Before the interview Sara stressed that 'I have never understood such people [lesbians]' and further on in the interview she speaks about her boyfriends:

> I had one disabled boyfriend. Otherwise, I've always had healthy boy-friends – if I can put it like that! It sounds a bit stupid, so maybe I should say 'not disabled'. … Well, I seem to have had a number of them. It's not exactly like that, but [laughs] I've had three or four of them that have been serious.
>
> (Sara, 19, interview)

Sara refers to her boyfriends as 'healthy' and presents herself as sick by con-trast. At the same time she approaches the norm – the healthy – by pointing out that she is heterosexual, and that she attracts able-bodied boys. This too is to be found in the interview as well as the video diary, in which she says: 'I've always had boyfriends, if that's what I wanted to.' Once again Sara stresses her sexual attraction, and thus her normality. She also portrays herself as active when she adds 'if that's what I wanted to'. That she brings this up in both the interview and the diary shows the significance this has to her.

On the one hand, Sara characterizes herself as on the respectable side when she notes that the number of boyfriends has been limited, implying that she has not simply been running around. This balancing was also present in the social anthropologist Fanny Ambjörnsson's (2004) study of gender, class and sexuality among girls in upper secondary school. To appear as a heterosexual object of desire, two negative poles have to be avoided: firstly, the slut, that is the morally loose and sexually too accessible woman, and secondly, the unattractive, unfeminine woman, according to Ambjörnsson often represented by the lesbian (2004: 117), whom Sara distances herself from too. It is also important to show that you are '*lagom*' sexy – that is to say, showing neither too much nor too little sexual desire. Having a boyfriend keeps the balance between being accessible and being respectable. Thus the young woman shows that she is feminine enough to get a boyfriend without being overly sexual (Ambjörnsson 2004: 125; see also Skeggs 1997).

On the other hand, Sara opposes the view of disabled young people (especially women) as passive, overprotected and lacking independence by relating that she goes to pubs, gets drunk, has sex and gets caught speeding. Presenting themselves as sexually attractive has a special function for disabled youth, since they often are regarded as genderless (Malmberg 1996; 2002; Marston and Atkins 1999: 89; Sandahl 2003: 45; Reinikainen 2004: 258; Grönvik 2008: 53). The ethnologist Denise Malmberg has interviewed women with visible physical disabilities, in their 50s and 60s. Those women tell about how they have been fighting against the picture of disabled women as genderless and asexual. They have tried to be accepted as wives, mothers and mistresses, contrary to the feminist struggle for women not to be defined as someone's wife, mother or mistress. Feminist disability researchers have criticized gender researchers for ignoring those subjects, thereby contributing to the oppression of disabled women (Malmberg 1996: 20; 2002; see also Morris 1995: 76). Thus, disabled young women may also represent the unattractive, unfeminine woman Ambjörnsson writes about. Helmius (2004) argues that establishing a sexual life of one's own is a way for young people to create their own identity and one step in the separation from parents. Boys and girls are socialized into different sexualities, and girls' sexualities are more problematized. What is more, Helmius emphasizes, disabled girls are often desexualized as they primarily are socialized as disabled and then as disabled children, instead of just as disabled girls (2004: 103). The question is whether it is desirable that children, disabled or not, are socialized in a gender-stereotypical way.

The cultural sociologist Angela McRobbie (2007) claims that since the 1990s young women have been depicted as privileged in the supposedly equal society. Their future has long been expected to comprise marriage, motherhood and economic dependence; but that is not the case anymore: 'The meanings which now converge around the figure of the girl or young women ... are now more weighted towards capacity, success, attainment, enjoyment, entitlement, social mobility and participation' (McRobbie 2007: 721). If they have previously been controlled by rules about 'what young women ought not to do', their lives are now regulated by an imperative concerning their possibilities: 'what they can do'. But the movement is double: with the young women's recently acquired freedom follows a promise not to make collective, feminist demands, and thus the gender order is restored (McRobbie 2007: 720). I regard this femininity as one expression of the emphasized femininity Connell (2014) speaks of, which complies with the subordination of women. This new type of femininity that McRobbie describes is visible in the three fields of consumption culture, education and employment, and it applies especially to the five oldest individuals in my material, those who have finished upper secondary school. But the picture of capacity, individual freedom and freedom of choice that is painted, with its strong impact upon media and the political discussion, can be regarded as a basis for comparison for young people as well as when adults are interpreting the life situations of the young. However, these values are far from the reciprocity that Sara describes, and they do not fit in with my interviewees' need of assistance, transportation service and other support, at least as long as independence is interpreted as the capacity to do everything by yourself.

The fields of reproduction and sexuality, according to McRobbie, are regulated by normative presumptions. While young or single parents are considered as examples of failed femininity and the well-being of their children is questioned, marriage and planned parenthood are considered as the ideal family norm. If a young woman clings to this ideal she is permitted 'a prominence as a pleasure-seeking subject in possession of a healthy sexual appetite and identity' (McRobbie 2007: 731–22). The 'phallic girl' or 'ladette' seems to have achieved equality since she has been given some male privileges, including an active and pleasurable sexuality. The position may seem bold and transgressive, but it is conditional. It presupposes that hegemonic masculinity is not criticized and that the position of the feminist and the lesbian is avoided. The risk of punishment is also significant (McRobbie 2007: 734). The participants in my study are not associated with failed femininity – their femininity is rather questioned as a whole. Hence they do not have the same access to the more active sexuality that the 'ladette' has. But the far too well-known punishments that follow can explain Sara's balancing act. In the video diary Sara says more about boyfriends and sex:

> I have never had any difficulties in opening up to boys. And I have never experienced any problems, when you have said all this about leakage anyway and about what this [diagnosis] implies. I remember my sexual debut. For certain it was a catastrophe, you could say. I was 17 and I had a boyfriend, who I then loved above all else, and we had sex for the first time and I felt *nothing* [nods]. Nothing. I could feel pain, I could, but

nothing that was directly pleasurable. But then I thought it was probably just the first time. You are a bit nervous and stiff. But I didn't feel anything the second, third, fourth or 79th time either and that was quite tough for me. ... When I told him that I didn't feel anything of all this he said: 'Then you almost have had sex for my sake, haven't you?' And what do you answer to that? I felt like certainly I need the closeness; you need the cuddling, kissing and caressing, and all this too. And *that* I feel! I'm probably highly hypersensitive in other places instead because I don't feel anything down there. ... But, as said before, it was a major disappointment that I couldn't feel anything.

(Sara, 23, video diary)

The disability does not seem to matter when meeting boyfriends. But when she had sex for the first time she felt 'nothing that was pleasurable'. She thought it could be due to her nervousness, but when she did not feel anything later on either, the characteristics of her body became manifest to her as well as to her boyfriend. 'It was a major disappointment', she explains. In addition to the fact that the impairment changes over time, the insight into the specifics of the impairment and its effects can deepen during different life phases. The focus on normative, penetrating sex and orgasm contributes to her disappointment, but when she gets older she realizes that she can get sexual pleasure through other parts of her body and through 'cuddling, kissing and caressing'. She begins, in disability scholar Tobin Siebers's words, to 'think expansively and experimentally about what defines sexual experience' for her, and other parts of her body become eroticized (2012: 47–9).

Femininity and other people's emotional reactions

Susanne, 22 years old, was involved in a traffic accident when she was 15 and has used a wheelchair ever since. She talks about the time after the accident:

It was a strange time. Because it was precisely at the age of 15, when you are supposed to get out and live. Being a teenager.
Which grade were you in then?
It was at the end of eighth grade. So it happened exactly one week before school broke up. It was a major accident. My whole family was in it, and one died. And I broke my back.

(Susanne, 22, interview)

During the two months when Susanne records her video diary, she and Anders, her boyfriend of two years, break up. 'I somehow didn't want to anymore. We had gone back and forth to each other for over a year now. And if we should invest now, we should invest whole-heartedly.' It is Susanne who broke it off and she seemed relieved: 'Now it's all about me. Now, you know, I sort of don't have to think about him anymore, and that feels good. I will take care of myself now.' After about a month she meets a new boyfriend:

> It feels quite good to have started afresh again and that I have met some-body who likes me for who I am and isn't afraid and ... . [Sigh] He isn't afraid of the wheelchair and he is curious about the life as a wheelchair user ... He's a gorgeous guy anyway [nods]. So we'll see what's going to happen. At least he seems to have ... . He probably has *more* feelings than *I* have. Because it has just been three weeks and ... I want to glide along [laugh]. And as I know him now, he's a really straightforward guy. But as his friends have said when he talked about me ... Because his friends obviously know who I am ... They said that maybe I can calm him down. I don't know how I should interpret it [laugh]. But ... maybe it's positive then if I can calm him down. He evidently needs to be calmed down. Anyhow, it's fun to be back on track again when it comes to meeting boys and love.
>
> (Susanne, 22, video diary)

While Sara in the quotation above speaks about her body's physical character-istics, Susanne implicitly brings up the expected reactions of surrounding people. She knows that boys can be 'afraid of the wheelchair' and her sigh implies some kind of weariness about this circumstance. However, her new boyfriend likes her 'for who I am', and hence seems to disregard her impair-ment. On the other hand, Susanne says that he is curious about life as a wheelchair user, which indicates that he nevertheless pays attention to Sus-anne's impairment and wheelchair. Maybe a certain fascination is hidden behind the curiosity? Perhaps it feels especially good to have met a new boy-friend when knowing that boys can find the wheelchair a deterrent, even though she feels less than he does and she was looking forward to looking after herself. Susanne also has an explicit function in relation to her boyfriend: his friends expect her to 'calm him down'. She says that she does not know how to interpret this. It could be about her personality, but also about the idea of men as 'wilder' than women, and about women who use wheelchairs as being even more passive. In educational research the idea that boys are noisy and can be calmed down by the more mature and responsible girls is well documented (Odenbring 2010: 118, 129; see also Ambjörnsson 2006: 61–2), which can be seen as part of the orientation of emphasized femininity towards meeting the needs of boys and men (Connell 2014: 296). Susanne undertakes the task with some hesitation, as she explains that 'maybe it's positive then'.

    If Susanne's narrative is about handling emotions of fear and perhaps fas-cination, 26-year-old Julia manages stares. She too began to use a wheelchair after a traffic accident, and speaks about the reactions of other people when she describes her life as newly injured:

> In the beginning it was very much about asserting oneself, showing that you still could, because you were treated in such an incredibly different

way, compared to before you got injured. From being a 19-year-old chick to suddenly, yes, you know … . So it was a tough period for a start.

(Julia, 26, interview)

Julia emphasizes that her experience of other people and their reactions to her and her body has completely changed since the accident. As a wheelchair user she has to assert herself – that is, actively make herself visible. It is taken for granted that she is incapable – the capacity that according to McRobbie (2007: 721) characterizes young women in an equal society is not applicable to those who are wheelchair users. Previously she was a '19-year-old chick' with an attractive body, but being a chick in a wheelchair seems to be a contradiction. The word 'chick' describes how others look at Julia's body, a body she simultaneously is and looks at from a distance (Bartky 1990: 40). Now instead Julia has suddenly become 'yes, you know'. What this means she explains later in the interview:

> You get a different kind of attention when you sit in a wheelchair. Then you have to make the most of it. You are seen, you know. And I utilize it as much as possible.
> *What kind of attention do you get then?*
> You are visible, in both a positive and a negative sense. And then you have to kind of choose, should I look down or should I look up and show that I am here? …
> *Can you give examples of positive and negative reactions?*
> Yes, of course there are negative one, there are some people who have the approach that you are stupid because you are sitting in a wheelchair, which was really tough in the beginning. Positive is that you show that you can anyhow. You maybe notice that this person doesn't really know how to react. But here I come, I smile. Then you notice like 'wow, what a girl!' That you can attract people, you know. There's quite a lot of people that think it's fun too when they see … . If you only show them that you are just like everyone else despite your disability.

(Julia, 26, interview)

The wheelchair means that Julia is seen. She has to handle the stares she experiences in her everyday life. Garland-Thomson maintains that impairment reduces women's feminine capital and gives rise to the stare instead of the male gaze: 'feminization prompts the gaze; disability prompts the stare' (1997: 28).[2] It is this shift from the male gaze to the stare after the accident that Julia describes. She is forced to be constantly aware of herself as well as the impression she makes on other people. Goffman suggests that when a visibly disabled person meets the 'normal', a common strategy is that both of them pretend that the disability does not exist (1963/1990: 57). But this is no alternative for Julia. The people who meet Julia do not regard her as a person. However, she is not passive, but meets and deals with their stares by showing them 'here I am', as a person. Garland-Thomson (2009) describes the positive potential in the interaction between the starer and the staree. While the gaze subordinates the person who is gazed at, the stare is curious. The starer wants 'to make the unknown known' and the staree gets an 'opportunity to be known' (Garland-Thomson 2009: 9, 15). Sometimes this potential is not developed. Julia thinks that at least some of the starers take it for granted that she has an intellectual disability too. The physical body becomes, in Ljuslinder's words, 'an index for the entire person' when reduced physical ability is supposed to affect both intellect and personality (2002: 117, author's translation).[3] Julia conceives the presumption of her having an intellectual disability as negative, a common reaction that can be explained by her thus being coupled with a category of disabled that is lower on the (often implicit) status hierarchy of disabilities (Deal 2003: 898, 906). But often Julia succeeds in taking the lead. She meets the stare, smiles and shows that she is 'just like everyone else' – that is, normal and capable but also an attractive, happy and positive girl. Thus Julia opens up for an empathetic identification and recognition. People notice 'like "wow, what a girl!"' and the starer goes from being curious to know (Garland-Thomson 2009: 92–4, 191–2). Julia describes how she makes a conscious choice every time.

The word 'despite' is present here too, even if it is not about the narrative of the hero (Ljuslinder 2002: 119). When Sara explains that she always has had boyfriends whenever she wanted to (and, besides, healthy ones) 'despite my disability' is implicit. Susanne actually did not want a new boyfriend, but nevertheless she is happy that she met a new one so soon again, a boyfriend who sees her as she is despite the wheelchair that often makes people afraid. Julia thinks it is impossible to be a chick in a wheelchair. She devotes a lot of energy to showing that she is a normal, capable and happy girl who 'can anyhow'– that is, despite a disability which makes people stare. Those stared at 'are sometimes reluctant participants in their starers' visual search for something new; they have their own lives to live', Garland-Thomson (2009: 7) writes. Julia could have devoted the time and energy she puts into handling the stares to something else, and in this way the stares constitute an obstacle for her.

Meeting others in the same situation: From exclusion to inclusion

Thus, in the empirical material the wish to appear normal is manifest. But the participants in this study also give evidence of the importance of the disability sports movement, in which meeting other people with similar experiences has made a great difference. Several of the interviewees tell how, during adolescence or even during childhood, they were sad, depressed and, in one case, had an eating disorder. This can, in part, be due to their being alone during the years when they were growing up. Certainly they had friends, but they did not know anyone else who was disabled. Previous researchers have paid attention to the isolation disabled people often experience (Garland-Thomson

1997; Sandahl 2003: 37). Garland-Thomson emphasizes the reactions they often meet as the only disabled person in a family or a community:

> Most disabled people are surrounded by nondisabled families and communities in which disabilities are unanticipated and almost always perceived as calamitous. Unlike the ethnically grouped, but more like gays and lesbians, disabled people are sometimes fundamentally isolated from each other, existing often as aliens within their social units.
>
> (Garland-Thomson 1997: 15)

From the isolation also follows a lack of a historical background that makes disabled people differ from, say, ethnic minorities. Stories about things such as the disability movement's struggle against institutionalization and independence are not part of the family history.

The interviewees also give several examples of how they have been excluded or singled out. In the interview guide a number of questions about previous physical activity were included, in addition to questions about organized sports. I asked the interviewees whether they participated in unorganized physical activities in leisure time or during breaks in school and about their experiences of the lessons in physical education (PE). The question about PE distinguished itself particularly since six of the interviewees, that is, all except two of those with congenital impairments, talked about problems. It is also illuminating that several gave long answers to this question, as for example did Ingela, who went into detail on just a few occasions during the interview.

Previous research shows that disabled pupils are over-represented among those who run the risk of not passing PE in grade eight (Bråkenhielm 2008). Almost 2 per cent of the pupils are 'excused' from the subject in grade seven to nine (Skolinspektionen 2010). The reasons that are given are chiefly sickness, disability or psychosocial problems (Larsson et al 2010: 41–2). Researcher in physical education and sport Håkan Larsson and co-authors point out that it is not only the pupil who is excused, but 'the school management also "excuses" the PE teacher from responsibility, in terms of both teaching and grading' (Larsson et al 2010: 78, author's translation). However, to be 'excused' can, from the pupils' perspectives, be experienced as exclusion. This was shown in three research studies directed towards young people with physical impairments, despite the fact that none of them explored young people's experiences of PE as such (Barron 1995; Taub and Greer 2000; Asbjørnslett and Hemmingsson 2008). The 'visibility' of bodies during the lessons and in the dressing rooms and showers, with the ensuing experience of vulnerability, is pointed out (Barron 1995: 52). Ingela, who began a sports school for young people in a disability sports club when she was seven years old, trains wheelchair basketball two or three times a week and does weight training; she is one of those who have negative experiences of the lessons in PE:

It has been like: 'Well, you do the programme that you have been given by the physiotherapist.' But sometimes I have been able to participate in the Physical Ed, but that's really, really, really, really seldom. ...

But what do you think about that?

I think it's really bad, because I think we... I think we should also have a... chance to be included, like everybody else.

(Ingela, 17, interview)

The teachers seem to have excluded Ingela almost completely during PE – she repeats the word 'really' four times to underline how seldom she can participate. In a class in which will and ability vary greatly, Ingela succeeds. That she is an engaged young sports woman in her leisure time, and probably quite all-round after eight years in the sports school, makes no difference. Ingela criticizes this and claims that 'we' ought to be given the same opportunity to participate as all classmates. By 'we' she probably refers to the category of young disabled people, despite the fact that from first to seventh class, she was the only one in school with a visible physical disability. But Ingela obviously identifies herself with this category. In Barron's (1995) study a young man, who otherwise doesn't normally identify with the group of 'disabled', gets into a conflict with his personal assistant. When describing the difficulties in even bringing up the possibility of changing assistants, he shifts from 'I' to 'we'. Barron argues 'when confronted with certain problematic situations ... disabled young people may identify with others, i.e. disabled peers, whom they envisage having similar experiences' (1995: 82). One explanation could be that Ingela thinks that she is not the only one who is being excluded. Ingela may have friends in the disability sports association who also have experiences of exclusion. But by using 'we' Ingela also avoids the victim position, thus describing the incident in collective terms; the problem comes to be a question of disabled people in general and how they are treated in PE. Ingela also has a suggestion for how the problem could be resolved: 'I could very well tell the teachers what I can do. But it depends on what they want to take in too, you know'. The resources that Ingela has in the form of knowledge about her own body's possibilities and about doing sports in a wheelchair are not utilized.

Hanna, as mentioned before, was physically active during the years when she was growing up. She says that PE was really good throughout her first six years in school. Firstly, 'it was more play' during these years. Secondly, the teacher 'understood that I really wanted to. ... She was also an ice hockey coach, not for my team, but she knew I was playing hockey.' The teacher knew about Hanna's huge interest in sports, and that she was active in her leisure time. At the age of 12 Hanna began to train table tennis at a disability sports club in the closest city. After six months in the club she took part in a table tennis competition for disabled people for the first time. 'The national team manager began talking to me, and then it wasn't difficult to choose.' Hanna received immediate acknowledgement, and chose to go in for table tennis. But during the last years of compulsory school PE did not work out as well. Hanna had the feeling of lagging behind and of being treated with ignorance by the teacher:

> He [the teacher] didn't take notice of my impairment at all. When I couldn't take part, I got bad grades. And it was things that I absolutely couldn't do. ... I can't hang on rings or run in the woods, it has to be flat ground ... . At that time I began to feel that I always got behind. ... I fought and fought, but I could never be as good as the rest. ... I had an eating disorder during the whole period of senior level [of compulsory school]. In retrospect I think it was my way of trying to be good... at something, because I fought all the time to look and be like everybody else. And I can't.

> (Hanna, 25, interview)

Hanna's yearning for normalization is strong. She remembers how she struggled to achieve the same results in PE as her classmates, and to look like and be like them. Hanna was probably as good as or better than her classmates in several physical activities – she was a hard-working and versatile sports woman in her leisure time; but some specific parts of PE were difficult or impossible to carry out because of her impairment. The teacher did not seem to consider Hanna's circumstances – her impairment and her dedication and talent for sport – neither when planning the lessons, nor when grading. The teacher lowered her grade at the same time as Hanna was recognized as a table tennis player. Hanna internalized the teacher's view of her as less capable, and turned the disappointment inwards. Afterwards, Hanna regarded the teacher's attitude as a contributory cause to her eating disorder. When the teacher disqualified her body, Hanna found another way to take control. According to the evaluation performed by the Swedish National Agency for Education, PE can lead to reduced self-confidence among girls, especially those in the last year of compulsory school (Eriksson et al 2003). This is confirmed by my study. Hanna no longer felt like 'the others in my class', as she describes at the beginning of the interview, but that she 'always got behind'.

The special treatment during PE can also result in feelings of being singled out. Maria, who is 17 years old, walks short distances without assistive technology when indoors, but in most cases she uses a wheelchair outdoors. She has been playing a team sport in a disability sports association since she was around ten, and is a national team player as well. She has been swimming in the same association since she was 14, and a few months ago she also began swimming four times a week with 10- to 12-year-old kids in a swimming club for the non-disabled. The following quotation comes from the beginning of the interview, when I have asked her about how she experienced PE:

> Junior level, in those days it was mostly play. It wasn't anything serious. But, there have been problems, like teachers who were uncomprehending and quite insensitive.

And how could that show itself?

... I don't know, I'm quite stubborn I think, but...

Is it anything special you remember?

... Maybe it was a bit wimpish. But I am standing at one end of the gym and the teacher is at the other end. And she has just given us the instruction for the class. Then she calls out to me, 'You, you do your best'. Or no, no. She says, 'You do it in your own particular way', or something. ... And I remember how everybody turned around, and they looked at me and like: 'Oh, yes.' It really wasn't anything she [the teacher] said to be mean. But, yes, it made an impression.

(Maria, 17, interview)

Maria's narrative takes place during a lesson in PE during junior or intermediate level of compulsory school. The teacher has just given instructions for the lesson, and then, from her side of the gym, she calls out to Maria at the other end of the room: 'you, you do your best', 'you do it in your own particular way'. Maria seems not sure if she remembers the exact wording, but the essence of the two versions is the same: the teacher's remark is derogatory. It implies that Maria is not fully capable of following the teacher's instruction. In front of the class the teacher constructs Maria as the one who deviates. Probably the task will be performed in a number of different ways by the other pupils, depending on factors like their capacity and will, but Maria is the one who is singled out. She is also left to work out all by herself what she should do during the lesson. Maria then recalls how her classmates reacted by turning around and looking at her. The derogation occurs in front of the class, and with their 'Oh, yes' Maria imagines that they have no objections to the teacher's depreciation of her. Maria shows a double consciousness when she alternately looks upon the situation from her own and her classmates' perspective (Du Bois 1903/2007: 8).

Maria's story is lined with what I interpret as a number of reservations. To my introductory question Maria answers, 'it wasn't anything serious'. This can, on the one hand, refer to the junior-level PE in general, when 'it was mostly play'. On the other hand, it can refer to Maria's situation during these lessons. In the latter interpretation Maria's denial of the seriousness of the situation works as a reservation concerning the rest of the narrative. Next Maria says that there have been problematic situations after all. Her first explanation is that the teachers were uncomprehending and insensitive. The lack of comprehension can be interpreted to mean that the teachers cannot really be held responsible for their actions. When I ask Maria to specify how the problems could be manifested, she hesitates once again when she says, 'I don't know' and 'maybe it was a bit wimpish'. Finally Maria evaluates the situation, stating with emphasis, 'It really wasn't anything she [the teacher] said to be mean.' Why then this hesitation, these reservations in a narrative that, with its wealth of details, has been established as credible and that is concluded by Maria explaining that this episode made an impression?

When Maria talks about a vulnerable situation, she risks, as a woman, being seen as a victim. Women's resistance against being regarded as victims has been discussed by the sociologist Donileen Loseke (2001). Loseke notes that although the position of the victim leads to support and sympathy for the woman, at the same time she is regarded as weak, powerless and as being out of control of her own life (2001: 123). Maria's disability reinforces the picture of her as passive and helpless – someone to pity. Thus, when confronting me, an unknown, able-bodied interviewer, it seems of great importance to her that she distances herself from the subordinate categories she constantly risks being cast into. When Maria instead points out that the situation is not so serious but, rather, wimpish, she dissociates herself from the subordinate position, and thus succeeds in bringing out the discriminatory treatment she has been given without becoming a victim. Before Maria begins the narrative, she calls herself 'quite stubborn'. This may seem completely irrelevant to the request to give an example, but becomes comprehensible in the light of my interpretation. Emphasizing the stubbornness functions as a way to make resistance against the role of the passive victim as well as the moral stigma that is often associated with a physical disability.

Stares play an important role in the quotation. Maria describes how the rest of her class turned around and looked at her, when the teacher told her to do it 'in her own way'. Hughes (1999) uses the term the non-disabled gaze, which I interpret as a stare that does not lead to a positive interaction. Hughes claims that this gaze imagines itself to be 'pure' and neutral (1999: 164). When Maria's classmates stare at her they probably believe that they are only registering the deviant, while it is their staring that constructs Maria as the deviant Other (Garland-Thomson 1997: 26; Hughes 1999: 165). I interpret the teacher's belittling as a kind of patronizing pity. The stereotypical view of disabled people as tragic is behind this emotion.

When I ask Maria what function sports have had in her life, she tells me that as a child she was depressed:

> I think, when I went in for sports it really helped a lot to meet other disabled people. It really helps to meet other people who are in the same situation, you know. Because I had some kind of depression when I was eight, nine. I don't think it only was due to me being disabled, even if that's why I was sad. But I think that if I hadn't been so lonely and if I had known other disabled persons, if I had become a member [of the sports club] earlier, that is to say, I don't think I would have needed to be sorry for that. Because then I would have seen that it could work out anyhow, you know.
>
> (Maria, 17, interview)

Her depression was not only a matter of her disability, Maria explains. That she was alone and did not know other disabled people was important too.

Loneliness can have several causes, and is not a characteristic of Maria but arises in the interaction between Maria and the people around her. Likewise, the fact that Maria did not know other disabled persons is not due to herself or her disability. In this way she shifts focus from her physical impairment to the social situation.

Sara is the only one in my empirical material who tells about experiences of bullying. She recollects her time at the senior level of compulsory school:

> They wrote a lot of things on my locker, I remember, nicknames. Everything from whore to cunt, sorry for the language but that's how it was, you know [smiles]. And of course it was awful. I was feeling *so bad* and it ended up with me behaving really badly towards my parents because I blamed them for what it was like for me in school. I always attended the lessons, it's true, but I began to mix with the wrong people. ... I did everything that my parents thought that I shouldn't, I got a mohawk, had clothes that I looked really awful in. Piercings, listened to music that was simply horrible [little laugh]. ... It was enormously tough to accept that you had a disability. The most difficult part was of course the incontinence.
>
> (Sara, 23, video diary)

Sara 'was feeling *so bad*' and reacted by revolting against her parents. In part, she protested with or on her body, through hairstyle, clothing and piercings, but also through her choice of music. She brings up her difficulties of accepting her own disability once again. At the age of 12 Sara began to train in a disability sports club, after some opposition from her father:

> It took quite a long time before I could go there, because my dad didn't accept it. Seeing me with a gang of disabled children. I know how he imagined people who probably were both mentally and physically disabled, with Permobil and respirator and all that stuff. ... [But] it was great for me! There you had several people to speak with about your disability. ... I speak with my parents, to be sure, but they can never feel how I feel. They can know everything about my disability but they can't feel as I do. ... I also became calmer in myself then. I began to dress normally. I stopped listening to that music that I didn't like anyhow. I simply began to find myself.
>
> (Sara, 23, video diary)

Sara describes her father as having had a rather stereotyped picture of disabled people, mixing up different kinds of disabilities and reducing disabled people to their physical and/or mental state; most importantly, he did not consider his daughter to be one of them. In the sports sociologist Ian Brittain's words, he follows 'a tendency within society to ... attribute the same meaning (usually that of the person with the greatest level of impairment) to people with all types of impairment' (2004: 443). While Maria clearly locates the cause of her depression outside her own body in the social situation without specifying it, Sara is concrete: on the one hand, she was bullied and, on the other, her father's attitudes hampered her contact with the disability sports movement.

In the following quotation the opposite occurs. Jenny, who is 20 years old, has related her situation in compulsory school. She explains that during this period she had 'good pals … they haven't cared so much about it', that is to say, her friends have not paid attention to her disability. Jenny continues: 'During the breaks you were mostly sitting and talking and walking around. … When the weather was good there was always something, you could play catch.' Apart from some practical problems with the lessons in PE, such as the lack of a shower chair, everything around Jenny was fine:

> *It seems as if it has worked out well, on the whole. Can you remember anything that has been problematic, for example in teacher's attitudes or anything like that?*
>
> No, actually it hasn't been so bad after all. It has been quite good. It's more my own attitude. … That I haven't been feeling good and things that sometimes happen when you are at a certain age. You begin to be conscious of a number of things. So, it was about fifth or sixth grade that it began.
>
> *And what was it then, for instance?*
>
> It was all sorts of things. But I got a bit of depression… and didn't want to go to school. … It was before I started with basketball. The basketball has lifted me up incredibly much. … [You] got better self-confidence and you got to meet others in the same situation. … During all the years when I was growing up it was only me, so to speak. So it was nice coming to a place where you were the same.
>
> (Jenny, 20, interview)

Jenny does not give any examples of the 'all sorts of things' that she became conscious of when she was in fifth and sixth grade, despite my direct question. But she herself makes the connection between the depression and her disability when she says that during childhood 'it was only me' and that the disability sports club was 'a place where you were the same'. However, she states that the depression was due to her own attitude. In spite of this I pose the question once more:

> *You say that in fifth or sixth [grade], it became tough. Was it some-thing … ? There's always an interplay between the surrounding and oneself, I believe. Was there anything that they, the surrounding, could have made different?*
>
> No, I don't think that really, it was a bit pals also, so … . It was mostly oneself I think. Actually.
>
> (Jenny, 20, interview)

Jenny indicates that her depression could have had something to do with her friends but does not expand on this. Eventually she puts the responsibility for feeling bad on herself, which differentiates her from the other interviewees. By now, playing basketball seems to give Jenny an opportunity to give vent to her feelings in her everyday life: 'I think when I play basketball I get an outlet for so many feelings too. ... Joy, anger and sadness and everything.'

My interpretation is that it is the process of stigmatization – in the form of bullying in Sara's case – combined with growing up isolated from other disabled people, which cause Maria's and Sara's depressions. Barron (1995) maintains that some of her interviewees have been socialized to see themselves as 'normal', like their able-bodied peers. They have not been performing activities where they could meet other disabled children. But at the same time they have participated in extensive training and they use assistive technologies, and thus an identity as disabled has been created nevertheless. In addition, some of them have had few opportunities to play with non-disabled people of their own age. When they get older they feel confusion – they are alone with some experiences, but yet they hesitate about contacting other disabled young people (Barron 1995: 119). Sara resembles the youth Barron describes in so far as she was socialized as normal. Maria, Sara and Jenny had no contact with anybody else who was disabled. Maybe they were received as unanticipated calamities, in Garland-Thomson's words (1997: 15). However, the participants in my study do not react with confusion, but relate to the meeting with the disability sports movement as a new turn in life. Maria describes how she realizes, as she meets other disabled persons, that 'it could work out anyhow', despite other people's attitudes. Sara says that her parents can gain knowledge about her disability, but they cannot fully feel what she feels. The complex emotional experiences of subordination that they share with other members of the disability sports clubs are hard for an outsider to take in entirely and translate into other situations, as Narayan points out (2004: 220). A collective identity is created and the experiences that are directly associated with a life as disabled are emphasized at the expense of other experiences that differentiate the members of the sports club (see Brah 2001: 473).

Concluding discussion

In this chapter the independent, capable individual appears, expressed as 'I can', as well as the desire for normality, expressed as 'I am like everyone else.' In both of these cases there is an implicitly expressed 'despite' my disability. Several of the participants dissociate themselves from the subject position assigned them as dependent or weak. In their attempt to gain autonomy and normality a dichotomy arises between strength and weakness. Autonomy is linked to masculinity when one of the interviewees – as well as the male leader and the coach – speaks about girls whose mothers are overprotective. Distancing oneself from weakness and dependency can be understood in the light of, on the one hand, the frequently occurring discussions about overprotective parents, and, on the other, the accounts in the media and in the political debate in which the image of the free and independent women is reproduced (Garland-Thomson 1997: 26; McRobbie 2007). But the desire for normality can also originate from their parents' wish to normalize them. The interviewees, however, cannot achieve autonomy to the extent that they can do everything themselves and this fact makes them deviant. Sara, Susanne and Julia's femininity appears to be questioned due to their disabilities. They talk about their boyfriends and portray themselves as attractive and hetero-sexual young women who 'can anyway', despite their disabilities.

They thus emphasize their ordinariness, but they also tell of depressions during adolescence. At the same time as they describe themselves as normal and talk about their friends and boyfriends, they also describe how they have been stigmatized and, in one case, a young woman describes how she has been harassed. The encounter with the disability sports movement and with others with similar experiences is experienced as a turning point.

Of Young's (1990/2011) four faces of oppression that were presented in Chapter 2, we have seen examples of cultural imperialism in the form of stereotyping and othering (or stigmatization), as well as violence in the form of the bullying that Sara was exposed to. One of their resistance strategies is a negation of differences: I am like you (autonomous, capable, heterosexual), despite my disability. Sometimes dis-identification and othering is used as a part of this strategy: I am not like those who are overprotected or lesbian. Julia tells how she consciously chooses to meet the stares of others to avoid othering. Sara is the only one who speaks of a teenage revolt, which she expressed with clothing, her taste in music and the 'wrong' kind of friends.

Notes

1 One of the boys in my pilot study, 15-year-old Lars, used 'we' when he talked about his dumbbells: 'We bought [dumbbells] when we were in X-city. We caught sight of them, and then we thought it was a good idea. [Something] you could do in your leisure time', as well as when he explains how it happened that he began playing table tennis: 'It was my parents who met someone who gave a tip about [table tennis] in X-city, sometimes you can train with the A-team. And then we thought that I could go to the training.'

2 The gaze of the film camera is male, as the film theorist Laura Mulvey (2000) maintains. It lingers on women's bodies and the story is frozen for a moment. While the male gaze is active, the woman is made a passive object for the characters in the film as well as the audience in the cinema (Mulvey 2000). Bartky describes how the male gaze (outside the world of film) leads to self-consciousness and the coercion to 'see myself as they see me' (1990: 27; see also Young 1980).

3 Paterson and Hughes express the same phenomenon as the appearance becoming 'an omnipotent guide to competence' (1999: 607).

4 Bodily experiences

In this chapter I will explore different kinds of experiences in my empirical material that are more explicitly linked to the body: experiences of the operated body and the medical gaze, of the good-looking body and the teenager's dissatisfaction as well as the body as a source of pleasure and joy. Previous researchers have stressed that disabled people tend to be defined by their bodies (Paterson and Hughes 1999: 607; Ljuslinder 2002: 110; Malmberg 2002), among them Hargreaves:

> Disabled people ... are looked upon, identified, judged and represented primarily through their bodies, which are perceived in popular consciousness to be imperfect, incomplete and inadequate ... The emphasis in Western societies is on mastery and perfection and the disabled body represents a transgression of this ideal.
>
> (Hargreaves 2000: 185)

Disabled bodies are put up against the ideal in the form of the perfect and skilful body, Hargreaves argues. Garland-Thomson speaks of two separate narratives: 'the narrative of deviance surrounding bodies considered different is paralleled by a narrative of universality surrounding bodies that correspond to notions of the ordinary or the superlative' (1997: 7). According to Garland-Thomson both the ordinary and the extraordinary are included in the universal narrative – the latter is represented in this research project by the sporting body. Perhaps it could be seen as a continuum between the different bodies that are regarded as universal, which is interrupted by a distinct drawing of a boundary against the other narrative; the one that deals with bodies considered deviant. Garland-Thomson claims that there are many reasons to reject the sharp boundary between women with and without disabilities. Non-disabled female bodies are also among those who are considered deviant in relation to male bodies. Throughout history foot binding, corsets and female circumcision have been used as 'socially accepted, encouraged, even compulsory cultural forms of female disablement'. Cosmetic surgery makes women's bodies appear unnatural while the surgically changed body is considered normal and natural (Garland-Thomson 1997: 27). The female body is regarded as deficient as such and must be constantly supervised and 'done' by means of make-up, clothing, training, removal of some hair and dressing and dyeing of other hair to just be female (Bartky 1990: 40, 80–1; Ambjörnsson 2004). The disability, in contrast, works in the other direction:

> In a society in which appearance is the primary index of value for women (and increasingly for men), beautification practices normalize the female body and disabilities abnormalize it. ... Feminization increases a woman's cultural capital; disability reduces it.
>
> (Garland-Thomson 1997: 28)

A discussion about how female bodies considered deviant and pathological are distinguished from 'ordinary' bodies and from the bodies that are made female is found in an empirical study by the sociologist Kerstin Sandell (2001). Sandell made observations at plastic surgery clinics following breast reconstructions and burn injuries, among others. In addition, she conducted interviews with patients and surgeons. In both treatments the deviant appearance was regarded as undesirable, and the normal was what they were trying to attain. However, the plastic surgery had clear limitations when it came to burn injuries: it was not possible to restore the 'normal' appearance, that is, what the patient looked like before the accident. Parallel to the physiotherapists' training to increase mobility and stretch the skin, they were trying to get the patient to accept his or her new appearance (Sandell 2001: 174). When doing breast reconstructions, on the other hand, deformation was equated with mental suffering that could only be cured by normalization through surgery. Thus, when medical technology made normalization possible, no attempt was made to accept deviances in the form of scars or a reconstructed breast. Sandell criticizes the link between bodily deviance and mental suffering that is maintained within plastic surgery, which makes it impossible to understand how one-breasted and disabled people can live a life as 'deformed' without feeling bad (Sandell 2001: 202). She also criticizes feminists who strive for 'ordinary' bodies, those who have not undergone cosmetic surgery (such as face-lifting, breast or lip augmentation) to be considered normal. Disabled bodies are not included among the 'normal', but are pathologized. Those bodies require normalization through surgery. By only criticizing cosmetic surgery and leaving plastic surgery unquestioned, the latter appears accepted or even necessary (Sandell 2001: 48; 2003: 199–200).

The effects of the normalization of the disabled body, for instance through prostheses, have been described in autobiographical texts (Lapper and Feldman 2006; Collmar 2010). The journalist Lollo Collmar bears witness to her experiences of having a leg prosthesis as a child. It gave her a less provocative appearance and a way of moving that brought her closer to the norm. But the prosthesis was also the source of pain, worse functioning, dependence on help from others and a feeling that her body belonged to experts. Therefore, at the age of eleven, Collmar dropped the prosthesis (2010: 15–6).

In the following I will discuss the multiplicity of bodily experiences that is found in the empirical material.

The body as public property

The operated body

Several of the interviewees have repeated experiences of hospital treatment. When I chat with Natalie, who is 15 years old, during a break at the first day of the sports camp and ask her if she trains in any club, she tells me about her forthcoming surgical operations:

> I have a lot of problems now because I will have two operations, so I don't have much time. ... The first operation, then I will actually have an operation for my spinal marrow because it's squeezed. So I will be in hospital for a week. And then the second, it's because I am crooked. Then they will put in one of those struts.
> *But that the spinal marrow is squeezed, is it something you can feel; does it hurt?*
> Yes, I have a lot of pain in my back. It has an effect on my head too now. That's why I may not exert myself, because then I get such a strong tension, it's like headache but worse. I break out in a heavy cold sweat and become completely dizzy, and so on. And then the leg jumps, and sometimes the thigh. ...
> *So maybe you are looking forward to this operation?*
> Indeed!
> *Have you had an operation at any time before?*
> Yes, *a lot* of times!
>
> (Natalie, 15, informal recorded interview)

The pain in her back has been severe and has made it impossible for Natalie to be physically active during the last year, hence the surgery is much longed-for. Ingela, 17 years old, estimates that she has had surgery about 20 times. She has had several foot operations and two back operations. Sara, too, tells in her video diary about spending a lot of time at different hospitals during the years when she was growing up:

> There were operations almost each year, at least a couple of times. And it was everything from checking my bladder, such a routine check-up ... . They had to check the pressure of the bladder, the kidneys, X-ray and feet and orthopaedics and neurology, anything. So I was very, very much away and most often with my mum.
>
> (Sara, 23, video diary)

Different parts and functions of the body are controlled by different experts; sometimes it is only a 'routine check' to establish that everything is all right. The recurrent stays at the hospital interrupt everyday life as they take you away from family, friends, school and recreational activities. Susanne spent the first two years after the accident at different hospitals. 'Oh gosh, I've been everywhere. … I went to XX after the accident. Then I went back and forth, in all hospitals. Because I was feeling really bad, I was. I was feeling really bad.' Susanne still has to see the doctor quite often. Sitting at home, feeling a bit chilly with a big shawl wrapped around her neck in spite of the summer heat, she says:

> [Sigh] I'm so damn tired … I don't know if it might be a urinary infection [wrinkles her forehead] on its way. … I have it [urinary infection] quite often, because I can't … I use a catheter every four hours. So it may be that that is causing trouble again. It's quite a time since I had it. We'll see. [Sigh] Maybe I have to call the care centre and check it up, because it's unnecessary to feel bad if there's something you can be given for it.
>
> (Susanne, 22, video diary)

The three informants who make video diaries talk quite a lot about their diagnoses and their symptoms. In addition to what Natalie said spontaneously during our chat, this, as mentioned earlier, did not come up in the interviews. This was probably because I waited until the end of the interviews before I asked them about their diagnoses in an attempt to avoid defining them by their bodies and diagnoses. But when I asked them to depict their everyday life in the video diaries, this was a given part.

Loss of control and integrity

A more detailed account of the experience of a stay in a hospital is given by Maria, 19 years old. In her video diary we follow her at home before she leaves for the hospital, in the hospital before the operation, in the car on her way home and when she has got home. She expresses her feelings two days before the operation:

> Before I'm registered, I have to wash myself with some kind of disinfecting sponge that smells bad. I'm a bit nervous, because I remember when I had an operation on the same foot, the left foot, about three years ago. And even if it wasn't a major operation – certainly, it's larger this time – the days just after are rather tough. You are like stoned, and you are waking up and feeling sick at once and … . Oh, I dislike it so much!
>
> (Maria, 19, video diary)

Maria feels anxiety since she knows that the operation is followed by a certain discomfort. Once in the hospital, waiting for the operation, Maria starts the camera over and over again, in all recording four sequences. 'I can't leave the camera alone, I'm too nervy', she explains. In the next cut she sits in her bed and, with hand-held camera, shows the hospital clothes that are put out on the bedside table. In the background beeps can be heard from alarms going on and off:

> Here are some hospital clothes which I think they wanted me to put on. But I won't do it until they tell me to. They are *so* ugly! Look! Look! This is underwear. Like *hell* I'm going to put them on! Oh! *Jesus Christ!* And how the hell … . How big do they think I am? Are they kidding me? [Little laugh/snort] Okay. Yes, okay. And here we have the nightshirt. Large, yes, okay, but it's okay, long. But wear those panties, like hell I will, I'll have my own panties. They can be white, see, I have white you know, but. What the hell, I won't have these super panties.
>
> (Maria, 19, video diary)

While talking Maria takes the pair of briefs, which have two rows of four buttons each at the front, and lay them on her legs so they can be more easily seen. In the hospital her own scents are replaced by the smell of disinfectant and her own underwear with 'super panties' that look much too large for a dainty teenager. Painkillers make Maria feel sick and 'stoned' – that is, groggy and not completely present. She protests by telling the camera about the bad smell of the disinfectant sponge and by refusing to change underwear, at least if nobody tells her to. Maria continues:

> I'm *really* short-sighted. Besides, I only use contact lenses; I have had them since I was 12. So I don't have glasses anymore, because they are much too weak. So I will have to take my lenses out before having the operation, damn, I won't see anything. [Sigh] Before I fall asleep I mean.
>
> (Maria, 19, video diary)

Maria films close to her face, and turns her head repeatedly towards the door. That she cannot have her contact lenses means that she will lose control over her body in this sense too, as she will see badly before the operation and during the awakening. 'By the way, have I told you why I must have this surgery?' Maria asks and points at her stockinged foot and toes and explains in detail what is going to happen. She has put the wrong load on her foot and that has caused her pain:

> They will straighten my foot out; turn the heel so it becomes straight. So somehow I will be more flatfooted. But I will put a load on the whole foot instead of only this side. So that's good. … I want white plaster, I wonder if you could ask for that? I hope they haven't run out of it now. They had it once when I was small. Then I wanted some white plaster so people could draw on it. But I got purple plaster instead, because there was no white. I saw a girl the other day that had black plaster. There are probably all sorts of colours.
>
> (Maria, 19, video diary)

The alarms continue to bleep in the background when Maria points and shows her foot. Just like Ingela, Sara, Julia, Malin, Natalie, Felicia and Susanne, she has had surgery before. They are all accustomed to interventions in their own bodies and to being in hospitals. The intention is good, Barron stresses, but entails a particular approach to the body: 'While this interest in the young people's bodies can result in increased mobility and reduced pain, it also serves to portray an image of their bodies as "public property"' (1997: 37). The journalist Malena Sjöberg argues that the focus within care and habilitation is on what is considered wrong and not functioning; this should be fixed and trained. Furthermore, she describes the effects of the frequently recurrent meetings with these institutions in problematizing words: '[they lead to] a negative image of the self and the body. They have to endure, and get accustomed to the many hands that touch them, something that probably affects their development of self-reliance and integrity. ... The children often get confirmed that they are not good enough' (Sjöberg 1998: 42, author's translation).

The body becomes an arena for others to act in. Is normalization part of the surgical operations? None of the participants in the study brings up anything like this and it is hard to draw any conclusions from the material. Maria knows, like Natalie, that the operation will reduce her pain, but the uneasiness is still there. The beep from the alarm in the corridor and Maria's quick glances at the door strengthen feelings of anxiety. Someone can enter her room at any time. Maria shifts between different subject positions as she, on the one hand, gives a comprehensive account of the situation at hand: its routines in general and the coming intervention in particular. On the other hand, she gives expression – in words and pictures – to her nervousness about the operation, the feeling of sickness and the loss of control and bodily integrity, based on her previous experiences. Thirdly, she takes up the subject position as teenage girl when she talks about (un)pretty underwear and the colour of plaster, as if it was about the seasonal colours of pantyhose. I interpret this as a way for Maria to retain the feeling that her body still is hers, and that she herself decides over and is in control of it. Thus, the picture that Sjöberg paints of negative body image and undermined integrity does not get unequivocal support from my material.

Being carried

In the next video clip Maria sits in a car, resting her head on the head restraint. In the background her mother is seen and heard, loading the new rehabilitative devices that Maria has received. Maria speaks in a low voice, much thinner than it normally is:

> Mum and Ingemar are busy packing, and I'm in the back seat. Here is my parcel [turns the video camera so the plastered leg comes in view]. This is how it looks now. I actually wanted to stay at the hospital. It's

Sunday and I have been here since Thursday, but it's much easier at the hospital. You get everything done and painkillers too if you want.

(Maria, 19, video diary)

Maria blinks slowly and hardly looks into the camera. This is the only time she appears (in her own word) pitiful. At the end of the clip the mother says in a loud voice to someone outside the picture: 'Does it work like this now? I'll try. Otherwise I'll take everything out again.' There are many aids and they take up a lot of space; her mother struggles to get them into the car. Maria is very far from the capable individual she otherwise presents herself as, she wants to have 'everything done' and get the pain relieved. After this sequence from the journey home it is some time before Maria uses the camcorder again:

It's almost two weeks since I last filmed. But I … I went soft after the operation. I have really been rather down, to be honest. … Not being able to walk, that makes an enormous difference. Really. And I have never really understood that before, how fortunate I actually am, being able to walk.

(Maria, 19, video diary)

Now Maria wears make-up again and has a hint of a smile during the whole clip. Maria may not support herself on the newly operated foot, but uses a wheelchair or a walking frame, which she has as a support when she jumps forward on one leg. However, she cannot use these in her school, since it is located in a listed building. Maria explains: 'listed implies that you may not change anything. So they can't install a lift or any such things. And there's quite a lot of stairs everywhere, just because it looks nice.' She has spoken to the headmaster of the school, but without getting any response: 'I just wish he could help me a bit more than he does.' Maria's mother has an idea of why she has not got help: 'She thinks that if I had been a boy I would have got help immediately. That could certainly be correct.' Instead Maria and her friends have solved the problem by themselves, and it is this solution that makes her depressed:

I have to be carried everywhere. And it's … You could put up with it, and I do. But I hate it! Really! Oh, I don't know, but somehow you lose something when you can't take care of yourself in this way, when you have to ask people to *lift you*, because I can't do it. … [My friends] have to help me. A trick we have is that when we have a lesson on the second floor, I may hang with my arms over their shoulders. From the beginning my idea was that I could jump the steps one at a time. But, you know, the first time we did it like this they just carried me away. And of course, it was much easier than me jumping step by step.

(Maria, 19, video diary)

To begin with Maria has a weak smile on her face here too, which, as in the clip above, works as a way for her to maintain distance from the negative experience that she describes. Maria had worked out how she could get help to be able to walk by herself, but instead she gets carried. 'I hate it!' she declares, yet she realizes that she has to put up with being carried since it is easier and faster for everybody involved. She feels that something gets lost when she has to ask her friends for help. The temporarily lost capacity – that she cannot move herself – is a severe setback for her feeling of autonomy; 'you can't take care of yourself.' As when she had the operation, Maria expresses dislike but, simultaneously, accepts the situation. Maria's impairment, as for most participants in this study, is not constant; in some periods she is more impaired and sometimes less. Garland-Thomson claims that the same applies to the great majority of persons with physical impairments. 'The physical impairments that render someone "disabled" are almost never absolute or static; they are dynamic, contingent conditions affected by many external factors and usually fluctuating over time' (1997: 13). Both the impairment and the current situation influence how hindered Maria is, in this case her plastered foot in combination with a listed building without lifts and a headmaster who, according to Maria, has not stood up for her to solve the problem in the way she had hoped for.

Maria experiences her impairment as relative: 'I could almost go so far as to say that usually I am not disabled. I have a minor problem to walk. Because now when I can't walk, I'm not allowed to support myself on the foot and I'm so dependent on everybody else, now I am disabled, really.' Maria, like several of the others in my empirical material, is moving on a continuous scale and does not regard herself as disabled when she is at her 'normal' level, the one she is used to. Merleau-Ponty (1945/2012) states that the body consists of two 'distinct layers'. On the one hand, the habitual body, which is the one we are used to. On the other hand, the actual body, which is our present body. The stairs in school are manageable for Maria's habitual body, but not for the actual body that cannot handle it for the time being. The stairs have 'ceased being something *manipulable for me* and have become something *manipulable in itself*' (1945/2012: 84–5, italics in original).

It is also clear that Maria's disability is dependent on the context: on what she does and where she does it. If she had attended a school with a lift she would have been able to get on by herself. Ahmed contends that 'some spaces extend certain bodies', those who can manage stairs in this example, 'and simply do not leave room for others' (2006: 11). For those bodies that are not extended by the stairs in school, the inaccessible environment 'produces a vivid, but unwanted consciousness of one's impaired body' (Paterson and Hughes 1999: 603). Maria does not elaborate on the ideas she brought up when discussing with the headmaster, but it is possible that they could have solved the problem if the headmaster had had the will. If Maria's mother is right in her assumption, Maria's gender comes into play too: if she had been a young man she would have received help to be independent.

The medical gaze

Progress in medical science has of course made a great difference regarding the cure of chronic diseases, relieving pain and saving the lives of people who have been in accidents and bringing them back to everyday life (Garland-Thomson 2009: 28; Meekosha and Shuttleworth 2009: 57). However, researchers in disability studies as well as proponents of the disability movement have criticized the medical experts' power to decide which bodies are legitimate and which bodies are in need of correction and normalization, and put forward demands for demedicalization (Berg 2008: 85–6). The body is tested and assessed and, depending on the result, it is decided to what extent the applicant is entitled to assistance and technical and financial support from the welfare state (Shildrick and Price 1996; Edwards and Imrie 2003: 248). In this way, professionals in medical and social institutions exert control over disabled people and their daily life (Thomas 2007: 96–7). The medical gaze believes itself to be neutral, but, as Haraway points out, all vision is particular, embodied and situated (Haraway 1988; see also Garland-Thomson 2009: 28). The assessment of the body is based on an idea about the normal way of looking, being and acting (Hughes 2000: 561; Grue and Heiberg 2006: 240–2), and through that disabled people are constructed as abnormal and deviant. 'In this way, normalization, and its technologies, contribute to the reproduction of the differences and asymmetries that they seek to escape and undo' (Moser 2006: 388). Thus the compensatory strategy of the welfare states leads to a reproduction of boundaries between disabled and non-disabled bodies, between the normal and the deviant (Moser 2006: 374–5).

An example of this control is the assessment instrument for personal assistance that the Institute for Methods in Social Work (IMS), the National Swedish Board of Health and Welfare and the Swedish Social Insurance Agency developed on behalf of the Swedish government. The instrument was finished on 31 August 2011. In the test version the applicant's life was mapped out in detail. Help needed with such things as skin, face, tooth, scalp, nails and genital care was indicated on a scale divided into five degrees, together with estimated consumption of time and how many times per day this care needed to be carried out. Then the investigator had to assess whether the need for help and the consumption of time was reasonable. The aim of the new assessment instrument was to secure the legal rights of the individual; but the users' organizations left the commission as they considered that the questions violated the applicants' integrity (Socialstyrelsen 2010; independentliving.org 2011). In the final version the questions are reformulated and addressed to the Swedish Social Insurance Agency administrators rather than to the applicant. This allows the administrator to adjust the questions in the interaction with the applicant (Martinsson 2011).

In the next quotation Felicia tells about the annual 'gathering' at the Child and Youth Habilitation, when her physical status was to be discussed:

Did you have a lot of contact with the Child Habilitation?

Yes, at that time you had the physiotherapist that you met twice a week. And then the doctor that you met a couple of times a year. Then there probably was some welfare officer too. ... Then [you] had a gathering each year. ... They were maybe five physiotherapists, two doctors and a few more. So you were completely on your own there, and everybody was walking all around and, yes, they were talking over my head. It wasn't very pleasant. But you maintained constant contact with them.

What was the idea of it then? What was the unpleasant part of it?

Well, just imagine sitting almost naked and all those people, you don't know all of them, some of them maybe ... They are sort of discussing my physical status. 'Yes, look here, how you have the leg now', and things like that, and 'there the hip turns a bit outwards'. ...

Could any of your parents come with you?

I think my mother was with me. But there wasn't much she could do.

(Felicia, 28, interview)

Felicia relates an annually recurring situation in which she is at a disadvantage in many ways. Certainly, her mother is with her and was probably an important support, but 'there wasn't much she could do'. Felicia is at the centre of attention and a child surrounded by adults. She is alone while the adults are at least eight. She is there in her capacity as a patient while the others are there as professionals. Whereas she is almost naked, several of them are probably wearing white coats that emphasize their professionalism. Finally they do not talk *with* Felicia but *about* her body. The body is fragmented as they examine a leg or a hip. The medical gaze, a gaze that according to Garland-Thomson is a 'form of person-to-person staring that is highly impersonal, scripted, and asymmetrical' and 'seldom encompasses the whole person', makes the body into an object to observe and thus hinders the individual's agency (2009: 28–9). Felicia becomes, in de Beauvoir's words, a being that exists in itself, instead of existing for itself (1949/2011: 161). Sjöberg argues that there is a tradition of treating disabled people as objects: 'They have been non-gendered and deindividualized, and therefore it has been possible to make them into objects for care ... . Even when it has been done with the best intentions, it has resulted in infantilization and exclusion' (1998: 8, author's translation). Felicia does not know all those who are present, which contributes to the feeling of uneasiness. She knows that there tends to be a couple of doctors, about five physiotherapists 'and a few more' – maybe she does not know their profession? Later on Felicia adds, 'Yes, then there was staff and those who were going to be physiotherapists who were there to have a look.' In Barron's (1995) study several of the young people did not know who had decided which upper secondary school they should enter. They did not know their name or their profession. 'This implies a de-personalization of services, which means that these professionals have taken on an abstract identity for the interviewees', which in its turn leads to difficulties in raising objections to the decisions (Barron 1995: 79). In a similar way most of the people who participate at the Child and Youth Habilitation are unknown to Felicia and that makes it more difficult for her to oppose the situation at hand and any decisions about measures or interventions.

On one occasion, however, Felicia shows that she becomes sad and distressed. It is when she meets her doctor at an annual visit to the Child and Youth Habilitation:

> The second doctor shouldn't have been in charge of children. I have always had some problems with my hips. ... But I'm not in pain. Then once she felt my leg, it was sort of at the annual visit, and said 'Yes, we probably have to operate on the left hip.' And that has always been my *best* hip! 'Well, why?' Then I got a bit upset. I was 13. I got sad and that's not strange. You don't want to have an operation. So 'Oh no, I shouldn't have said anything, because now you got sad!' Oh yes, of course you should say something, but you have to have evidence for it. Then we brought in my physiotherapist who said 'Felicia's hips have always been like this.'
>
> (Felicia, 28, interview)

Felicia is critical of the Child and Youth Habilitation. 'It was not very pleasant' at the larger gatherings and her second doctor 'shouldn't have been in charge of children'. In the earlier quotation Felicia said that her mother used to come with her to the hospital. The 'we' that opposed the future surgical operation most likely stands for Felicia and her mother, and the latter appears as a necessary support when visiting the doctor. They had to call in yet another member of the nursing staff, Felicia's physiotherapist, to put a stop to the planned operation.

Increased control: 'Maybe you should be grateful'

Sara postpones her video diary several times, and afterwards she tells me that she got pregnant and had a really complicated pregnancy. 'It wasn't planned – but what happiness it was! ... I also wanted to be able to go into town with my nice belly and wonder how it feels to give birth to a child, how it feels when it kicks in the belly and such things.' Sara explains that in her early teens she experienced disappointment when she realized that she could not do the same things as her mates, but since the age of 15 she has been able to do all that she wants to do. Nevertheless, she has longed to be pregnant. In the video diary Sara speaks at length about her pregnancy: 'The beginning was good, so to speak. I threw up for three months. I was almost happy with that because most people do, that's at least what you have heard.' The feeling of sickness becomes a proof for Sara that, in this respect, she was just like other women. But after the first three months, complications begin to set in:

It was then all the problems began. First the kidneys, then began the leakage of urine, and at that time I had begun to get a small belly too and it pressed, the baby pressed on the bladder. So then I got a permanent catheter in the urethra that was terrible to walk with, I'd say. And from that date until the delivery in week 36 I was in hospital ten days a month at least, if not more. ... My bowels stopped working too. I hadn't been to the toilet in almost two months the day I gave birth to her.

(Sara, 24, video diary)

The complications are a consequence of Sara's impairment. She has repeated ultrasound scans and has nightmares about giving birth to a baby with the same diagnosis as she has herself. 'My dreams kept on for three weeks. Every night. I almost went completely nuts.' However the midwives cannot see whether the foetus has the actual diagnosis or not, and finally Sara gets angry with a doctor: 'Then I said like "Why should I take all these other tests [shrugs her shoulders]? It's better that I do them in week 18 just like everybody else, when you can't see anything anyway!"' One midwife also takes a test without Sara's knowledge: 'I think they took the nuchal scan to see if it was Down's syndrome or chromosome anomaly and it wasn't at all. And I hadn't ordered that, so I was quite angry: "Why should you do this? You have to ask me first!" Maybe you should be grateful.' Sara shakes her head a bit when she speaks, as if to stress her questioning of the scan. A nuchal scan is an ultrasound examination and part of the foetal diagnosis that is offered to pregnant women in some of the Swedish county councils. Like all foetal diagnosis it is voluntary. A nuchal scan is performed to examine the probability of chromosome anomaly and the higher the age, the higher the risk. The pregnant woman is recommended to carefully think through the consequences of having the scan before she makes her decision: what will it mean to wait for the result and the possibility that the result shows that there is a risk of chromosome anomaly (Dellgren et al 2008)? Sara has difficulties in understanding why the test is taken, since she has not asked for it.

The denial of civil rights regarding women's sexuality and reproduction in general and disabled women's rights in particular has a long tradition. 'Gender, disability and denial of citizenship rights come together most starkly in the area of sexuality, reproductive and marriage rights. People with disabilities have been seen in some cultures as potentially disruptive of the race and nation – they constituted a threat to the gene pool', as the disability researchers Helen Meekosha and Leanne Dowse point out (1997: 56). They write from an Australian perspective, where above all aboriginal women's rights have been limited, but in Sweden this has happened too, for example through the Sterilization Laws of the 1930s and 1940s and through abortion laws.[1]

The eugenic arguments are now gone, but still the ability of disabled women to take care of a child is called in question, even if this is rejected by several empirical studies (Garland-Thomson 1997; Meekosha and Dowse

1997; Sjöberg 1998; Alexander et al 2002; Gustavsson Holmström 2002). Sjöberg (1998) argues that women with extensive impairments are questioned to a higher degree than men in a similar situation if they want to have children. It is taken for granted that men get help to take care of the child. If both parents are disabled they are even more called into question by administrators as well as employees who give concrete support. Sjöberg asks if the reason for the treatment has its source in the view of disabled people, according to which they are not regarded as 'adult women and men with the ability to manage their own lives' (Sjöberg 1998: 50, author's translation).

Both Sara and her partner are disabled. Are they not considered adult people who can judge by themselves whether they are able to take responsibility for and look after a child? Perhaps the nursing staff regard Sara's body as 'unfit for motherhood' due to her disability (Garland-Thomson 1997: 26), at least for children who in some way deviate from the norm, and hence perform extra examinations. Sara reacts with anger to the many ultrasound scans and questions the nuchal scan above all. But her concluding remark discloses a certain ambivalence: 'Maybe you should be grateful.' Her ambivalence can be interpreted as an expression of her position as, on the one hand, included, since she receives good specialist medical treatment, and, on the other, excluded, since she is subjected to extra control and pointed out as deviant when existing rules are set aside.

The uncontrollable body

Bullying

Sara is the only one in my empirical material who tells me that she has been bullied.[2] When she was small she did not regard herself as a person with an impairment: 'Before I began school ... I can't say that I knew I had an impairment. ... I didn't see it as a big difference. It's like you are sitting here wearing glasses but *I* don't wear glasses.' The fact that Sara had an impairment was just one of many bodily variations among her and her friends and nothing that they paid attention to or to which they attached value. When starting school the feeling of being one amongst the others changes. 'It began when the headmaster wanted to put me in a special class or remedial class; I really don't know what to call it nowadays. After which my parents, sort of, "but hey, she has no special needs in that way! It is physical, not mental."' The headmaster of the school seems either to be unable to distinguish physical disabilities from intellectual disabilities, or he believes that if a pupil has a physical disability this also influences their intellectual capacities. The latter is not unusual, as we have seen – Julia too says that people she meets believes she is 'stupid' because she is a wheelchair user. Sara continues:

> Gymnastics was tough. I didn't dare shower with the others. ... My feet weren't shaped like the other kids, and my legs, and so on. ... I also had

to wear incontinence diapers until I was nine, and you could see them a little through my shorts. It was embarrassing as hell!

(Sara, 19, interview)

All of a sudden, Sara's body and bodily functions are negatively valued. She becomes aware that her body does not look like her classmates. Besides, she also differs in that she is incontinent and has to have diapers, which she now finds very embarrassing. She begins to use her impairment as an excuse to avoid exposing her body during the lessons in PE: 'I was smart enough to say: "I can't do this because of my disability."' The geographer Robyn Longhurst (2003) writes about the fear of the leaking body as well as the bodily fluid that threatens to trickle out. She regards the body and the intimate 'rooms' that it inhabits as close as well as 'close*t*' spaces: 'They are close spaces in that they are familiar, near and intimate. They are also close*t* spaces in that they are often socially constructed as too familiar, near, intimate and threatening to be disclosed publicly' (Longhurst 2003: 123, italics in original). The subject feels ambivalence towards both the body as space and the body's space, as they are both familiar and threaten to be revealed. The boundaries of the space are unstable and this creates anxiety (Longhurst 2003: 123–4).[3] Sara's body looked different from the other children's and became a 'close(t) space' – the body as space is close, familiar and intimate for herself, but she tried to conceal feet, legs and diapers. Sara continues:

I had a disabled toilet at school where I had a bench with my things – catheters and diapers ... and panty liners and everything, and an extra change of clothes, just in case I had an 'accident'. Then one day when I came in some kids had taken all those things and hung them all over the school. And they stood around the school yard, and they had found out, I don't know how they got to know, but when you scare me, when you get like frightened, then it's easy to wet one's pants. And they did that, so I did it [wet myself]. And then I got bullied.

(Sara, 19, interview)

The disabled toilet is Sara's intimate space and the diapers tell about her bodily fluids and the threat of leakage. The brutal disclosure of the body as space and the body's space is a fact. Sara goes home and asks her parents:

And they had to tell me that I was different from other kids, you will never be able to walk like everybody else, and you will always have more or less leakage. You will always need to use enemas and things like that. And it became sensitive to know that, you know. That I will never be like everybody else. I don't think they had put off telling me, I think they actually thought that I knew it.

(Sara, 19, interview)

Goffman (1963/1990) notices that parents sometimes protect their children from knowing about the stigma that can arise in the interaction with others. Hence the children become unconscious 'passers' in society (Goffman 1963/1990: 113, 120). This is the case for Sara, at least indirectly since her father refused to accept that his daughter was disabled. In such situations, it is common that the person becomes aware of the process of stigmatization when first starting school, when getting interested in meeting a partner or when it is time to look for work, Goffman points out (1963/1990: 46–7). For Sara it was through the experiences in connection with starting school and the violent interaction with the other pupils that she realized that she had an impairment. At that moment she became (socially constructed as) disabled. This insight influences her way of living in the world and future projects as well.

Managing emotions

Maria speaks about the uncontrollable body in her video diary too when she depicts what happened in school the same day. Initially she tries to fasten the camera on the tripod, but gives up and puts it in her lap instead:

> Today after the French lesson something disability-related happened [smiles]. I fell today. Ah, you know, I think it's quite embarrassing to do that when you're almost grown-up. I've always thought it is rather awful, but I handled it pretty well. I didn't become ... I didn't show it on the outside anyway. I tumbled with the entire wheelchair, almost at the front door steps. I was on my way out of the entrance hall and then I stumbled over the stair, over the carpet. And that's because I was tired. Then I thought 'Damn, lift your feet!' [Little laugh]. And so I fell. There were people of course, but there weren't so many, and they always become nervous, you know. But, yes, if you just smile and brush the dust off [smiles] they don't become so nervous any more. It's just the second, no, the third time that I've fallen in school I think. The first time it occurred *that* wasn't fun. I was in a hurry on that occasion too and I was quite upset with something. I think I had had French [smiles], so that's why. ... I was wearing rather bad shoes, sneakers that fit really bad, like Cheap Monday. They are drop-dead gorgeous but I can't have them because I can't walk in them. And then I stumbled, and it was so fucking awful. People rushed up to me, and they were just kind, but ... . Oh, God! At that time I had long hair that I used to hide myself under. It was really good. I don't know if it's a thing I have that it's more embarrassing for me to fall. Or if everybody thinks it's so awful. ... People get worried, they come up to you. ... 'Oh, there she fell, oh, poor girl!' I think it's terrible. I fell a lot when I was a kid, but know I only fall when I'm tired.
>
> (Maria, 19, video diary)

Maria looks out of the window as she speaks, and smiles from time to time, especially when she looks into the camera. She begins by saying that 'something disability-related' has happened during the school day. By that utterance Maria keeps a distance between herself and disability-related things. We understand that something unusual has happened – not everything she does is disability-related just because she is disabled. The distance is strengthened by Maria's smile. As a child she fell often. Now the falling disturbs the picture of her as almost being an adult; falling is associated with small children. Maria gets a forewarning as she often begins to stumble before she falls, but she does not always manage to sit down in the wheelchair in time.

The quotation is about the uncontrollable body, but also about managing emotions, both Maria's own emotions and those of others. It seems of great importance to Maria not to show negative emotions: 'I didn't become ... I didn't show it on the outside anyway.' Was she going to say that she did not become sad, afraid, in pain or embarrassed? Whatever she experienced, she at least did not show it outwardly. Maria is engaged in what the sociologist Arlie Hochschild (2003) terms surface acting, that is to say, what Maria expresses on the surface is not in accordance with her deeper emotions. This is a situation where she risks being pitied because of her lack of control over her body. People around her become concerned; perhaps they also worry about her having hurt herself. By concealing her own emotions she also relieves others' anxiety. This 'double duty' for one's own and others' feelings is something wheelchair users often have in public spaces, the sociologists Spencer Cahill and Robin Eggleston (1994: 303) maintain. When she was younger she covered her face with her long hair, but now she quickly smiles and tries to look unconcerned.

Once again Maria shows a double consciousness; she can see herself from her own point of view but is simultaneously conscious about how others perceive her. From this Maria works out her strategies, in this case hiding her emotions and looking unconcerned or even happy. De Beauvoir describes how the woman, standing in front of the man, does not apprehend herself as only a subject but, 'assumes herself as both *self* and *other*, which is a contradiction with disconcerting consequences' (1949/2011: 755, italics in original). The woman simultaneously becomes an object and a subject. When Maria attracts gazes she becomes an object for herself. In a study into how having asthma influences young people's everyday life, the ethnologist Kristofer Hansson (2007) explores how they handle the use of an asthma inhaler. When and where do they think it is okay to inhale openly and when do they feel forced to conceal it? Several informants explain that they tend to step aside, and they discuss the negative attention that they assume that they otherwise would get and imagined emotional reactions such as anxiety and pity from people around them (Hansson 2007: 127–8, 132). Hansson's interpretation is that they regard themselves from outside as objects and 'instead of being a subject who defines himself, there was a danger that he [one of the interviewees] would have been defined by other people' (2007: 132–3, author's translation).

Pity, which is the emotion other people above all exhibit when Maria falls, has its origin in the view of disabled people as tragic. When Maria smiles and pretends that nothing happened it is to avoid being defined as tragic.

Bodily pleasure and strength

The body also gives rise to feelings of delight. In the interviews these feelings are connected to physical activity. Here I will give two examples of this and then I will come back with another two in the next chapter that deals with technology as an extension of the body. The first quotation is taken from the interview with Susanne:

> *How does it feel at the very moment when you are on the go and really extend yourself?*
> Yes, it feels, it's gorgeous you know. It is ... this persistency, which may appear. I like boxing, because there you can really get everything out, and I like that. Yes, I like being on the go.
> (Susanne, 22, interview)

Later on I ask Susanne if she has any good memory from doing sports. She first wonders, with a little laugh, if I mean 'as disabled or as not disabled'. I suggest that she begin with a memory from the time after the accident, and she relates an episode from the first girls' group she joined, in which they above all did strength training and boxing:

> It was the boxing. Maybe it wasn't good, but the leader praised me anyway. I happened to punch someone ... on the jaw. ... But we just laughed, you know. And it was tremendous fun! [little laugh] So there she got herself a knock! It was actually great fun, it's a really good memory I think.
> (Susanne, 22, interview)

Indeed, Susanne unintentionally hurt one of the girls during the boxing; but this is also a memory of physically tough training of the kind that Susanne had before the accident when she went to a school with a sports profile, and that she now has difficulty in finding. Furthermore, it includes the feeling of direct hit, praise and shared joy. The memory of the time when she was able-bodied also deals with direct hits, she says, 'Before the accident it was all the goals, all the goals in football. That feeling.' Susanne does not elaborate on what feeling she has in mind, but it is imaginable that the winner's feeling of being invincible, of pride and shared happiness are included. In this moment the unity of the body is at its clearest, as Merleau-Ponty argues:

> So the connection between the segments of our body, or between our visual and our tactile experience, is not produced gradually and through

accumulation. I do not translate the 'givens of touch' into 'the language of vision', nor *vice versa*; I do not assemble the parts of my body one by one. Rather, this translation and this assemblage are completed once and for all in me: they are my body itself.

(Merleau-Ponty 1945/2012: 151, italics in original)

Susanne does not have a body but is her body. When I ask Sara about the role physical activity has in her life she speaks about her physical ability in relation to her impairment:

> Without my commitment in sports I don't think I would have been able to walk as much as I can. … Normally I should be able to walk 250 metres, for example, but I can walk 10 kilometres if needed. I don't think I would have walked all the time, but would have used a wheelchair … . Then you feel that you can participate more. And I can do what my friends do. Maybe it sounds ridiculous but it's completely marvellous to get out on a fine day and just walk as far as I can. Other people would think 'Are you crazy, why are you walking?' But I think it's such a good thing that I can do it. … There are not many who can cycle, that is, on two wheels. I have never had any problems with that, because I learnt to ride a bike when I was five years old. And that was rather normal I think among others. I can swim, not well but I can at least keep my head above the water. I don't drown. … I can jump into a deep swimming pool alone, and I don't need anyone just staring at me all the time. And I can drive a car. Sure, I would have done that anyhow, with hand controls or something. But I have done it with an ordinary, manual car. And yes, it was a trying experience, but damn, I was determined to make it!
>
> (Sara, 19, interview)

Sara argues that if she had not done sports she would not have had the strength and ability to move that she now has. The capacity is central and related to two imagined groups: on the one hand, those who are 'normal' – that is, non-disabled; and, on the other, those who have impairments similar to Sara's. She talks about all the different things she is able to do: walk, ride a two-wheeled bike, swim, drive a car that is not adapted, and once again there is an implied 'despite' the impairment. 'Normally I should be able to walk 250 metres' refers to the capacity she thinks she ought to have given her impairment. She stresses that her physical ability does not make her different from her (non-disabled) friends and compares herself with the non-disabled when she says that she learned to ride a bike as a five-year-old child, in her opinion the 'normal' age for this. 'There are not many who can cycle, that is, on two wheels', she says, thus comparing her ability to others with her impairment. She is no good at swimming, but accentuates her independence instead: she is good enough to be able to swim without supervision. It is understood that other people with the same impairment need a car with hand controls and someone who watches over them when swimming.

Sara depicts herself as having a position between those who are considered normal and those who have the same impairment. She cannot belong to the social group of normal people, but symbolically she approaches them by accentuating her capacity and autonomy that differentiates her from other disabled people, with whom she dis-identifies. As when Sara spoke about those who are more dependent than her (Chapter 3), she now compares herself with others 'perceived to be less "fortunate"', thus enhancing her self-respect (Deal 2003: 904). Some of the boys in Barron's (1995) study use this kind of dis-identification (the opposite to identification) from other disabled people. Barron terms their strategy self-sufficiency. The boys are together with and identify with non-disabled persons of the same age and talk about other disabled people as more isolated and dependent. They do not talk about discrimination either. Barron, however, makes an important distinction: those young men may not distance themselves from people who are categorized as disabled, but from the consequences this categorization has (1995: 102–5, 129). If this is the case in Sara's story it is rather ascribed ideas of passivity and dependence that she dis-identifies with.

In the interview with Sara the capacity and the movement in itself seem to be filled with pleasure. Going for a simple stroll is so marvellous that it may sound ridiculous. Sara's situatedness in the world is determined by her body and physiological conditions, how she lives with her body in the world and how others live with her and react to her body (Moi 1999: 68). Sara experienced how her father denied her disability, which meant that assistive technology and adaptations were not available to her for a long time. This had an effect on her physical ability and – this is my interpretation – her attitude towards assistive devices and those who use them. Her body was exposed to bullying during the years in compulsory school, but has also been given national and international recognition in disability sports. Those experiences are part of her body, and make using the body pleasurable. The negative image of the self and the body that according to Sjöberg was the result of the many and long stays at hospitals is contradicted here too (1998: 42).

The appearance of the body

The beautiful body

In the interview with Julia I begin by asking her to talk about herself and her background. She says her name, where she lives, what she works with and subsequently she adds, 'I'm married to a wonderful, terrific man. Then I always smile', she laughs. Julia, who previously said that she was a '19-year-old chick' before the accident, brings up her appearance later on in the interview too:

How do you look at your body?

   Well, it's not the most beautiful body in the world, not if you compare with before. So that's tough, it is of course. But now I have found my husband nevertheless [laughs out loud]. Who has a gorgeous body, and that's fun [laughs out loud]. No, I find it tough it goes without saying. After all, I was tremendously pretty before [laughs out loud] so it was tough. Yes, it has been tough.

(Julia, 26, interview)

When I ask Julia how she regards her body she associates it with her appearance, not her strength, flexibility or capacity. She emphasizes that, obviously, it is tough that the body is not as beautiful as before the accident. The philosopher Sandra Lee Bartky (1990) stresses that the feeling of being a woman and an individual is closely linked to a body that is perceived as 'feminine':

> To have a body felt to be 'feminine' – a body socially constructed through the appropriate practices – is in most cases crucial to a woman's sense of herself as female and, since persons currently can *be* only as male or female, to her sense of herself as an existing individual. To possess such a body may also be essential to her sense of herself as a sexually desiring and desirable subject.
>
> (Bartky 1990: 77)

Consequently, for Julia, who has perceived herself as 'tremendously pretty', the disability implies that the experience of being woman, individual and a sexual subject and object is questioned. That Julia couples the beautiful body with being sexually attractive becomes clear when she quickly gets on to the man she has met 'nevertheless'– that is, despite her disability. Besides, he has a gorgeous body compared to hers. Ambjörnsson's (2004) study of girls in upper secondary school points out that having a boyfriend shows that you are heterosexually attractive, which in turn gives status. However, it is important to be able to get the 'right' boyfriend with reference to appearance, class and 'race'/ethnicity to achieve status as a successful and normal girl. The limits are narrow and the risk of failure is considerable. The boyfriend's bodily constitution, hair and clothes influence the girl's own self-image (Ambjörnsson 2004: 110, 113). When Julia talks about her husband's gorgeous body it gives her status; she shows that she is attractive and more normal. It almost seems as if his beautiful and able body can compensate for the status she lost in the accident. She objectifies her husband's body, just as Ambjörnsson's informants objectified boys' bodies when they discussed their possible suitability as boyfriends (2004: 114). Julia also says that she has entered a modelling competition abroad, and I continue:

Do you model? Have you joined any agency?

   … I can't keep as thin as you should be [laughter]. And then when I'm training I get too big muscles, the agency thought. They just go, 'Your

arms are somewhat fat' [in snobbish dialect]. I just, 'Yes, I play basketball.' 'Well, that's not so good.' 'No, but then I may just as well quit this
agency', I said. And they just, 'Eh, but we don't want you to do that.'
'No, but then you have to take my arms', I said [laughter]. And they go,
'But don't you want to be a model, isn't that your primary goal?' 'No, it's
not', I said. ...

  How did you get there then?

There was a girl [that I met through sports] who had been a model for
this agency who said, 'But you look pretty, you can be a model.' So, 'Yes,
sure!' And I applied and then I was selected for the final from a group of
about 210 in wheelchairs.

(Julia, 26, interview)

Julia accentuates that she dictated the terms as she refused to stop playing
basketball and explained to the agency that if they wanted to work with her
they had to put up with her muscles. By telling me that the agency complied
with her terms and that she was chosen out of 210 young women using
wheelchairs, she shows that she still has the power of attraction even though
her body is not 'the most beautiful in the world'. The philosopher Susan
Bordo observes that women take part in the sexualization and objectification
of their bodies (2004: 28). This can also give a certain delight, de Beauvoir
remarks, as a woman 'often derives satisfaction from her role as *Other*'
(1949/2011: 10, italics in original). I interpret Julia's story about her own
muscular model body and her husband's 'gorgeous' body as filled with
delight. Simultaneously Julia explains that a model career is not her highest
wish. The girls in Ambjörnsson's study were, on the one hand, entirely
familiar and partially agreed with the critique against popular culture's
unattainable ideals and demands about what women's bodies should look
like. On the other hand, they tried to attain precisely these ideals by means
of make-up, hairstyle and clothes (Ambjörnsson 2004: 156, 182–3). Maybe
Julia's repeated laughter when she speaks about her and her husband's bodies
indicates a consciousness about and a distance to the sexualization and
objectification she takes part in.

The teenager's dissatisfaction

In a video clip Maria complains about having put on weight and that she
ought to train more. But she also tells that she and her little sister have baked
three chocolate cakes during the last four days, and cheerfully shows the
snack she is eating: ice cream with Nutella, shredded coconut and cacao. In
the following quotation Maria speaks about her acne. She has watched the
video she made earlier that day and noted that her acne is visible. Maria is
now very close to the camera, she stretches the upper lip to show a pimple
under her nose, puts her hair behind the ear, bends the chin and points with
her finger along the line of her jaw:

> I need help. Look, I have fat, disgusting things here and here! This is inhuman! You shouldn't have to put up with this. I have had it since I was 11. ... I know that this has nothing to do with this, but I am so terribly upset about this. I don't *want* it anymore, it's so awfully unfair. It's no *teenage* period, hell, this is a disease. I think I should have some powerful medicine, that's for sure!
>
> (Maria, 19, video diary)

The acne appears worse than Maria's disability. She uses strong superlatives: the acne is 'inhuman' and that she has been subjected to it is 'so awfully unfair'. To express dissatisfaction over one's body in this way was common among the middle-class girls that Ambjörnsson (2004) studied. Ambjörnsson argues that since the mid-1990s there has been a public discourse about young women, appearance and the pressure they are exposed to from society, a discourse that the participants in her study were well aware of. Among the middle-class girls the talk about dissatisfaction, or what Ambjörnsson calls 'bad body talk' (expressed between girls in the homosocial intercourse), appeared as the norm, as a way of constituting themselves as girls. It is a discourse that girls must show that they can handle. To say that you are satisfied is unthinkable; you would stand out as too cocky (Ambjörnsson 2004: 177–80, 308). When Maria, a small and slender teenager, complains about her fatness and acne it can be interpreted as a way to present herself as a normal teenage girl. She shows that she can master the talk about the unsuccessful body. According to Ambjörnsson, the interaction follows a pattern: the dissatisfaction expressed is answered with a compliment, which in turn is dismissed. But, as Ambjörnsson adds, 'a girl who really is overweight, has sagging breasts or a potbelly seems less ready to express herself' (Ambjörnsson 2004: 181, author's translation). This explains how Julia in the previous paragraph could talk about her body as less beautiful – the modelling competition has proved that in comparison with other young disabled women she is still pretty. That Maria would talk about her disability as 'inhuman' or 'unfair' is not likely either. Then her way of speaking is completely different:

> I'm actually not so sad because I'm disabled. Of course, if someone had offered me a pair of sound legs I would have taken them immediately. But I don't think you should bury yourself in that sort of thing even if it's quite easy to do that for me too. But in principle I don't do that. And my pals don't think about it either as far as I know [shakes her head]. They say that if you have got to know me it doesn't matter a damn.
>
> (Maria, 19, video diary)

Maria admits that she could easily have been absorbed in her situation as disabled, and earlier she talked about her sadness after the operation. But she seems to have arrived at a decision in principle about which approach she should have to her life: you should not be sad. Consequently, her disability is nothing she or her friends pay much attention to. This can be understood as a dis-identification from the tragic or even the self-pitying position that is ascribed to disabled persons.

Concluding discussion

In this chapter the ambivalence towards medical care, which is part of Young's (1990/2011) marginalization, has been explored. The participants in the study meet a large number of social and medical professionals who assess and define their needs, and they risk being exposed to integrity-violating treatment in the form of objectification and increased control. Operations are performed with the interviewees' best interests in mind; but at the same time these interventions in their bodies lead to a loss of control and integrity. I interpret Maria's refusal to wear the prescribed underwear provided by the hospital and her discussions as to which colour of plaster is most attractive as attempts to guard her personal integrity in a situation in which her body is entrusted to others. Sara feels that her ability to make decisions regarding her own life is called into question, when hospital personnel conduct a nuchal scan during her pregnancy without acquiring her consent. She objects imme-diately by protesting against the test and the number of ultrasound examinations.

The changing nature of impairment is illustrated. The experience of one's own impairment is relative. The habitual body appears capable and normal while the newly operated body stands out as disabled.

Interviewees describe how they have experienced cultural domination (Young 1990/2011) in the form of stereotyping and othering when those in their environment assume that physical impairment is associated with an intel-lectual impairment, and with others treating them with pity. Maria and Sara describe how they control or hide their bodies to avoid stigmatization. Maria expresses a double consciousness – from previous experience she knows how others usually view her and define her on the basis of her impairment. When she falls down, her strategy is to smile instead of showing her real feelings, in order to avoid others' pity. When Sara begins school, she gets bullied (which again is an example of violence) and that completely changes her experiences of the body.

Furthermore, the participants describe the joy they feel when they exhaust themselves or when they score a goal. Sara describes the pleasure and thrill she experience when she takes a walk, cycles or swims, at the same time as she dis-identifies from other disabled people – or from the categorization of them as passive and dependent – as she claims that those others need more help and aids and that she is as capable as 'normal' people.

The accident and the impairment that have resulted from the accident have, according to Julia, made her body less attractive. When she describes her husband's body as 'gorgeous' and that she got to the finals in a modelling competition for women in wheelchairs, she shows that she still has (sexual) appeal. Maria, on the other hand, complains about her acne and about gaining weight. Expressing displeasure over the body in such a manner, they represent themselves as 'normal' young women.

Notes

1 There were three indications for sterilization, according to the 1941 law: firstly eugenic, which also included severe bodily disease and severe bodily defect (physical disability). Secondly a social indication. An asocial way of life was considered as grounds for not being able to take care of children. Finally a medical indication that included disease, bodily dysfunction or weakness of the woman. The implementation was clearly gendered. Between 1935 and 1975 more than 90 per cent of those sterilized were girls and women, even though sterilization of men would have been more logical, considering both surgical methods and the genetic theory of the time (Broberg and Tydén 1996: 120). Female low-income earners ran a greater risk of being sterilized than high-income earners. For a discussion regarding Swedish abortion laws, see, for instance, Maud Eduards (2007).

2 At the sports camp 13-year-old Petter also talks about being bullied. Petter, who alternates between a prosthesis on one leg and crutches, likes to play football but his classmates 'prefer me not to join'. Sometimes, he explains, 'I have happened to use the crutch, and then they get so angry.' Petter's classmates say 'that I'm just so lousy and things like that. … But I'm not. When I get within shooting range when it's football, then I shoot and I can score a goal.' Once they started fighting, and Petter gives a vivid portrayal of the situation: 'they were bullying me, and I said, "What the hell are you saying?" Then they go, "Are you looking for a fight?" … So I said, "Yes, come on!" Then he just hit me, he gave me a blow in the stomach, and then he hit me here. Then he took a chair and beat me on the head. Then I got so bloody angry so I hit him on the head with the crutch.'

3 Longhurst takes the philosopher and psychoanalyst Julia Kristeva's (1982) notions of abject and abjection as her starting point. The abjection arises from the child's ambivalent struggle to separate from the mother's body, which simultaneously is the body that nurtures and comforts (Young 1990/2011: 143). Kristeva claims that the self must expel the abject in order to secure a clean, proper and socialized body. 'It is thus not lack of cleanliness or health that causes abjection but what disturbs identity, system, order. What does not respect borders, positions, rules. The in-between, the ambiguous, the composite' (Kristeva 1982: 4). The movement is a twofold one: the subject is fascinated and attracted to the object, then overcome by disgust or fear and retreats from it. Hughes (2009) claims that the strength of the two concepts lies in their uncovering of the fantasy of the normal ideal body that only exists with the help of cleaning, training and repression. While the theory of the personal tragedy can explain pity, emotions such as disgust and fear, which also colour the relation between disabled and non-disabled persons, can be theorized by means of the abject (Hughes 2009: 408). However, the notions are seldom used within disability studies and need to be further developed in future research.

5   Technology, gender and the body

In my empirical material several types of technology, such as wheelchairs, rehabilitative devices and sports equipment, are mentioned in different contexts. Ingunn Moser (2006), researcher in science and technology studies, points out that the role of technology is largely unexplored in disability studies. This can be explained by researchers' attempts to replace previous medical models of explanation and their focus on the individual and normalizing measures, with social and cultural analyses of disability (Moser 2006: 375). Assistive technologies represent the medical professionals' endeavour to compensate for individual impairments and have as such been of little interest (Blume 2012: 349). However, in disability sports research the difference between everyday technology and the technology that is used in disability sports contexts has been emphasized. Hargreaves argues that 'the wheelchair, normally a symbol of weakness, of dependency, of neediness, when used for track races is transformed into a symbol of power, speed and muscularity' (2000: 190). It should be added that these are two quite different types of wheelchairs differing in appearance and function. Wickman (2007a) claims that sports technology, for instance prostheses, can challenge the boundaries between bodies with or without impairments by reducing physical differences and contributing 'to the production of "super sportsmen" and "super sportswomen."' But no matter how good the sports results are, the disabled body is still considered 'different and … inferior to the non-impaired body' (Wickman 2007a: 7).

Phenomenology offers analytical tools to explore the functions of assistive technology. Merleau-Ponty (1945/2012) compares the blind person's stick with the gaze. The former 'has ceased to be an object for him, it is no longer perceived for itself; rather, the cane's furthest point is transformed into a sensitive zone, it increases the scope and the radius of the act of touching and has become analogous to a gaze' (Merleau-Ponty 1945/2012: 144). The stick becomes an extension of the body and a utensil with which the blind person perceives the surroundings. In this way the habit – that is, knowledge that only can be obtained through the body, and thus not objectively mediated – can incorporate new instruments or aids and by these extend our 'being in the world'; the stick is one example of a perceptual as well as a motor habit (Merleau-Ponty 1945/2012: 145, 153). Merleau-Ponty's example has certain similarities to

Haraway's (1999) use of the metaphor of the cyborg, as described in *A Cyborg Manifesto: Science, Technology, and Socialist-Feminism in the Late Twentieth Century*. Haraway's cyborg is, just like Merleau-Ponty's blind man with a stick, a hybrid of an organism and a machine. But Haraway politicizes the cyborg, describing it as a female figure in the borderland that questions the whole, normal body with her mere existence. The cyborg is a conscious actor who actively disturbs order and crosses boundaries. According to Haraway we all are cyborgs who use information technology and modern medicine but, she adds, 'Perhaps paraplegics and other severely handicapped people can (and sometimes do) have the most intense experiences of complex hybridization with other communication devices' (1999: 178).

Haraway only mentions disability once in *A Cyborg Manifesto*, and cyborg theory has mostly engaged disability metaphorically (McRuer 2006: 224). But Moser (2000) applies Haraway's notion of the cyborg as an alternative to prevailing rehabilitation discourse and as a possible figure in theorizing about a marginalized position – that of the disabled. Moser writes about Olav, a man who lost his faculty of speech after a stroke and became partially paralysed on his right side. By means of computerized technology, Olav maintains contact with the world around him and with his life before the stroke. The computer gives Olav a voice and makes self-representation possible. In this way he becomes an agent instead of a passive recipient, and restores his dignity. The computer has become 'an ally and an opponent. It is both a friend and an intimate part of him' (Moser 2000: 230). Moser argues that Olav's subjectivity comes into being in the relation between body and machine – that is, through the heterogeneous cyborg. However, Moser does not discuss gendered aspects of Olav's use of technology in his self-presentation.

The sociologists Diana Mulinari and Kerstin Sandell (1999) problematize the idea of crossing boundaries as they stress that the opportunities to cross look different depending on social position: 'The transcendence beyond the body is the ancient patriarchal dream, and moving across boundaries out of pleasure speaks to experiences of privileged subjects and elites' (1999: 293). Haraway also depicts the crossing as free from conflict, while several researchers insist that such action in fact implies a personal risk-taking that is often followed by punishment (Pratt 1991; Mulinari and Sandell 1999: 293; Bordo 2004: 298).[1] That said, I will now use Merleau-Ponty's description of the significance of bodily knowledge for using assistive technology, in combination with the metaphor of the cyborg to explore how the hybrid machine-human being can problematize the idea of the whole, homogeneous body. To begin with, however, the role of technology when the participants in the study are made the Other will be explored.

Othering

Assistive technology can reduce impairment effects (Thomas 2007: 135; Reeve 2012: 103), as when Sara got her first wheelchair at the age of 20 and could move around more easily and without having pain (see Chapter 3). It can also have negative effects, causing soreness, repetitive strain injuries and increased pain (Reeve 2012: 96). Jenny says that all the wheeling when she plays basketball has its price: 'It takes its toll on the shoulders and arms. Those are the main disadvantages.' When in pain, Jenny is reminded of both her body and her wheelchair. The body that tends to disappear from our awareness in everyday life 'dysappears' again in a dysfunctional way (Paterson and Hughes 1999: 602), and the wheelchair is no longer experienced as an extension of the body. Several of my interviewees also discuss their experiences of the wheelchair becoming a negative sign of difference, and of themselves being 'marked out as different and subject to stigma' (Reeve 2012: 97). Ingela claims that the students in her first school wished to exclude her as one of their classmates because of her wheelchair:

> They [the classmates] haven't really accepted me. ... In my first school I was the only one sitting in a wheelchair. And then, they didn't really want to ... They stood in front of me and said, 'Oh, she pushed me' and sort of 'ran into me' and such things. So, you see, they didn't want me at all. I was pretty much alone.
>
> (Ingela, 17, interview)

The wheelchair becomes a hindrance in the interaction between Ingela and her classmates, both literally and metaphorically. Ingela describes it as a lack of will among the others in the class, which makes it difficult for her to get friends. As we saw in Chapter 3, Julia observed that people she met noticed her in a new way when she became a wheelchair user. She described how she handled the stares and often succeeded to create meetings that gave rise to empathetic identification. Two more interviewees talk about how able-bodied people focus on their wheelchair. Nathalie and Malin, both 15, recalled strangers in town asking them questions about why they used a wheelchair. They have developed slightly different attitudes and put time and energy into answering the questions. Malin explains that it is mostly children that approach her:

> You notice it sometimes when you go and look around the shops or go into town. In most cases there are small kids that approach and some-times ask. I just say that I have an impairment that I was born with, so I must sit in a wheelchair. And they tend to be sort of satisfied with that.
> *And how does it feel?*
> It feels quite good actually. Yes, it doesn't bother me so.
>
> (Malin, 15, interview)

Malin does not care much about the questions. She gives a simple answer that satisfies the wondering person, and is thus left alone. Gazes or stares from the child precede the questions. Garland-Thomson (2009) notes that people who are 'stareable', due to the use of a wheelchair for instance, often develop a number of strategies to handle the staring. The strategies vary depending on several situational aspects, including who the starer is and in which way he or she stares, but also depending on the staree's form of the day. Adults' sometimes furtive glances can be difficult to meet. Other times adults can feel entitled to stare intrusively and pose too intimate questions. In Malin's case it is mostly children who stare. They have not yet learnt that staring is considered impolite. They stare with wonder and curiosity and do not turn their eyes away when discovered, but pose questions that Malin answers. Previous research reveals that the staree more often has indulgence with those, or feels responsibility for teaching them how to look or for answering them (Cahill and Eggleston 1994: 303; Garland-Thomson 2009: 88–9, 95). 'It feels quite good actually', Malin explains, which I interpret as the staring being transformed into a rather positive and productive meeting. Natalie on the other hand explains, 'When I go into town people approach and ask me a lot of things. … [It feels] a bit tiresome. I don't want to answer people I hardly know, whom I never have met before.' However, she is ambivalent towards the questions: 'Somehow it's good that they ask, because then they get to know.' Nathalie thinks it is good that people get knowledge. But often the questions feel troublesome, and then Natalie has another strategy to handle the situation. 'I'm not always in mood for answering. Then I just say, "Yes, but it's so and so and so." And then I leave.' By giving an abrupt answer and then leaving the spot she escapes the situation and further questions. In both cases it is the reason for Malin and Natalie to use wheelchairs, that is to say, the injury or diagnosis, which makes other people curious.

Nathalie also speaks of how people stare at her in situations where she is the only one using a wheelchair:

> If there are lots of people that are able to walk, and then I come to the group, using a wheelchair. It gets so embarrassing. … When I am going horseback riding for instance, then someone has to put me up on the horse, because I can't get up by myself. Then people may be staring. …
> *How does it feel then, people watching?*
> It's really annoying!
>
> (Natalie, 15, interview)

When Nathalie is seated on the horse, it is not her impairment as such that constitutes the hindrance, but the non-disabled gaze or stare (Garland-Thomson 1997: 26; 2009; Hughes 1999: 165; Guthrie and Castelnuovo 2001: 18). The stares seem more difficult to manage than the questions. The staring does not directly encourage answers, as the questions do. It is going on from a certain distance and when Natalie is busy mounting her horse. Hence she cannot choose to answer by meeting the stares either. Simultaneously she becomes self-conscious and her agency is hindered (Young 1980: 154; Bartky 1990: 27). 'Instead of coinciding exactly with herself, here she is existing *outside* of her self' (de Beauvoir 1949/2011: 349, italics in original). The body 'dysappears' (Paterson and Hughes 1999: 602) in this situation too, not because of pain but due to the stares. In both cases the wheelchair is central in the othering of the young women and in reducing them to being defined by their diagnoses. 'The prosthetic is endowed with cultural and social meanings which in turn impact on identity and subjectivity', as the disability studies theorist Donna Reeve states (2012: 105). The same could be said about all technology.

For Sara, who is 19 years old, the reverse sometimes happens. She becomes irritated when she hears comments like:

> "Oh, you are disabled and you can still do things!" I hate when people say things like that, and when they get really impressed just because nowadays, for instance, I can drive a manual car; or they say, "Oh, even though you have that, you can drive a car!" Why shouldn't I?
>
> (Sara, 19, interview)

This is an example of positive discrimination due to her disability. When Sara, despite impairment, uses the technology of 'normal' people – a car not adapted with accessibility features – the boundary between the deviant and the normal is transcended, and Sara is met with astonishment. However, the underlying assumption is that Sara, because of her impairment, is incompetent.

Falling in love with a wheelchair

Felicia, 28 years old, needs a new wheelchair and talks about what is important:

> It must be light in weight and easy to wheel, of course. And [it is important that] you sit well. You should sit well but not comfortably, you know, you shouldn't sit like in an armchair. There are many who have armrests, high back and almost a headrest. There are those who need it, they should have it. But I can also see an ignorance, at least when I was younger, among physiotherapists but above all the occupational therapist, maybe, 'Yes, you should have support for the back.' They didn't give the person a chance to feel.
>
> (Felicia, 28, interview)

The function of the wheelchair, its comfort and how easy it is to handle is important to Felicia. But the wheelchair, which is meant to increase the user's mobility, can also promote passivity if the comfort is too good or the wheelchair begins to resemble an armchair. Felicia speaks in general terms and is critical of occupational therapists who suggest wheelchairs that are too comfortable and, besides, are not sensitive especially to the younger users' needs. Thus she concurs with the critique in the disability movement and disability studies of how professionals in medical and social institutions create and worsen dependency and passivity among disabled people (Thomas 2007: 97).

When Julia, who is 26 years old, speaks about her present wheelchair she also looks back to the time when she was newly injured:

> *How do you look upon the wheelchair? You have this and then you have a training wheelchair.*
>
> Mm exactly. It's an aid that I notice when there's snow, otherwise I don't think so much about it. … I don't think that it exists. In the beginning I didn't like it but now I do.
>
> *Though you'd rather have had a wheelchair that weighs 2.1?*
>
> Yes, that's right yes! But that's just because you'll be cool, it's important what image your chair has so you don't come with some great big thing. You should have a nice chair, that's important, you know. … I have silver hubs here, there aren't many who have silver hubs for instance [laughter]. Rather slim-lined, yes, rather nice tyres here. Yes, but that's important!
>
> *When you chose this chair there were such demands?*
>
> Yes, absolutely, I would never… Yes, Good God, I would never have a chair that was ugly, that's for sure! It's nonetheless a part of me that I bring along everywhere I go.
>
> (Julia, 26, interview)

As newly injured Julia did not like her wheelchair. Now she describes the wheelchair as 'a part of me' that she likes but does not think of. In Merleau-Ponty's words it has ceased to be a thing, and 'is only given through a bodily effort' (1945/2012: 145). She is not reminded of it until such things as snow hinder her. Appearance and image are important when Julia chooses a wheelchair. The lightweight chair is primarily desirable because it is 'cool', not because it is easy to handle. Silver, slim-lined and nice tyres are what she wants. The negative opposite is the 'great big thing' that, just like an armchair, evokes the picture of something heavy and clumsy that can hardly be moved, and is in poor accordance with their well-trained bodies.

Susanne, who is 22 years old, explains in her video diary that she too had difficulty accepting new technology linked to the body as newly impaired. She was offered a standing aid after the accident, she explains, while showing the stander and how it works: 'Directly after the accident I had one of these too, but at that time I *refused* to sit in it. So I returned it.' Now she has contacted the local authority and received one again, 'It's really good for my muscles to stretch out thoroughly.' Goffman argues that people who are exposed to processes of stigmatization when they are older, if they acquire an impairment, for instance, can have problems redefining their identity, and disapprove of themselves initially (1963/1990: 48). Perhaps assistive technology symbolized negative difference, passivity and dependence for Julia and Susanne before the accidents, and when they needed them themselves they disliked them. The non-disabled gaze that they had turned towards those others in wheelchairs was suddenly directed towards themselves and their aids. However, in the course of time the habit, that is, the bodily knowledge Merleau-Ponty (1945/2012: 144–5) describes, has resulted in Julia incorporating the wheelchair as a part of herself and Susanne accepting the stander. As the aids have become an extension of their bodies the appearance and function become all the more important.

This is even more manifest when Maria shows her wheelchair, twirling around in front of the video camera:

> This is my favourite wheelchair ever. … It is so tremendously fine! It is really *gorgeous*! It is so easy to handle, and it is *really* pretty! … [Turns the camera downwards and rotates from side to side to allow the wheelchair to be seen.] It is sporty in a pretty way. Otherwise, I don't like the word sporty, but … . It is pretty because it is not the chair you see when you see me. But it's, so to speak, *me. Precisely*, just like it should be. Yes, it was love at first sight! [Comes close to the camera with her face.] There is room for improvement, absolutely, but yes. I'm simply in love [with it].
>
> (Maria, 17, video diary)

My interpretation is that Maria's expression of love for her wheelchair is part of a conscious strategy against pity. She calls herself a fighter. Criticizing the treatment she gets from people in everyday interactions, she claims that:

> The worst thing you can do is pity someone. … If you pity someone you regard that person as being inferior. As if that person doesn't get along. And I do. … I have no, I see myself, you know, I am disabled, but I can do anything that's demanded of me to go along in this society.
>
> (Maria, 17, interview)

Maria expresses herself in general terms about how it is when you pity someone: you regard that person as inferior and incapable. Garland-Thomson stresses that pity functions to diminish, creates distance and thus counteracts reciprocity (2009: 93), a description that fits well with Maria's picture. Next Maria emphasizes that she does not belong to the category of incapable, and hence dissociates herself from the view of her as being hit by a personal tragedy. Even if the retakes in the last sentence are incomplete, they show the extent of her capacity: I have no, I see myself, I am, and I can. She argues that the person who is being pitied is simultaneously made inferior. By talking about her wheelchair as pretty and by claiming it was 'love at first sight', Maria opposes the view of it as a negative sign of difference and personal tragedy. Moreover, Maria accentuates that the new wheelchair brings her out as a person, not as belonging to the category of wheelchairs users. Thus, Maria turns the reasoning upside down – the technology that is said to define disabled people instead becomes a resource for the opposite.

Assistive technology and sports equipment: Femininity, pleasure and strength

The next quotation is about Ingela's basketball wheelchair – a purpose-built wheelchair that is lighter than an ordinary wheelchair and has skewed wheels that makes it easier to turn around. Wheelchair basketball is described as one of the fastest and toughest of the disability sports (Malmö Open, 2015) and rough collisions that overturn the chairs are common. Ingela's feeling of not being completely accepted by her classmates changes as soon as she arrives with her basketball wheelchair:

> When I bring my basketball wheelchair and they [my classmates] have been playing basketball, then they are sort of like, 'Wow, I want to try!' And then they become completely different.
>
> *The mates?*
>
> Yes. And when I am with my older brother ... they change. It is hard to explain. ... [It is as if they are saying] 'I am your best friend!' Because they probably wanted to try it. ... Then, the next day, they are just the same as before.
>
> (Ingela, 17, interview)

Ingela moves from a position of rejection (the subject position as disabled) to acceptance as a young sporting woman and the owner of a piece of desirable sports equipment. The basketball wheelchair temporarily gives her the status she otherwise lacks, and opens up for a possible identification. The presence of her older brother, a top-level football player, contributes to the rise of status. On the one hand, in the field of sports the boundaries between the two categories disabled/deviant bodies and able/universal bodies (the latter including both the normal and the extraordinary) are strong. Swartz and Watermeyer stresses that the idea of the perfect, sporting body does not comprise bodies considered deviant:

> The idealized, mythic valuing of the perfect body, with its associations of personal virtue, carries as its counterpoint the denigration of persons with different bodies. The unspoken assumptions about these bodies, and their inhabitants, relate to undesirability, psychological damage, abjection and failure.
>
> (Swartz and Watermeyer 2008: 189)

Inclusion of disabled people would threaten to destabilize the construction of the normal, human body and the boundaries between the two categories (Swartz and Watermeyer 2008: 189; see also Brittain 2004: 438). On the other hand, sports equipment and assistive technology are two fields close to each other. Shoes for different sports, specially designed canoes and custom bicycles are used to perform more easily, faster and smoother. Assistive technology of different kinds, such as wheelchairs, prostheses and crutches, are also used for the same purposes. Ingela does not actively and explicitly fight against being categorized as disabled as Maria does. However, as female wheelchair basketball players they both challenge the view of disabled people as passive, deficient and subjected to personal tragedy, by being active and capable. They also oppose the gender regime in sports by showing themselves to be young females who play a tough contact sport involving strength, endurance, danger, risk-taking and violence (see Koivula 1999: 54). Technology is of vital importance in this effort.

Maria, in the earlier quotation, illustrates the link between sports equipment and assistive technology by characterizing her wheelchair as sporty, thus relocating it from one field to another. She also shifts her wheelchair from a masculine field of technology to a feminine field of accessories when talking about it as 'tremendously fine', 'really gorgeous' and 'sporty in a pretty way'. Previous research (Mellström 2004; Holth and Mellström 2011) has shown that even though women use technology as much as men do and are as technologically skilled as men are, technology is seen as a cultural expression of masculinity. Early on, boys are socialized into the pleasures of technological tinkering, develop an embodied relationship to machines and form male bonds to earlier generations through this tinkering in homosocial environments (Mellström 2004; Holth and Mellström 2011). Maria's talk is a way for her to construct femininity despite sitting in a masculinely coded wheelchair.

Garland-Thomson points out that the cultural image of disabled women disturbs two opposed paradigms: being seen 'as the opposite of the masculine figure, but also imagined as the antithesis of the normal woman, the figure of the disabled female is thus ambiguously positioned both inside and outside the category of woman' (1997: 28–9). Maria counters the image of the disabled woman as non-gendered and asexual in the way she talks about her wheelchair, thereby constructing a more traditional femininity that complies with the emphasized femininity of the time.

Haraway's cyborg is a female figure who questions the normal. She is what Moser calls a 'bad girl' who refuses to be a woman (1998: 215). Those interviewed do not refuse to be women, but they are 'bad girls' insofar as they do not accept the ascribed subject position as being non-gendered and as defined by their disabilities. Ingela recounts her sheer delight in physical activity:

> I was scheduled for an operation on Tuesday, but we had a training camp scheduled in Stockholm from Friday to Sunday [the weekend before]. So it was my last basketball training session, you could say. It was rather fun. I drove like anything that Sunday. And then on Thursday I lay completely flat and couldn't move.
>
> (Ingela, 17, interview)

The contrasts in the quotation are strong. The memory of how she 'drove like anything' during the training camp gave her pleasure and strength when she lay immobile a few days later after having back surgery. When the interview took place, Ingela had not been in training for almost a year because of her operation. Telling me about her capability and skill as a basketball player became important for her self-representation, so that it was in accordance with her self-image, and in this self-representation technology played a significant part.

Susanne eagerly related how she loves driving at high speed in her wheelchair, her dog running at her side, and sweating heavily. 'It is fun. And it's high speed. It's not strolling. … If you have been out on a really long walk with the dog and you come home, like completely sweaty, you know, it is a marvellous feeling'. Susanne's focus on joy and having fun counters the negative approach to disabled people as well, or what health researchers Naomi Sunderland, Tara Catalano and Elizabeth Kendall call 'missing discourses of joy and happiness in relation to disability' (2009: 703). When Susanne accentuates that 'It's not strolling' it is also possible that she distances herself from and belittles non-disabled people's way of taking their dogs on the walk, and instead 'up' values her own considerably faster wheeling.[2]

In Ingela and Susanne's stories about how bodily feelings of speed, strength and pleasure arise, technology and body are inseparable. They are their bodies, and technology is incorporated in these bodies. As for Olav in Moser's study, technology is 'a friend and an intimate part' of their lives (2000: 230). The boundaries between body and machine dissolves. During physical activity they also transcend the embodied limitations that, following Young (1980), characterize the emphasized femininity: they fulfil the movement, they do not doubt their capacity and they use their whole body together with the wheelchairs.

Concluding discussion

Several examples of cultural imperialism (Young 1990/2011) have appeared in this chapter. The wheelchair has a central role in the othering of the participants. While Ingela's wheelchair seems to stand between Ingela and her classmates in a double sense, Malin and Natalie tell about strangers who stare and pose questions, thereby contributing to them being defined by their diagnosis or injuries. But especially the curious questions from children seem easier to handle. Malin and Natalie answer them, and hence satisfy the children's search for knowledge. Positive discrimination is also coupled with the use of technology, as when people are impressed by Sara driving a non-adapted car 'despite' being disabled.

However, those interviewed make use of their wheelchairs when constructing their identities as young women and active subjects. The wheelchair has become an extension of their bodies. As such, its appearance and function are important. The armchair represents passivity and immobility, and hence is rejected. In talking about pleasure and strength they oppose the view of disabled people as passive, needy and pitiful. They also challenge the gender regime in sports by displaying toughness, strength and risk-taking, while constructing a more compliant femininity when they oppose the view of disabled women as non-gendered and asexual. Like heterogeneous cyborgs, they question the dichotomies between organism and machine, natural and artificial, able-bodied and disabled, active and passive, normal and deviant, female and male, as well as the idea of the essentialist wholeness of the human body.

Notes

1 In *Identity: Skin Blood Heart* (1991), the feminist scholar Minnie Bruce Pratt describes how moving across boundaries resulted in her being severely punished when, as a lesbian, she stepped out of the white heterosexual woman's 'circle of protection': 'Raised to believe that I could be where I wanted and have what I wanted and be who I wanted, as a grown woman I thought I could simply claim my desire, even if this was the making of a new place to live with other women. I had no understanding of the limits that I lived within; nor of how much my memory and my experience of a safe space was based on places that had been secured for me by omission, exclusion, or violence; nor that my continued safety meant submitting to those very limits' (Pratt 1991).
2 Thanks to the historian Helena Tolvhed, who pointed out this interpretation to me.

6 Sporting bodies and gender

Friday evening.
Snow outdoors. I walk to the Baltic Hall [a sports centre in Malmö, Sweden]. My intention is to watch two matches this evening: one with each team out of which I will interview a player. On Saturday morning I will return and interview at least one of them. I have spoken to one of them over the telephone and have had e-mail contact with the other one and told them that I will come and say hello on Friday evening. First I go up to the janitors and ask for a room where I can do the interviews. I get the phone number to the janitor that works on Saturday. A stand in the entrance advertises catheters, there are catheter samples for free and a bowl of toffees. … There are only a few spectators. I sit down behind one of the teams to be able to hear what they are talking about. … At my side three young women take their seats, together with a small girl. I understand that they know a boy in the team. … A few more people drop in on the grandstand, I count up to 26 people altogether. One more girl sits down some seats beyond the others, and occasionally they ask her a question and I understand that they know each other too. I get the same feeling as in previous years when I have attended matches in wheelchair basketball, wheelchair rugby, sledge hockey or table tennis: everybody knows each other because they are either relatives, functionaries or employed. And, true or not, everybody wonders who I am.

As last year, I think to myself that the possibility to block the opposing team with the wheelchairs really gives the game its character. It also makes the game considerably tougher than basketball. Sometimes the confrontations are forceful and the chairs overturn. But they are always quickly on their wheels again; it very seldom leads to calling off. A couple of times the wheelchairs get stuck together and a functionary has to take off a wheel – but it is quick work.

XX is heard during the match. For instance, she calls out which number she is blocking and warns if someone is coming close to the goal area and needs to be stopped. She is the one who takes the throw-ins. Several times I think that I should only follow her, but my gaze over and over again slips over to the player who has the ball, and that is never XX, except for the throw-ins.

Saturday morning.
[I see two matches] …

Saturday 2: 00 pm.
I am actually finished for today but feel like watching the semi-final and am curious about the outcome. I also think about my credibility as a researcher, but, above all else, the game has really captivated me. I persuade my daughters to come along, promising them Saturday sweets from the closest grocery store. […]

Saturday evening.
Once again it is a mixture of excitement and my desire to be credible that makes me put down the dinner cutlery five minutes to eight and then jog along in the falling snow to the Baltic Hall. To my own astonishment, on a Saturday when I had been looking forward to a lazy evening in the TV sofa! The away team was so skilled; it was really fun watching them play, and it will be exciting to see them meet the home team. I buy a ticket and enter a crowded hall, just as Calaisa [a local band] begins to play. Afterwards I read that they have taken a break from their gramophone recording in London for this gig. The hall is full of people and expectations. Functionaries stop me. The seats at the end of the rows are reserved for disabled spectators, but the girl finds a seat in the upper part of the grandstand. However, I want to sit further down, and finally she finds a seat in the third row. People with wheelchairs sit on the other side of the boards; some young people have assistants with them. A large screen shows close-ups of Calaisa. The spectators shout with joy and after three songs two women dressed in brown blouses with puffed sleeves and black skirts enter and give them a bouquet of flowers each. After Calaisa a *compère* informs us that Silvia [the queen of Sweden] didn't have time to come so the Swedish king will give a speech instead. A dressed-up comedian plays the king and it is really funny! Everybody laughs. A young girl and talent-hunt winner sings a pop version of the Swedish national anthem. Then the two teams enter the hall and begin to warm up while the house band plays covers from a small stage in one of the corners. I have already seen the home team warm up twice; it really looks nice, and more professional than other teams I have seen. The game begins. It is incredibly thrilling! The first two periods the home team leads by a few points, then the other team catches up, but the home team takes the lead again. I am happy, because the only woman in the two teams gets to play quite a bit. As usual her task seems to be to hinder the antagonists and do the throw-ins. I am fully absorbed by the game, applaud and cheer with the rest of the audience. This is something completely different from the matches I have seen earlier during the day or during Malmö Open on the whole. It is professional, well-organized, a party, and I am part of an enthusiastic crowd. The commentator explains the rules, gives current goal statistics for individual players and makes it easier to follow

the game. The house band plays electronic organ during longer stoppages in the match. During the breaks two rigged-out characters enter and dance around the court: an elephant and an inflatable man with a top hat that makes him about three metres high. Malmö All-star Cheer wait at one of the short sides, dressed in purple and white miniskirts and with purple and silver bows in their hair. They go in and dance and do some gymnastic tricks between the periods and during longer breaks.

When two periods are played there is a longer break. A woman takes the microphone. She is going to hand out a sports award. This is when my way of seeing shifts. The award goes to a male sports leader. The women in puffed sleeves bring in flowers again. The cheerleader girls enter the court and show their panties once more. Suddenly I catch sight of Malmö All Star Cheer's leader at one side of the court. It is an adult woman with long, brown hair. She too has a big school-girlish purple bow with long ribbons in her hair. The third period begins. There is a male commentator, three male judges and four male coaches. The female player, who has won the ball once, gets, as far as I know, the one and only pass during this match. I hear her name being shouted at the very moment she misses the ball, of course, since it is entirely unexpected. Halfway in the third period the away team takes the lead and the distance between them and the home team increases inexorably. They are simply better at scoring. Afterwards Mona Sahlin [then chairman of the Swedish Social Democratic Party] gives medals to the winners. There are even more flower girls now, and, as a matter of fact, at the end there is a boy with a bouquet. But he does not need to have puffed sleeves.

And why should it be different? Why should disability sports be more gender-transgressive, less macho? Because of the mixed teams somebody may say. But as long as there are only one or two girls in each team no change will occur. Perhaps the need to stay close to a hegemonic masculinity is even greater among disabled men, as compensation? Maybe the able-bodied men who play wheelchair basketball are the transgressive ones.

(Written down after observation, based on field notes)

Gender, sports and able bodies

In this chapter I explore how young women with physical impairments negotiate their position in a traditionally male, able-bodied context. That ideas about gender and sexuality are (re)produced in sports has been elucidated from many different angles in social science research (Hargreaves 1994; Dworkin 2001; Dworkin and Messner 2002; Fundberg 2003; Larsson 2004, 2006; Connell 2005; Fagrell 2005; Andreasson 2007). Within mass culture sports have become 'the leading definer of masculinity', Connell writes (2005: 54). On the other hand, being too strong and athletic a woman is considered inappropriate and unfeminine (Hargreaves 1994: 146; Dworkin 2001; Larsson 2004; 2006: 218). The sociologists Shari Dworkin and Michael Messner point out the often exaggerated picture of sporting men that is put up against sporting women:

> Organized sport has overblown the cultural hegemony of heterosexualized, aggressive, violent, heavily muscled male athletes and heterosexualized, flirtatious, moderately muscled female athletes who are accomplished and competitive but expected to be submissive to the control of men coaches and managers.
>
> (Dworkin and Messner 2002: 24)

The conception of men and women as two entirely distinct and mutually homogeneous categories is strengthened, as is the subordination of women as a group. The field of sports is one of the few in Sweden in which grouping based on gender is permitted, and men and women are regarded as two completely separate categories, even in sports where gender has no significance.[1]

The idea of the perfect and highly achieving male sporting body does not include disabled bodies (Swartz and Watermeyer 2008: 189). Consequently, male sporting bodies are considered superior to female, and able-bodied superior to disabled bodies. There is also a hierarchy within the latter group, according to which sportspeople with acquired or slighter impairments are placed above those with congenital or more severe impairments (Wickman 2004: 29; 2007b: 159–60; Deal 2003: 905).

Sports' potential for change?

Several researchers maintain that women internalize and embody historical, social, cultural and economic limitations as well as negative expectations of their physical capacities (Young 1980; Bourdieu 1998/2001; Fagrell 2005: 66). This begins while they are still small children. Sports researcher Birgitta Fagrell (2005) has a phenomenological perspective as she explores how seven- to eight-year-old boys and girls look upon the gendered body. The children thought boys were better than girls at sports, although research has shown that at this age their physical capacity is of equal merit. They regarded the physical body as male, and coupled it with characteristics such as activity, courage and strength, that is to say, characteristics necessary to triumph in sports. The female is associated with calmness, fear and weakness, qualities that counteract sports success. However, those approaches had not yet materialized in the children's bodies. The children enjoyed physical activities and were happy to jump, swing and play, irrespective of gender. But Fagrell noticed that the gender coding of physical activities was on its way. Some of the boys were aware of the expectation of the physical body to be strong and achieving (Fagrell 2005). The negative expectations of girls' physical capacity are manifest in their bodies and incorporated in what Bourdieu calls habitus and become part of the body in the form of permanent dispositions. Women, in Fagrell's words, 'can come to have more difficulty making the most of their bodies' full capacity due to the experiences a gender-impregnated life world have inscribed in their bodies' (2005: 66, author's translation). However, women's sporting, Bourdieu argues, may change this: 'intensive practice of a sport leads to a profound transformation of the subjective and objective experience of the body. ... Instead of being a body for others it becomes a body for oneself' (1998/2001: 67).

Results from a previous study about how femininity is constructed among girls who play football support Bourdieu's thesis (Apelmo 2005). During autumn 2004 and spring 2005 I followed a football team for talented girls aged between 15 and 18. I combined observations of training and matches, documented with field notes and video filming, with one-hour long semi-structured interviews with seven of the players. My empirical material revealed that the orientation towards relations that is ascribed to sports-women (Olofsson 1989: 181; Larsson 2006: 224) was not natural but rather was taught by the coaches of the girls' team through their emphasis on solidarity instead of competition and individual achievement. As a matter of fact both interviews and observations showed that the young women had become more physically tough, fearless, determined and aggressive by playing football and that they had learned to cooperate and communicate in a loud voice and with distinct body language on the football field. The football practices were embodied and they themselves said that they brought with them what they had learnt to contexts outside sports (Apelmo 2005).

However, the idea that sports in itself are strengthening and challenge dominating definitions of women as passive, docile and weak is criticized by Dworkin and Messner (2002). They argue that sports are new ways of producing what Foucault terms 'docile bodies' (1975/1991). It has become the white middle-class woman's 'third shift', after the two discussed by Hochschild: paid employment and unpaid household work (2003: 217–18). Instead of becoming involved in collective political work to change dominating social institutions, a 'radical turning inward of agency' is the result, Dworkin and Messner contend, and women's energy is devoted to the shaping of the individual body in accordance with prevailing ideals (2002: 23).

Sports can probably work both to liberate and to passivize, depending upon the circumstances. One factor that seems to influence the outcome is which sport is practised. In a study on women attending fitness centres Dworkin (2001) demonstrates how ideologies of femininity create an upper limit or a glass ceiling for women's muscular strength. What seem to be biological differences are rather 'women's conscious negotiation with a historically produced upper limit on strength and size' (Dworkin 2001: 345); a fear of appearing too strong (Young 1980: 144). This can be regarded as an example of how docile bodies with moderated muscles are created.

Women's paradoxical position in a competitive sport that requires strength is explored in Larsson's (2004) study on teenagers who are active athletes. The adolescents – of both genders – described young women as in need of formidable strength. At the same time they thought that the women did not want to exercise and had difficulties becoming strong. In this way the young female body was constructed as problematic. Positioned between the discourse of 'the achieving body' (whose ideal type is male) and the discourse of 'the beautiful body' (which could be male or female), the teenage girls were constructed as unsure of their own capacity (Larsson 2004: 63–4; see also Larsson 2006). However, in a later article Larsson (2005) is hopeful and maintains that in sports that are considered gender-neutral, like athletics, tennis, golf, skiing, biathlon and downhill skiing (see Koivula 1999), there is room for changes in the gender regime – and it is in these sports the big Swedish female sports stars are to be found. Here women can be competitive and serious and in these, Larsson envisages, women can also challenge men in the future (2005: 131).

Hence, if fitness, aerobics and rhythmic gymnastics strengthen ideas of emphasized femininity, the more gender-neutral sports as well as 'masculine' sports would have potential for change. But what is the situation for young women in disability sports?

Disability sports and gender

One measure of gender equality in disability sports is the gender distribution of participants. The Swedish governmental Local Activity Subsidy is directed towards supporting sports associations' activities for young people aged between 7 and 20. Disability sports are the one exception since activities for all age groups can receive the subsidy. This is based on the number of meetings per year multiplied by the number of participants on each occasion. The statistics for 2013 show an under-representation of girls and women. In the 7 to 12 age group, 35 per cent are girls; among the participants aged between 13 and 16, 32 per cent are girls; while in the 17 to 20 age group, 29 per cent are girls and in the 21 years and over age group, 34 per cent are women. These statistics include both sports administered by SHIF and those integrated in the specialized sports federations – traditionally feminine sports such as riding and wheel-chair dance, as well as traditionally masculine ones like wheelchair rugby and sledge hockey (Svenskidrott.se 2015). An even more uneven distribution is to be found in sport at the top level. The Swedish Paralympic team at the London Summer Games 2012 included 40 men and 19 women, while the team competing at the Sochi Winter Games 2014 consisted of 15 men and four women (Sveriges Paralympiska Kommitté 2014).[2]

Quite a lot has been written both internationally and in Sweden in recent years about how gender is constructed in sports. However, the whole, normal, able body is often taken for granted. In disability sports research, the lack of both a gender perspective and a critical approach to sports is noticeable. For instance, in a qualitative interview study on identity development among sporting teenage girls with physical impairments, the sports and leisure researcher Denise Anderson argues that 'sport is an ideal avenue of participation for both men and women to overcome barriers and acquire both physical and social skills' (2009: 428). Anderson regards gender (just like age and type of impairment) as 'personal attributes' and gives expression to ableism as she describes one of the participants as 'confined to a wheelchair' (Anderson 2009: 430, 439; see also Apelmo 2010). A recurring theme in existing research about women's position in disability sports is the observation of double sub-ordination: they are women and have disabled bodies in a context in which male bodies and able-bodiedness are celebrated (see Olenik et al 1995: 54; Taub et al 1999: 1481; Wickman 2007b: 163). To talk of a double sub-ordination indicates an additive approach and risks creating 'demarcated analytical spaces' (de los Reyes et al 2003: 23, author's translation). The question is, rather, how different axes of power are created and changed in relation to each other in specific historical and spatial contexts.

As we saw in Chapter 5, the sporting body is regarded as a body of per-fection, while the disabled body is viewed as incapable and 'as a major form of biological imperfection' (Brittain 2004: 438; see also Swartz and Watermeyer 2008: 189). This influences disabled people's self-perceptions, Brittain argues, and hinders their involvement in sports (2004). However, the situation for men and women differs. The sociologists Diane E. Taub, Elaine Blinde and Kim-berley R. Greer (1999) explore how disabled men's participation in sports and physical activity can function as a strategy for dealing with the stigmatizing processes they risk being exposed to. They interviewed 24 male colleges stu-dents, aged between 20 and 51, with physical impairments. For men a physical impairment implies that their masculinity is called into question. As sports are considered masculine activities it comes naturally, according to the researchers, to choose sports to handle the stigmatization. By doing sports the interviewees thought they could develop and demonstrate masculine qualities and char-acteristics. They were often met with astonishment when they showed physical prowess, fitness and health, and thus counteracted stereotyped ideas about them as passive, sick and weak. The men also felt that their bodily appearance was improved: they developed muscles and lost weight. Furthermore, they were able to show that they were in control of their appearance, body and movements (Taub et al 1999: 1477–9). Paradoxically, the men identified with the same norms of physical prowess and beauty that actually oppress them. Finally, the authors emphasize that the situation for sporting disabled women is probably completely different (Taub et al 1999: 1481). In *Heroines of Sport: The Politics of Difference and Identity* Hargreaves (2000) devotes one chapter to disability sports. Like Taub et al, Hargreaves argues that disabled men can compensate for lost physical capital with sports. In contrast, disabled women are affected by 'commodified anti-athletic stereotypes of femininity' that do not make the sporting body into a physical capital to the same extent (Hargreaves 2000: 186–7). This can partly explain why women are underrepresented in disability sports. In one of four studies in her thesis, Wickman (2004, 2008) explores how discourses of disability, competitive sports and gender interact in female Australian wheelchair racers' talk about themselves and their sport. The semi-structured interviews with five top-level wheelchair racers revealed that they were concerned about describing themselves in terms of a competitive sports discourse, while other people sometimes viewed their sporting as rehabilitation or exercise. These top-level sportswomen actively tried to change how outsiders viewed the sport they were doing (Wickman 2004: 30–1).

If Swedish research on disability and sport in general is limited to only a small number of studies (see Östnäs 1997, 2003; Kristén 2003; Bolling 2008), research on how gender and disability interact is even more uncommon. In another study Wickman (2007b, 2008) interviews nine Swedish wheelchair racers, five of them men and four women. The interviewees had experiences of being treated as second-rate sportsmen and sportswomen. They talked about their bodies as controlled, strong and capable and stressed that they, as wheelchair racers, were 'real' sportspeople, not just doing disability sports. In their aspiration to get closer to the 'norm' they distanced themselves, according to Wickman, from those more severely disabled who do sports (2007b: 157–9). In this way these wheelchair racers too reproduced the ideas of normality that oppressed them.

'This is something completely different'

Before I began the fieldwork at the sports camp for children and young people in the summer of 2006 I had a meeting with one of the employees at the regional disability sports federation that organized the camp. When I told him about my earlier research on young women playing football, he said, 'This is something completely different.' Of course, his remark could have referred to many different things: the participants at the camp were younger and on another level than the football girls who were aiming at the elite, for instance. Maybe he thought I would be disappointed, but I was well aware that I was not going to an elite camp.

At the camp two table tennis players, both competing at the top level, volunteered as coaches in their sport. The training included warm-up and stretch exercises that the participants took turns in leading, as well as exercises to improve strength, speed and technique. The degree of difficulty was raised with every day that passed, and elements of competition were introduced to get the participants to exert themselves to the utmost. Oskar, one of the coaches, explained his idea behind the training:

> I want each exercise to be a bit competitive. You have noticed that I do the two-minute exercise. Yes, it becomes an inspiration for them. You know, they want to compete. Then I just tell them something, 'Yes, now we have the record, it's this many hits in two minutes.' The next time they want to beat it, and the next time again. So they become better and better because I put pressure on them. ... Everybody wants to be the last one who is the king of goals. ... They just scream, 'Yes, we want to do it again, we want to do it again!'
>   *They put on the pressure then?*
>   They put on the pressure. And then many times I can terrorize them. On purpose, when I get to know them a bit.
>
> (Oskar, coach, interview)

The two-minute exercise that Oskar tells about was a competition in which the two players that made most hits in two minutes won. The 'terrorizing' consisted of punishments: the players who did not win had to run or drive around the table ten times or do push-ups.

In the other sports the rules were explained by way of introduction, nothing more. Day after day boules were thrown in the hot sun, curling-stones were delivered and new floorball teams were put together every morning and afternoon and matches were played. In all sports youth with different kinds of disabilities were mixed and several of them tried many sports, so the disparity in how the activities were planned was not due to the participants' physical or intellectual capacity. My interpretation is rather that it was an expression of differences in attitude to the young participants. I asked the table tennis coach why the training differed so much:

> Actually, there should have been one who was in charge of floorball, one in charge of athletics and one in charge of football. That is how it was meant to be. ... I think in a way it's a pity there wasn't a leader for each [sport]. Then there would have been even better speed on the whole thing. But it is their ... their [the people from the disability sports federation] job to fix leaders. They have had a year at their disposal.
>
> (Oskar, coach, interview)

In my field notes I write that Oskar 'sounds mildly irritated' when he speaks about this. Maybe the arranger's utterance, 'This is something completely different' concerns the view of disability sports and disabled young people? I will get back to the observations below, but first I will go through the other empirical material.

To dabble and pamper

Two of the young women in my study have acquired impairments. Julia, 26 years old, had been playing a tough team sport for 14 years when she had a traffic accident. 'So it was quite natural to find something new', she says. But the three disability sports associations she turned to appeared to have very different approaches to disability sports. First Julia tried floorball in a local club:

> I played floorball for a start. But I didn't think it was much fun, because they mixed people with mental disabilities with us, who had no mental disabilities. And all of a sudden, just because you had a physical disability, I don't think I should need to, from having awfully tough training in third division [...], to suddenly this namby-pamby thing. That wasn't quite my style.
>
> (Julia, 26, interview)

Julia tries swimming in the same club and meets a similar attitude:

> It was the same thing when I was trying to swim. Then you just got there, 'Yes, we have swimming for the disabled on Mondays.' So I went there so,

well, there were me and those with Down's syndrome who were dabbling
and I just, 'Let me see, is this the swim training?' I think it's humiliating
to do like that.

How was the ambition?

I don't know if they had any level of ambition. It was probably more
being kind to everybody.

(Julia, 26, interview)

Instead of training, Julia was offered a 'namby-pamby thing' and 'dabbling'. She
questions not being able to continue with the tough training she is used to
because she has become physically impaired. She associates the lack of seriousness with the club's mix of physically and intellectually impaired people in both
sports. If she previously objected to the way in which people around her regarded
her as intellectually impaired just because she used a wheelchair (Chapter 3),
now she protests against the training (or more precisely the 'namby-pamby
thing' and 'dabbling') together with persons with this kind of impairment. It is
unclear whether the humiliation lies in the mixture, the 'namby-pamby thing'
and 'dabbling' or the combination of the two. In this situation Julia does not see
herself and the other members of the club as part of the larger social group of
disabled people, but as belonging to different impairment groups, with nothing
in common. From a political perspective the former would possibly be pre-
ferred – by distancing herself from others, lower down in the hierarchy of
impairments she 'is likely to further isolate those perceived as less accepted by
society, creating a further level of social oppression' (Deal 2003: 907). But Julia
clearly marks that training with people with intellectual impairments is nothing
for her. Julia's interpretation is that the leaders do this because they want to be
'kind to everybody', irrespective of type of impairment.

Before the accident 22-year-old Susanne went to a school with a sports profile, played football, rode on horseback and had her own horse as well. 'It was
my great passion, it was sports', she explains in the past tense, which hints that
this is no longer the case. She says that she has always been stubborn and adds:
'I must always win.' After the accident she took part in two girls groups in a
sports club. She does weight training at home, and, as we saw in Chapter 5,
drives daily rounds with her dog. Four or five months ago she resumed the
riding. But before the accident there was 'more freedom' in the riding: 'I like to
feel independent when I do things. And … now, when riding, I can't feel that.
She holds the horse and in the beginning she holds me, and things like that.
But it's just a safety thing, you know.' Susanne thinks that it is difficult to feel
free and independent as long as she needs help to mount the horse, for instance.
For Susanne, being independent is about being able to do everything by herself,
not about getting assistance to be able to do what she wants. However, Susanne
plays down the assistance she gets when she says that it's 'just' about safety.

The first girls' group Susanne took part in was discontinued when the
leader left the club. Now, after a couple of years, a new group has been started.
Initially, Susanne was not satisfied with the new group: 'I told them I want my

tough training. After all, I drive all the way to X-city to get my training, not to play Chinese whispers, for instance, that they do with the others in the younger group. So after that they divided up the group.' The leaders were sensitive to Susanne's wish and started a new group for older members. Unfortunately, in most cases Susanne is the only one in her group, together with the leaders. But she prefers exercising together with other disabled people to training with non-disabled people:

> I even live next door to a health club, but I drive to X-city because there are disabled [people]. I somehow want to have this feeling of togetherness with them. I don't meet disabled people otherwise, in school or anywhere. ... I think it's more fun to train with people who are in the same situation.
>
> (Susanne, 22, interview)

At present Susanne only exercises individually. But she would like to 'join a team or ... I miss matches especially.' She describes how she becomes happy and alert, and feels better both physically and mentally by doing sports. 'Without it, yes, it would, it would simply not have been fun to live.' If sport was her passion before the accident, it now seems to be vital for her survival. At the end of her video diary a few months later Susanne tells about the years at senior level of compulsory school:

> I went to a class with a sports profile, so there was PE each day. We had ordinary lessons too, but PE took up more time. And I miss 60 metres and 100 metres, running that. I miss it enormously. That kick. Really. And football, to kick a ball about and run on the grass. Marvellous. So it's a bit... So I must have sport in my life, I know that I must have it. And I haven't really found my thing yet. I don't know if it's handball or if it's basketball that is my thing, I don't know ... Maybe it's simply 60 and 100 metres that is my thing.
>
> (Susanne, 22, video diary)

Again, the pleasure in physical activity is emphasized: the 'kick' it gives and the marvellous feeling of running and playing football. At the same time the interview with Susanne, like her video diary, is characterized by the search. She wants to continue doing sports and she wants tough training. She also wants to do sports together with other disabled people. But she has a hard time finding the right sport – should she train individually or in a team, only with girls or in mixed teams? When football and short-distance runs are not alternatives any-more, there are many choices. She vacillates back and forth during the interview and contradicts herself over and over again. Her remark about how she misses short-distance running and her concluding comment, 'Maybe it's simply 60 and 100 metres that is my thing', suggests that she may still regret the loss of mobility in the lower part of the body too much to make a choice. 'Impairment *is* a predicament and *can* be tragic', as disability studies researcher Dan

Goodley puts it (2013: 634, italics in original). If a person acquires an impairment he or she can also have problems redefining the identity (Goffman 1963/1990). As disabled Susanne must, in Ahmed's words, 'reinhabit space … . It puts some things "out of reach" that I didn't even notice when they were in reach' (2006: 101–2).[3] The able body and the spaces it inhabited were self-evident to Susanne before the accident. Now these spaces and objects are no longer accessible, instead everything is new. Goffman notes that those who have been disabled for a long time can play an important role in explaining how the newly injured can get on physically and mentally, but the feelings towards equals can also be ambivalent (1963/1990: 50–1). Maybe this ambivalence contributes to Susanne's difficulties in finding a new sport. Besides, she has not yet found a sport in which she simultaneously can get hard training, competition and a feeling of togetherness with 'people who are in the same situation' as she is.

It is not only those with acquired impairments who ask for serious and tough training. As we saw in Chapter 3, Maria, who is 17 years old, swims four times a week in a group for able-bodied children aged between 10 and 12. While Susanne has been seeking a disability sport, Maria has tried to get away from it (at the time of the interview she still trains with the team in the disability sports club). Maria explains why she likes to swim in a club for able-bodied:

> *Does the training differ a lot?*
> Above all else, there are more of us. That's what happens, you are urged on more by the others. And … yes, maybe the training is a bit more professional, in a sense. And then they can't pay as much attention to you, since they have a whole group to think of. I think that's good, because then there isn't time for so much pampering.
> (Maria, 17, interview)

Maria distances herself from 'pampering' and amateurishness in disability sports. In the swimming club the group is larger. Maria gets inspired by the others and feels that the coaches do not have time to pay her any extra attention, something she appreciates.

To sum up, Julia, Susanne and Maria talk about training in which you do a 'namby-pamby thing', 'dabble', 'play Chinese whispers' and 'pamper'. All three of them use expressions that make one think of children's play rather than the tough and hard training they want. Maria considers the swim training for 10- to 12-year-old non-disabled children – that is to say, children who are five to seven years younger than her, to be 'more professional' than the training in the disability sports club. Julia thinks the situation in the first disability sports association is humiliating, and regards the low level of ambition and the mix of people with different kinds of impairments as an expression of the leaders wanting to be 'kind to everybody'. This manifestation of well-meaning inclusion obviously does not suit Julia. Where then is the problem?

One possible explanation can be how the category of disabled is constructed 'as *any* departure from an unstated physical and functional norm … In other words, the concept of disability unites a highly marked, heterogeneous group whose only commonality is being considered abnormal' (Garland-Thomson 1997: 24, italics in original). Perhaps it is this idea that causes some sports associations to bring together all those who are not regarded as 'normal' despite large differences between them.

On the other hand, the table tennis training at the sports camp shows that it is not impossible to have physical and technical training just because people with different physical and intellectual impairments come together. Sometimes it can of course be about being too few to divide into different teams or groups. At the camp it worked because of the coaches' devotion. Oskar also mixes children and young people with different impairments in the club at a small village where he works as a leader:

> You can't always make it work. Someone who is running around, shouting and hitting with the stick and then one who has a physical impairment, he wonders, 'Why does he do such things?' ... You have to tell those who have a mobility impairment that they [those with intellectual impairments] work like that. ... They have got to know each other over a long time. It doesn't work the first day. ... Through this we have won a lot in our club. We have mixed most sports, just to get groups. Otherwise we would never get a group, because there aren't enough [people].
>
> (Oskar, coach, interview)

Oskar stresses that there is a lot of work behind the success of the club. But without including young people with intellectual impairments, the club, which originally addressed people with physical impairments, would never have acquired full teams. Perhaps it is also easier when it concerns small children for whom play and competition are more mixed – those that I interviewed at the camp were aged between 10 and 15, while Julia was considerably older when she turned to disability sports.

Yet another explanation is to be found in the view of disabled people that is expressed, for instance, in the *Disability Sports Policy Programme* (SHIF 2006). If they are considered weak and passive people on the fringe of society, hit by personal tragedy, and the main goal of sports is to give them rehabilitation and social integration (Apelmo 2012c), it is possible to understand the low level of ambition in the other sports at the camp and in the association in which Julia tried floorball and swimming. In such a case, the extra consideration that Maria objects to and the wish to be, as Julia puts it, 'kind to everybody' is all about pity. Thus, the camp organizer's remark, 'This is something completely different' (in contrast to the able-bodied football players in my previous study) could also be an expression of this stance. Oskar, who is disabled, does not have this approach, which explains his success as a coach. My interviewees' aims do not coincide with the ones in the SHIF policy programme. Just like the Australian top-level sportswomen Wickman interviewed (2004), they go against the image of people with physical impairments as needy and deserving pity.

Felicia, 28 years old, however, stresses that disability sports can have a function as rehabilitation too, in addition to the competitive part:

> I have taken part in many of the Recruitment Group's [RG Active Rehabilitation] camps both as participant and as leader. There you learn really good wheelchair technique and that you should help yourself as much as possible. And I support that, also rehabilitation through sports. Because if you are in good form, you get on better in ordinary life. And I think that's an awfully good philosophy. Then it may not suit everybody. ... They tend to have two sports sessions each day. But in between you can be together, get experience. It's not just sports; there are wheelchair sessions too. If you are newly injured you learn to manage to jump up from the floor or to a sofa and back again and to manage the new world. Get tips and tricks.
>
> (Felicia, 28, interview)[4]

For those who are newly injured or have recently undergone a major operation, rehabilitation and physiotherapy are enormously important for learning techniques for using the body and any assistive technology that may be needed. Besides sports, Felicia also brings up sessions that are devoted to learning how to handle the wheelchair in everyday life as well as the importance of 'tips and tricks' – that is to say, learning from others' experience. But this is something quite different from the aims and activities in disability sports clubs.

Being a woman in a male context

Julia did not continue with floorball or swimming but began to play a team sport in another club instead. 'Somehow it was tremendously elevating to get to know other disabled people, who showed that you could still have an ordinary life.' The other players seem to share their experiences just as at the RG camp that Felicia talked about. This sport suits Julia better, 'It is tough and there is no ... . No mercy. That's what I like about it.' She does not want 'mercy' or pity just because she is disabled. But it is not only the sport that is tough:

> There can be quite a lot of sexual comments.
> *What kind of sexual comments?*
> Well... Just in general, so to speak ... . When you circle up, then you can, yes, but bring your hand a bit up and I just, 'No, stop it!', such things. You have to be quite tough as a girl; you can't be a softy. I often put on a mask when I go and play basketball. ...
> *But do the leaders ever react against you getting sexual comments?*
> ... It's just as much the leaders as the others.
>
> (Julia, 26, interview)

Julia tells about both verbal and physical sexual harassment from male players as well as leaders. She presents herself as tough, and continues, 'I don't think they are like that with the other [women]. They know that I can put up with it a bit too.' Thus, she gives a picture of herself as more uncomplaining than most women. Yet, the harassments are so trying that she begins training in a third club. That team, she says:

> ... is more professional because there aren't these [harassments]. But there I didn't get any playing time, so it wasn't fun in that regard. ... [I] didn't get any playing time even if we could have had a great first team, which I could be part of. ... It's just that it's a girl. No, 'Girls should play with girls', that's the mentality there.'
>
> (Julia, 26, interview)

The fact that Julia was not allowed to play matches was especially remarkable since she had just been abroad for a long period of time and had been competing successfully in wheelchair basketball. Hence Julia chose to go back to the team she played with initially, in which she now plays in the first team. I ask Julia if she has discussed the harassment with other women in the team, and she answers:

> No, I have talked about it with other guys, so that they notice it too. Who I have confidence in, and I know never would do it. Because I say, 'Now you know that I think it's tiresome and that it is like this. If you see it you may if you like, sort of...'
> *React?*
> Yes, react. And there are many guys who think it's wrong, you know. It's just some who have this way of talking. So it feels good, because then you have support from them. Somehow you think the sport is such fun, and you think that... For me it's not that tough. I think there are others who have a harder time.
>
> (Julia, 26, interview)

Julia is not completely alone; she has support from some of the men in the team. At the end of the quotation she contradicts her earlier statement as she says she believes others 'have a harder time'. But the effect is the same – Julia stands out as tougher than other women. The situation in the team has also been improved:

> They have really become much better, because now almost all have become fathers of small children [laughter]. So now, I think, they are not like that anymore. They are not such poor little fellows who, yes, [laughter] just assert themselves sexually because they don't get anything [laughter]. And now I'm also married, I think that too [laughter] has its little due share.
>
> (Julia, 26, interview)

Julia calls the men who pawed her and made offensive comments: 'poor little fellows' who 'don't get anything' – that is, sex. By talking about them as frustrated small boys and presenting herself as more enduring and tougher than other women she avoids the position of the victim. The recurrent laughter in this concluding quotation also works as a way to keep distance from the serious subject. She gives two reasons why she is not harassed anymore: several of the men have become fathers and do not have the same need to assert themselves and she has married. This implies that the men are no longer sexually frustrated and Julia is not regarded as available anymore.

In the article 'Research on Sexual Harassment and Abuse in Sport', the sports sociologist Kari Fasting (2005) notes that very little has been written about the occurrence, causes, characteristics and consequences of sexual harassment in sport. However, several studies have been done on working life and education, and the results indicate that harassment is more common in male-dominated professions in which women are under-represented. 'Since men, masculinity and traditional male values heavily dominate most sport organizations and most of the sport sciences, this raises the question of whether sport is a particularly risky location for sexual harassment', Fasting asserts (2005: 3). This could indicate a heightened risk in disability team sports, in which women are in the minority. A Norwegian quantitative study of the subject was carried out, in which 572 sportswomen who were competing at the top level, aged 15 to 39, and a control group of 574 women answered a questionnaire about experiences of sexual harassment. The results showed no differences in prevalence when the sports world was compared with the control group's experiences of school and working life. But there were more cases of harassment from male authorities in sports than in education and working life (Fasting 2005: 7–8). Hence, the leaders in Julia's team are no exceptions.

When I ask 19-year-old Sara if she has ever thought that it has mattered that she is a girl in sports, she answers, 'No, I have always mostly had boys as friends so I have never felt that.' As she develops her answer she gets on to the under-representation of women in disability sports, which she thinks is partly due to the lack of women's teams:

> It's hard for a girl to get into a team and feel that she has an important, major role. Because there's a difference between a boy's body and a girl's body. Men are stronger than girls, and often a bit more … mentally too. And then it's difficult for a girl to take the role as a leader in a team sport for instance. Then you remain in the background. … You may feel a bit lonely if the boys talk about their things and you are a girl. And then you don't have any other girl to talk with. I think that's a major reason why there aren't so many girls. You probably have to find a large group of girls who want to begin, so they can play together and develop together. And then, when you are good enough, if you are a girl who is much better than other girls, you can move them to the men's team, to get even better training. That's how I have done.
>
> (Sara, 19, interview)

According to Sara, young women have a lonely position on teams. She thinks that it is partly because men are physically and mentally stronger, but also that there is banter that the young women (or girls) cannot take part in. It makes it hard to take up space at the sports ground, and to become a leader. As a beginner it is best to play in a girls' or women's team, Sara believes, while the truly talented can train with the men's team later on. Like Julia, Sara assigns all these problems to other girls and women – she herself has not encountered them.

Julia emphasizes the feeling of having a crucial role in a women's team: 'The difference between a girl's team [and a men's team] is that you get much more responsibility. ... [In the men's team] it's not like: "Julia, if you don't score we won't win." But that's how it is when you play with the girls.' In Julia's case it is, as we have seen, about being *given* responsibility. Not even being permitted to play a match makes it impossible to score a goal. But even when you get playing time you have to be given space and possibilities. Furthermore, Julia says that she does not get together with the members of the team outside the basketball, and I ask her if the rest of the team see each other:

> Yes, the boys do it more I think, they go to the pub and such things. But it's often like you miss what's going on in the locker room as a girl, since you are playing with the boys. The social thing. ... Maybe it's there fun things happen that you miss as a girl. That's why you really have to think that the sport is tremendous fun in order to keep playing.
>
> (Julia, 26, interview)

The reason Julia does not associate with the team outside training and matches is partly that she lives in another city, partly that she is a woman. She thinks much of the social and 'fun' goes on in the locker room, which leads to further intercourse outside sports. The locker room's social significance in team sports has been written about in previous research (Fundberg 2003; Andreasson 2007). In this gender-segregated and closed room where private clothes are replaced with the uniform team dress, a particular intimacy and solidarity are created (Fundberg 2003: 73–5), and a sense of togetherness is developed (Andreasson 2007: 107). Julia points out that to continue with the sport, 'You really have to think that the sport is tremendous fun', as a compensation for the feeling of togetherness between the men.

Hanna, 25 years old, also points out that it is hard to feel one belongs as one of few women in a men's team:

> No girl in the rugby. Two girls in the basketball. There they [the boys] get this feeling of belonging and togetherness at once in the team, the feeling of togetherness that I missed. ... And the similarity. That you see that there are others in a similar situation. That you don't always need to feel one step behind. It's probably easier for boys to get into the team.
>
> (Hanna, 25, interview)

Hanna believes it is difficult for girls to get into team sports as well as individual sports where they risk being in the minority. She herself has never felt quite at home in the male sodality in disability sports. Like Jenny, Maria, Sara and Susanne, Hanna speaks of the importance of meeting others with similar experiences, so 'that you don't always need to feel one step behind'. While the three other interviewees have found this feeling of belonging in disability sports associations, Hanna has found it outside her club. For her it is not just about meeting other disabled people, but also about gender. In addition to the training in the disability sports club, she trains together with two able-bodied young women of the same age as Hanna, who also play table tennis. When they see each other, Hanna says, 'we do some really hard training, and then we go out and eat something nice and have a beer. ... I have never had that before, the social aspect together with the table tennis.' In contrast to Julia, Hanna gets both tough training and social intercourse.

Language that excludes

Hanna trains an individual sport, but since she also works as a leader in the association where she is active I ask her what positive and negative effects the gender-mixed teams in disability sports have, in general. Hanna answers:

> Ah, it's really hard to see what's good and what's not good. There is a language in sports that has always been there. There are also boys and men who don't stand this language. But if a girl gets into a team with this language ... I couldn't cope with it. The only girl, away on the national team camp, competitions. I was feeling so bad when I got home. ... This, you know, making jokes about girls, this talk you know about appearance and girls and this coarseness and toughness.
>
> *And you have encountered this in table tennis?*
>
> Yes, yes! Oh yes, indeed! Many want to start a discussion, and they know what's sensitive to me, where to push. They know it has been really worthwhile somehow. It is precisely these injustices, and the close-minded approach. I don't know how many times I have told them, because we have been sitting kind of, and watching TV. And, it is just a typical example. There were many of us who had been attending before, and then there was a group of new, young boys. Then there are two men who kiss each other on TV and they just, 'Oh God, so disgusting, what on earth!' blah-blah. And I almost hit the ceiling, 'But please, we are a minority, shouldn't we be a bit more open for other minorities? Do we have to oppress? Wouldn't it be better if we tried to accept, since we're a bit strange according to some?' I mean indeed we really ought to understand what it's like to be viewed in that way shouldn't we? And ought to be more open-minded. But what the hell, they have no idea. Here comes a new group of boys, damn, what if one of them is homosexual?
>
> (Hanna, 25, interview)

After initially hesitating, Hanna only brings up the negative effects of the gender-mixed teams. She begins by talking in general terms about the language 'that has always been' in sports. Men can also have problems dealing with this, but Hanna thinks that it especially affects women. And, she adds, 'I couldn't cope with it.' Next she tells about personal experiences with the language. She seems to refer to a use of language known by all when she says, 'This, you know, making jokes about girls, this talk you know about appearance and girls and this coarseness and toughness.' She also makes clear that it commonly occurs by answering 'Indeed!' when I ask if she has encountered this language, and by explaining, 'I don't know how many times I have told them' and when she takes a 'typical example'. Consequently, there are more examples. Hanna's protests against the language seem futile. Her presence rather seems to strengthen it. The men know 'where to push' to start a discussion with Hanna. The language is both sexist – like the language Julia told about – and homophobic. In previous research about sexual violence, several authors claim that this ought to be considered as a continuum from verbal abuse and molestation to rape (Lundgren et al 2001; Andersson 2005: 72; Fasting 2005: 4). Fasting suggests that this can explain the process in the relation between a leader and a sportswoman or sportsman that often begins with trust building, and then grows into a state of dependence and eventually leads to increasing degrees of sexual harassment (2005: 4). This approach also couples Hanna's stories about sexist language with Julia's experiences of physical sexual molestation.

The sexist and homophobic language in organized sports has been dealt with in previous Swedish sports research. Cultural sociologist Mats Trondman establishes that boys' team sports have problems with expressions of aggressiveness, as for instance a tough locker room culture, sexism and homophobia (2005: 214–6). In a qualitative study of how masculinities are constructed, the ethnologist Jesper Fundberg (2003) follows a boys' football team from the white Swedish middle class. The boys and their coaches look upon themselves as individuals instead of representatives of a category. They are what Fundberg calls bearers of normality. They formulate their self-understanding by recurrent jokes about the weak 'old woman', the threatening intimacy of the 'queer' and the 'immigrant's' exaggeratedly self-confident masculinity – the boys and their coaches are what these three figures are not (Fundberg 2003: 182, 185–8). Their jokes are examples of what Bourdieu calls symbolic violence in that they are directed downwards (Fundberg 2003: 159). Hanna's fellow sportsmen are not bearers of normality and are forced, like the young women in my study, to relate to the category of disabled that they often get to represent. However, when they talk about women and their appearance they joke down, since they joke about the women who are subordinated in disability sports. At the same time, they construct themselves as heterosexual men both by their sexist jokes and when they dissociate themselves from homosexuality.

Questioning the potential for change in disability sports

The gender-mixed teams in disability sports have sometimes been considered to have a positive, transgressive potential. In the health researcher Steve Robertson's critical study of the relation between masculinity, sports and health, he takes the mixed teams in disability sports as an example of a pheno-menon that can challenge the hegemonic masculinity, and more specifically the 'macho culture' to be found in much male team sports (2003: 712, 714). But in my empirical material, the inclusion of one, two or three women in a men's team has not changed the gender regime in the actual sport. To sum up, the problems that are brought up in the team sports are verbal and physical sexual harassment, the crude sexist and homophobic language (the latter can affect men too), that women are not allowed to play matches, that it can be difficult as a single woman to take up space at the sports ground or become a leader and, because they are in the minority, that they remain outside the social intercourse. According to Hanna, the language and difficulty of feeling belonging and togetherness exist in the individual sport she is doing too.

Julia works as a coach for one of few Swedish women's teams in her sport and tries to start a women's national team. As the situation is now she has no reason to train more intensely: 'Why should I train more, what goal do I have? Now I play from the start in my present team. Where should I proceed? I have no national team to train for.' Instead she sits on the grandstand at international tournaments and supports the men's national team. She recalls the last European Championship: 'We [Julia and another sportswoman] were at the European Championship together when the boys won, and sat cheering and shouting. It was terrifically funny! ... Each time Sweden scored a goal they filmed us, so we just, "Yeah!"'

The results of my earlier research project on young women who played top-level football support the idea of women's intense sporting as a means to change embodied limitations (Apelmo 2005). Beate, one of the football players I interviewed, illustrated how sports can be conducive of change:

> You become sportier, you maybe don't stand one hour in front of the mirror and prepare yourself. ... Maybe you think other girls are a bit ridiculous. ... If we see a group of people playing football, we can perfectly well go there and play with them. Other girls would never do that. Instead they like to sit and look as nice as possible so the boys will check them out.
>
> (Beate, 16, interview, quoted in Apelmo 2005)

Instead of sitting beautifully at the edge and being 'merely a thing that is made to be looked at' or standing in front of the mirror and being something 'which one has to look at in order to prepare it to be looked at' (Bourdieu 1998/2001: 67), Beate related how they chose to take part in the game. Thus, she and her team-mates went from being passive objects of others' (male) gazes, as Bourdieu (1998/2001: 67) and Young (1980: 154) describe, to become active and acting subjects (Apelmo 2005). The only imaginable possibility for Julia to go abroad on international competitions is as a passive spectator and an object for the television viewers' gaze. Thus, the potential for change that Bourdieu emphasizes is limited in the disability team sports.

At the end of the interview I ask Julia if she wants to add something, and she answers:

> Girls in disability sports … definitely need much more support, that people believe that we should be able to do something. Because that doesn't exist right now. Now you have to fight an uphill struggle, the whole time. … In teams too… but mostly at the level of federation I think, more support is needed.
>
> (Julia, 26, interview)

Julia argues that women are subordinated in disability sports and need more support both in the clubs and from the federation. From what I have found in my empirical material I am inclined to agree with her.

However, not everybody is negative about playing in men's teams. Jenny, Felicia and Ingela are more positive. Ingela talks about the team sport she plays:

> *What is it about wheelchair basketball that you like?*
> I don't know. Team sport, a bit, and…
> *You said that you are quick.*
> Yes, I think so [laughter]. Now I have for certain lost a bit, but… I probably am. I don't know. It's really difficult. I like… Then it's quite unusual, you know, wheelchair basketball with girls … you kind of think that it's for boys, like that… But we are three girls in the team, so we are not so many. But it's, no it's great fun. I don't really know what makes it such fun, but… Yes, it's just fun.
>
> (Ingela, 17, interview)

Ingela hesitates about the question of why she likes wheelchair basketball. 'It is really difficult', she says and repeats three times that she does not know what to answer. But she thinks it is positive – at least 'a bit' that it is a team sport. Besides she stresses that it is a sport that is associated with boys and that is rather unusual amongst girls. Maybe playing a sport that is considered masculine gives Ingela heightened status. As we have seen earlier, Hanna expressed a similar idea as she felt that her sporting together with boys prevented her from being bullied. To sum up, Ingela points out that it is simply 'great fun' to play basketball.

Sometime in the middle of the interview I reflect on how Ingela seems to have difficulty answering questions about organized sports. It is as if she has not thought about sports in that way before, or as if the questions are bothering her. She began in the club as a small child and may think it is hard to look upon sports from a distance. Are disability sports a free zone that she does not question or reflect on? Ingela has previously told me that her classmates never accepted her and about bad experiences of the lessons in PE. In the sports club she meets people with both a common interest in sports and shared experiences of living as disabled. Brah maintains that when a collective identity is created, some experiences are emphasized while others are not (2001: 473). I interpret Ingela's silence regarding organized sports as a sign of this identification with the collective. From her perspective, the major differences are not within the group, but between the group and the others, the able-bodied.

Jenny, 20 years old, also likes to play in a mixed team. She explains, 'It's tougher somehow with the boys, because then you have to exert yourself, it feels like that. ... There's more pressure so to say. You have to think that it's boys and you have to be on a level with them.' The pressure to be on the same level as the boys in the team urges Jenny to try even harder.

Finally, 28-year-old Felicia brings up both pros and cons regarding playing in a team in which she is at present the only woman:

> It gets a bit tougher. Since I am competitive I think that's fun. We tried to start a girl's team some years ago and it became much more technical, not so physical you know, more thinking up here [in the brain] about how to play and pass and such. The disadvantage is that I am not as physical as the boys. I'm not as fast; I'm not as strong. Then you get a bit behind almost always. ... And the language, you get used to it.
> *How is the language then?*
> It can be quite tough. Tough but cordial.
>
> (Felicia, 28, interview)

Felicia also gets motivated by playing together with men who are physically stronger and faster, and stresses that she likes tough play and competition. On the other hand, the feeling of getting 'a bit behind almost always' is negative. Like Julia, Sara and Hanna, she brings up the language, which she terms as 'tough but cordial'. Felicia says that she has got used to it, which hints at some initial difficulties. The dis-identification from women's way of playing and the acceptance of the language could be interpreted as a necessary adaptation to the male community that she is part of. Yet, when Felicia plays matches and there is a woman in the opposing team the loyalty to her own team wavers:

> It's almost as if you cheer on the other girl [in the opposing team] when you meet that team (laughter). You do it automatically. You cheer on each other. ... If you, as a girl, when you play and succeed in knocking over especially those tall guys who have high points, they get really pissed

off. 'A tiny little girl on the pitch shouldn't stand in my way!' I think that's extra enjoyable, really! Another girl, when we were playing in the Swedish championship, commented on another team, 'Yes, they don't notice that you are there. They just try to push but get nowhere.' Then I'm standing there. That I think is fun!

(Felicia, 28, interview)[5]

Felicia is not afraid of showing her strength. Just as she could beat all the boys in her class and in the class above at arm wrestling when she was a girl, she enjoys being able to knock over a tall man who has 'high points' – that is, who is classified as having high functional capacity. She feels an affinity towards women in the other teams and they are pleased with each other's success on the court. The women's struggle against the men appears as a match within the match, of which only one partner is aware. Felicia argues that the men do not expect anything from them, they do not look upon her as a dangerous antagonist, but as a 'tiny little girl', if they notice her at all. She and the other female players have to prove their capacity to the male players in the same way as to able-bodied people.

Mobilizing for change

Girls' groups

One positive effect of sports is the possibility to go together and 'mobilize for collective political purposes' – as opposed to the risk of 'turning inward of agency', as Dworkin and Messner point out (2002: 23). Since disabled persons often grow up in families in which they are the only one who is disabled, they do not have access to how they have been constructed historically as a group in the same way as other subordinated groups, for instance ethnic minorities, may have. As Garland-Thomson maintains, 'because disabled people tend to be scattered among the nondisabled, political unity and consciousness-raising have emerged primarily as a result of traditional segregation or the self-imposed segregation that often accompanies positive-identity politics' (1997: 35). Paradoxically, the often-criticized separation of disability sports from other sports can make political change possible.

Hanna and Sara work as coaches in disability sports clubs and are also leaders of girls' groups in their clubs. Both speak with dedication about the rights of disabled people. They stress that disabled sportsmen and sports-women are like everybody else: they are capable people who can speak for themselves and there are no reasons to pity them. The reason for starting up the groups was the sexism some of the women had encountered in pursuing disability sports, and the fact that women are in the minority, especially in team sports in which they often only are one or two in each team. The groups strive for equality, try to raise each member's consciousness and self-confidence, and introduce the young women to various sports. Hanna says that several of the participants have experiences of not getting a chance to give their opinion. She relates the story of a colleague to explain the importance of raising the level of one's consciousness and working for enhanced self-confidence:

> You never got a chance to speak your mind. She [the colleague] said that 'When I was younger and they were going to try out a leg prosthesis, no one ever asked me if it was a good fit. They asked my parents if it was good, and they said yes or no.' And that's the way it has been ever since. Making up one's mind about the smallest things becomes really difficult.
>
> (Hanna, 25, interview)

A prosthesis may be compared with a pair of glasses. They are both an extension of the body that you bring with you every day. They must be comfortable, functional and look good. Nevertheless, Hanna's colleague, who is the one who is going to use the prosthesis, is not asked how it feels and functions. Hanna says that several of the participants, when growing up, had similar experiences of not getting a chance to speak for themselves, which has led to difficulties in making decisions, in general. However, this does not hold for everybody, which is important to highlight when it concerns a strongly categorized social group.

In addition to discussions, group exercise, sports and movie going, other traditionally feminine activities are arranged, such as a session at a cosmetics store. They also look outwards, aiming to change how other people view young disabled women, as when the group organizes a fashion show with women in wheelchairs as models. Some of the young women have had training in leadership and new groups have been started in other cities. The make-up class and fashion shows are ways to construct a more compliant and normative femininity, closer to the emphasized femininity, in opposition to the stereotypical view of women with physical impairments as genderless and asexual.

Disabled women's use of organized sport to advance social justice was also found in a study by the sports researcher Sharon R. Guthrie and the political scientist Shirley Castelnuovo (2001). They interviewed women with physical impairments about their approaches to managing disability through physical activity. Some of them argued that physical activity served as a means to improve their physical and mental capacities (they became more self-determined and self-confident), but 'it also served the political purpose of deconstructing their own internalized ableism, as well as that of others' (Guthrie and Castelnuovo 2001: 15). However, Guthrie and Castelnuovo do not report any activities directed to the world outside sports, such as the fashion show organized by the participants in my study.

About taking back the body's designation: Corpse, cripples and invalids

Hanna points out that the language in disability sports is not just sexist and homophobic, but can also turn against disabled people too:

This language you know, precisely this view of us, as disabled. That you have this coarse, tough [way of talking], that you call yourself a corpse, that you are a cripple [*skruppel*]. I'm very much against this entire thing. It happens so much ... everywhere. For me it's incomprehensible that they keep on like that. I don't understand it at all, and I think it should go away. If we are to be regarded the way that we want in society, we must influence how... We must think of something, nobody else does. I think it is like a tough shield you show to someone, so that it won't get too close to you. The acceptance of your own ... disability. So you build up a defence instead.

(Hanna, 25, interview)

In the quotation Hanna strengthens her argumentation by using words such as 'so much', 'everywhere' and 'incomprehensible'. Hanna links together the language with a lack of acceptance of one's own impairment. Furthermore she thinks that terms like 'corpse' and 'cripple' are used as a protection against other people. However, Hanna sees the language from another perspective. She thinks the initiative for a change of societal attitudes towards disabled people has to come from the disabled themselves. Exaggeratedly ironic comments about one's own body's presumed deficiency are not, according to Hanna, a way forward.

Hanna fights to change the view of disabled persons both in disability sports and in society, as a whole. I understand this as her strategy to deal with the discrimination she meets. In sports she works against the negative self-image which she thinks is manifested in the use of terms such as 'corpse' or 'cripple'.

The reversed position regarding the language is taken up by Sara as she discusses the Swedish sports movement's reluctance to support sports for disabled persons: 'The Swedish system is not built to accommodate those of us who are cripples [*skruppel*]. ... I was about to say invalids [*invalider*]. You had better write "disabled" [laughter]!' As earlier, when she says that she only had been going out with 'healthy boyfriends', she shows that she is well aware of how politically charged terms are.

The designation of disabled persons is discussed in an article in the journal of the former Swedish Institute of Assistive Technology (now the Swedish Agency for Participation), *All about Assistive Technology*.[6] Terms such as cripple are, according to the author, in frequent use among disabled people.[7] Björn Jidéus, formerly managing director of STIL, claims that it is an expression of 'black humour, you must be permitted to release the pressure'. In the article these terms are compared with similar language used by other subordinated groups such as immigrants or homosexuals as a way 'to take control, to challenge the people around you by strengthening and bringing out their differences'. Choice of words mirrors attitudes and changes the world (Huldt 2007, author's translations). At the Internet-based discussion forum *funktionshinder.se* the use of these terms is considered, too.[8] Some agree that these terms may only be used by disabled people as a sign of self-distance with humour or as an ironic provocation. Others use the terms to dis-identify themselves from their own group. However, many see the internal use as objectionable and depreciating, just as Hanna does. Something that is widely discussed is the difficulty of finding a good term on the whole. Garland-Thomson (1997) suggests several possible interpretations of the self-naming as cripple. It can be regarded as a way to celebrate the position as Other, to recapture and change a word's derogatory meaning but also as a way to pay attention to bodily difference (Garland-Thomson 1997: 25). The philosopher Ian Hacking associates the designations with the categorizations of social science:

> Many of the kinds that have emerged in social science are kinds of deviance, typically of interest because it is undesirable for the person to be of that kind. Such social sciences aim at providing information to help people in trouble. Classifications evaluate who is troubling or in trouble. Hence they present value-laden kinds, things to do or not to do. Kinds of people to be or not to be. … Classifications can change our evaluations of our personal worth, of the moral kind of person that we are. Sometimes this means that people passively accept what experts say about them, and see themselves in that light. But feedback can direct itself in many ways. We well know the rebellions of the sorted. A classification imposed from above is rearranged by the people to whom it was supposed to apply.
>
> (Hacking 1999: 131)

Hacking takes the gay movement, that took over the categorizations that had been imposed on them, as an example. Other examples are the terms 'queer' and 'crip' that have been used derogatorily, but are recaptured – as in Sweden the term 'black skull' in postcolonial and anti-racist research – to mark political resistance (de los Reyes and Mulinari 2005: 61; Mulinari and Neergard 2005).

Concluding discussion

In this chapter the young women's experiences of the sports movement, and, chiefly, the disability sports movement have been analysed. Several of them reject the exaggerated consideration taken in some sports associations and the almost infantile training that is offered. The 'pampering' in disability sports can be understood as an extension of the view of these people as victims of personal tragedies. This way of looking at things is highly present, for instance, in SHIF's policy programme, in which sportspeople are portrayed as weak, dependent and passive as well as in need of rehabilitation and social integration. This depreciation is yet another example of how cultural imperialism (Young 1990/2011) can manifest itself. This may also be mirrored when the organizer of the sports camp points out that 'this is something completely different' and fails to find coaches. The participants wish for hard and 'professional' training, but the problem is, rather, lack of variation. There ought to be room for several different levels in disability sports – playful children's sports, fitness sports as well as competitive sports for those who want to play more 'professionally'.

In Swedish disability sports there are no women's teams, with only a very few exceptions. Girls and women are offered the chance to participate in men's teams, where they are in the minority. While Julia did not get any playing time at all in the team with which she trained for a period, several others describe the problems they encountered in taking (and being given) a place and responsibility on the playing field or as a leader, and the feeling of being continuously kept one step behind others. I interpret their situation in the disability sports movement as to some extent characterized by powerlessness (Young 1990/2011). The interviewees who want to do competitive sport have few choices. They have limited chances of recognition and experience disrespectful treatment in team sports. Moreover, the participants document what Young (1990/2011) terms violence: homophobic and sexist language in disability sports, with (in one case) even incidents of sexual harassment from both team-mates and coaches. They also find themselves excluded to a certain extent from the social context in the men's team. Nor does the social integration that SHIF has as one of their main goals work satisfactorily for the young women. Taken together this leads to a limitation of the young women's possibilities of moving from the position as an object for others to an active subject through sports.

However, it is only in the men's teams that those who are interested in team sports can get the physically demanding training that they desire. My interpretation is that Ingela feels that she gains a share of men's higher status in sports, and Felicia enjoys bringing down tall men during matches. But, as Julia put it: 'you really have to think that the sport is tremendous fun in order to keep playing'.

Resistance is expressed as a form of active work for change, which the young women themselves have begun. Julia's struggle to create a women's national team is one example. The girls' groups that have been formed in several associations and that work to make the young women's voices heard are another example.

Notes

1 In riding and motor sport, amongst others, men and women compete together; the Swede Helen Johansson won in 1995 against all the male drivers in the French Prix D'Amérique. The Chinese woman Zhang Shan won the gold medal in the mixed Olympic Skeet Shooting in the Olympic Games in Barcelona in 1992. In the 1996 Olympics women were no longer permitted to compete in Olympic Skeet Shooting. Four years later a female skeet event was introduced (Jönsson 2003; Wegerup 2005: 24).

2 Sometimes male dominance amongst those who have a spinal cord injury is mentioned as an explanation for the uneven representation – about 80 per cent of 5000

people living with a spinal cord injury in Sweden are men. But even if all these men were active in disability sports it would not be sufficient to explain the imbalance.

3 Ahmed (2006) writes about the experience of the shift from being heterosexual to becoming a lesbian, which, like acquiring an impairment, leads to a 'reorientation'.

4 RG Active Rehabilitation is a non-profit association that, according their website, aims to 'motivate people with disabilities, especially people with spinal cord injuries, to lead an active and independent life. We motivate people through sports and we also use successful people with spinal cord injuries as role-models' (RG Active Rehabilitation nd).

5 In wheelchair basketball, all players are classified on a point scale of 1 to 4.5. Athletes with high functional capacity on the basketball court have the highest classifications, while players with lower functional capacity have lower classifications. The total number of points allowed on the court at one time is 14.0.

6 *Allt om hjälpmedel.*

7 Other terms discussed are, for instance, the Swedish *funkis, mungo* and *mupp.*

8 The website is presented as a 'meeting place, discussion forum and body of knowledge for everybody that is interested in disability' (funktionshinder.se 2015, author's translation).

7 Final discussion

Four faces of oppression and its resistance

In the young women's stories there are many examples of *cultural imperialism*. They are stereotyped and marked out as the Other as they are met with infantilization, patronizing benevolence or pity and are ascribed deficiency and weakness. One variation of the stereotyping is the positive discrimination that is to be found in the material, as when people are impressed by the interviewees and what they can do 'despite' impairment – that is to say, despite their alleged weakness and incompetence. Sometimes they are treated as feeble-minded. The visible physical impairment is assumed to entail an intellectual impairment. The young women make resistance against all this by accentuating their capacity, strength and normality in interviews and video diaries. This can show itself directly, as when they talk about their own muscular strength, skilfulness and abilities. Sometimes they emphasize their own capacity by relating it to boys' or men's capacity, as for instance when Felicia proudly tells about how she beat all the boys in her class and in the class above at arm wrestling, or when Hanna, Sara and Ingela describe how they have played and trained with boys and men. The resistance can also be indirect as they distance themselves from the position of the victim or dis-identify themselves from other disabled people or from the characteristics ascribed to these others. The discussions on the overprotective parents and the picture of the new, young woman – independent, free and with an abundance of choices – in the media and the political debate, contribute to a dichotomy between, on the one hand, weakness and dependence and, on the other, strength and autonomy.

Processes of stigmatization are also present in the young women's everyday life. These are manifested in surrounding people's staring and questions. The wheelchair is in several cases central in the stigmatization, which leads to the young women being deprived of the possibility to define themselves. Everybody has to deal with this, but they do it in different ways. However, curious questions sometimes lead to productive meetings. While strangers' questions do not bother Malin, Natalie is often embarrassed, gives an abrupt answer and then leaves. Julia chooses to meet the gazes, smile and show that, 'despite' her wheelchair, she is 'just like everyone else'. This way she takes back the right to self-definition. When Maria falls in school she hides her actual feelings and smiles instead, to avoid pity.

Yet another example of stereotyping results from the view of disabled people as non-gendered and asexual that has been documented in previous research. The young women's resistance against this stereotype is expressed in their compliance with the ideals of the emphasized femininity. At the same time as they challenge the gender regime in sports by doing tough team sports, several interviewees are eager to present themselves as precisely young women and as (hetero)sexual, in one case by dissociating from lesbian people. Here too an implicit 'despite' is to be found in their stories. They explain that they can easily get boyfriends, even men without disabilities and who may have 'a gorgeous body'. This shows that they are still sexually attractive 'despite' disability or wheelchair. However, the sexuality that is depicted is carefully kept within the limits of respectability.

The participants in this study are also made the Other as they are excluded or pointed out in compulsory school during the lessons in PE. There is a discrepancy between those well-trained, persistent and committed young women's successes in disability sports, and the lack of understanding and curiosity that the teachers of PE manifest. The evaluation conducted by the Swedish National Agency for Education in 2002 states that it is 'unusual that pupils feel out of it' (Eriksson et al 2003: 27, author's translation). However, the young women in my study belong to this rare group. In the interview situation Ingela shifts from 'I' to 'we' when she talks about the exclusion from PE. Instead of standing out as a lonely, vulnerable individual she presents herself as being part of the collective of young disabled people. Ingela has a suggestion for how to improve PE: in dialogue with the teachers she could contribute with her experiences of sporting in a wheelchair.

The importance of disability sports clubs is emphasized. The interviewees have met other disabled people in the clubs. They have not been without friends throughout childhood and adolescence, but, as Jenny says, 'During all the years when I was growing up it was only me, so to speak. So it was nice coming to a place where you were the same.' The emotional experiences of oppression are, as Narayan points out, difficult to fully understand for an out-sider, no matter how empathetic one is (2004: 220). In the clubs, on the other hand, there are others with similar experiences who 'feel as I do' and a collective identity is created. However, the participants talk about problems in sports. The possibility of engaging in different kinds of sports on different levels seems to be limited in disability sports. The young women want hard and 'professional' training, but find that in some disability sports clubs they are met with patronizing and infantilizing consideration. They are offered 'dabbling' instead of swimming training and they are 'pampered'. This can be explained by the theory of personal tragedy, according to which these individuals are grievously afflicted, and hence ought to be met with special tolerance and benevolence. This view also permeates SHIF's policy programme (2006), which portrays the sportsmen and sportswomen they organize as pitiable and in need of social integration.

The lack of choices in the Swedish disability sports movement give rise to some degree of *powerlessness* and a difficulty in fulfilling one's projects. The same could be said about the situation in team sports. The young women accentuate the problems with the gender-mixed teams, or what I prefer to call the men's team. The women are in the minority and participation is often on the men's terms. In one team women are not permitted to play matches and several of the young women say that it is difficult to take or be given place in the men's teams. Thus there are few opportunities to gain recognition. They also remain outside the social intercourse. However, the men's team is the only alternative for those who want to play team sports. The positive changes that the young women in disability sports have initiated are tangible. Several of the interviewees are leaders in and have been active in starting girls' groups in different sports clubs. Here sports activities are mixed with discussions and exercises that aim at increased consciousness about their own situation. They also turn outwards to change the attitudes towards young disabled women. Julia is also working to start a women's national team in her sport.

Examples of ambivalence towards the institutions of the welfare states are also to be found in the material. This is part of what Young calls *marginalization* (1990/2011: 53–5). The participants of the study are dependent on these institutions to be able to lead an autonomous life. Through this dependency medical professionals are given insight into and control over their lives; hence they run the risk of being subjected to objectification and integrity-infringing treatment. This is evident in the care contacts, when Sara feels she is subjected to extra control during her pregnancy, when Maria defends her bodily integrity before an operation, and when Felicia talks about the annual 'gathering' at the Child and Youth Habilitation, and the examination of her almost naked body leads to fragmentation and objectification. At the same time the experiences are ambivalent. They gain access to specialist medical care and know that the operations are performed in their own interest. 'Maybe you should be grateful', Sara concludes.

Finally they give evidence of oppression in the form of *violence*. Sara tells of recurrent bullying in compulsory school. Until the start of school she experienced her body as one of many bodily variations. As her leakage was brutally disclosed at the junior level of compulsory school, she became socially constructed as disabled. She resists, on the one hand, by not attending the lessons in PE during which her body is exposed, and, on the other, when she gets older by choosing friends, clothing, hairstyle, piercings and listening to music that her parents dislike.

Sexism and sexual harassment exist in disability sports just as in other sports. Thus, the genderlessness and asexualization of disabled people are not as obvious here as in the rest of society. What makes the situation for young women in disability sports specific is that there are no women's teams. The women in team sports who are subject to harassment either have to endure the harassment or stop playing the sport in question. Julia avoids the position of the victim by ridiculing the men who harass her and by portraying herself as being more able to endure than other women, while Hanna argues against sexism and homophobia.

The different forms of resistance can be interpreted as part of their struggle over the legitimate vision and classification of the world, in general, and of their own bodies and minds, in particular (Bourdieu 1987/1990).

A weak 'we' versus a strong 'I'

Thus, in the empirical material a paradoxical polarization is apparent between the weak, which is manifested through the expression of belonging as 'we', and the strong individual. The subject position as strong, positive and capable – as a reaction towards the weak, the negative – is one of the few positions available to them. With a positive and strong attitude, as with a distancing from the position of victim, the consequence is the difficulty not only of complaining but also of expressing pain, despair or discomfort in one's everyday life. In this study many critical voices are raised, and they tell of stumbling and urine leakage. At the same time, the answer 'it's fine' is given in many different forms. I interpret it as an unwillingness to express negative emotions.

In the phrase 'I am like everyone else' and the many variations on the same theme in the empirical material, a wish for normality is contained. Using the same logic – that attributed weakness leads to the expression of strength – the deviance that is attributed results in a nearly extreme expression of normality. The question is whether it is possible to deviate in more than one way. The lack of gender attributed to disabled people appears to imply that if functionality is not 'normal', there is no room for any other categorization. The endeavour for normality seems almost complete. One interpretation of my material is that disability is seen in the family and in society as a different landscape, in which vulnerability needs to be compensated for by normality, which in turn results in the interview persons' socialization into a compensatory normality.

The body and its pleasures

The participants have varying impairments. They have experienced a number of surgical operations that sometimes lead to prolonged stays at the hospital and lengthy convalescence, but also to reduced pain or increased functionality. Both disability and impairment appear relative. The habitual body – that is, the body we are used to – is experienced as capable and normal, while the actual body is sometimes experienced as more impaired or disabled depending upon the current state and context (Merleau-Ponty 1945/2012: 84–5). The body's actions can be hindered by a listed building, a snowfall or a reluctance to understand, as well as by the examples of cultural imperialism, powerlessness, marginalization and violence given at the beginning of this chapter.

However, the empirical material does not only contain experiences of oppression and resistance. The young women also speak about pleasure and joy in physical movement. It can be pleasure-filled play during childhood or a direct hit in boxing, tiring oneself out and getting wet through perspiration alone or together with others in fast-moving wheelchair races, during training or matches. The wheelchair, both the ordinary one and the one that is used in wheelchair basketball, often has an important role in these feelings of pleasure and becomes an extension of the body. Felicia accentuates the feeling when she, as a 'tiny little girl', succeeds in knocking over tall men during a match. She is glad when women in the opposing team score a goal, and the fight against the men stands out as a match within the match.

Able bodies

The aim of this book was to expose the young women's lived experiences of the body that, on the one hand, is considered deviant and, on the other, is powerful. I regard this as my contribution to the four research fields: the sociology of the body, feminist research, the sociology of sports and disability studies. During the work with this text, however, the able body has been very present too: as a philanthropist in the disability movement and later as a charity supporter, as the strong worker or the media consumer who pities the victims and admires the heroes who succeed despite disability. The able body is also to be found in parts of the research world that study the exposed and dependent group and – in an especially strong, healthy and achieving version – within the sports movement. Even more important is its presence in the interviewees' self-presentations, in which it is manifest in the phrases 'I can' and 'I am like everyone else'. My hope is that making the able body visible will also contribute to a shift of perspective in the four above-mentioned research fields.

Abbreviations

CDS	critical disability studies
DHR	Association for a Society without Mobility Obstacles
HSO	Swedish Disability Federation
IL	Independent Living
LASS	Act Concerning Compensation for Assistance
LGBT	lesbian, gay, bisexual and transgender
LSS	Act Concerning Support and Service for Persons with Certain Functional Impairments
PE	physical education
RF	Swedish Sports Confederation
SHIF	Swedish Sports Organization for the Disabled (Swedish Parasports Federation)
STIL	Stockholm Cooperative for Independent Living
SVT	Swedish Television
WHO	World Health Organization

References

Adkins, L., 2004. Gender and the post-structural social. In B. L. Marshall and A. Witz, eds. *Engendering the social: Feminist encounters with sociological theory*. Buckingham: Open University Press, pp139–154.

Ahmed, S., 2006. *Queer phenomenology: Orientations, objects, others*. Durham, London: Duke University Press.

Alexander, C. J., Hwang, K. and Sipski, M. L., 2002. Mothers with spinal cord injuries: Impact on marital, family, and children's adjustment. *Archives of Physical Medicine and Rehabilitation*. 83(1), pp24–30.

Ambjörnsson, F., 2004. I en klass för sig: Genus, klass och sexualitet bland gymnasietjejer. PhD. Stockholm: Ordfront.

Anderson, D., 2009. Adolescent girls' involvement i disability sport: Implications for identity development. *Journal of Sport & Social Issues* 33(4), pp427–449.

Andersson, B., 2005. Mäns våld blir kvinnors ansvar: Riskkalkylering i det offentliga rummet. In T. Friberg, C. Listerborn, B. Andersson and C. Scholten, eds. *Speglingar av rum: Om könskodade platser och sammanhang*. Stockholm: Östlings Bokförlag Symposion, pp69–85.

Andreasson, J., 2007. Idrottens kön: Genus, kropp och sexualitet i lagidrottens vardag. PhD. Lunds universitet.

Apelmo, E., 2005. 'Från det att jag var liten har det alltid varit boll': Om konstruktionen av femininitet bland elitsatsande fotbollstjejer. *Idrottsforum.org*, [online] http://www.idrottsforum.org/articles/apelmo/apelmo051005.html [Accessed 21 September 2015].

Apelmo, E., 2010. Kortrecension av 'Adolescent girls' involvement in disability sport: Implications for identity development' by D. Anderson. *Idrottsforum.org*, [online] http://www.idrottsforum.org/archive/2010/100127.html [Accessed 21 September 2015].

Apelmo, E., 2011. Att bli kär i en rullstol: Kropp, kön och teknologi. In H. Tolvhed and D. Cardell, eds. *Kulturstudier, kropp och idrott: Perspektiv på fenomen i gränslandet mellan natur och kultur*. Malmö: Idrottsforum.org, pp211–277.

Apelmo, E., 2012a. Crip heroes and social change. *Lambda Nordica*, 17(1–2), pp27–52.

Apelmo, E., 2012b. Falling in love with a wheelchair: Enabling/disabling technologies. *Sport in Society*, 15(3), pp399–408.

Apelmo, E., 2012c. (Dis)abled bodies, gender, and citizenship in the Swedish sports movement. *Disability & Society*, 27(4), pp1–12.

Arnfred, S., 2002. Simone de Beauvoir in Africa: Woman = the second sex? Issues of African feminist thought. *Jenda: A Journal of Culture and African Women Studies*, 2(1), pp1–20.

Arnhof, Y., 2008. Vanligare med dålig hälsa hos funktionsnedsatta. *Välfärd*, (2), pp18–19, [pdf] http://www.scb.se/statistik/_publikationer/LE0001_2008K02_TI_09_A05TI0802. pdf [Accessed 21 September 2015].

Asbjørnslett, M. and Hemmingsson, H., 2008. Participation at school as experienced by teenagers with physical disabilities. *Scandinavian Journal of Occupational Therapy*, 15(3), pp153–161.

Barnes, C., 1998. The social model of disability: A sociological phenomenon ignored by sociologists? In T. Shakespeare, ed. *The disability reader: Social science perspectives*. London: Continuum, pp65–78.

Barron, K., 1995. *The transition from adolescence to adulthood for physically disabled young people*. Uppsala: Uppsala Universitet.

Barron, K., 1997. Disability and gender: Autonomy as an indication of adulthood. PhD. Uppsala Universitet.

Barron, K., Michailakis, D. and Söder, M., 2000. Funktionshindrade och den offentliga hjälpapparaten. In M. Szebehely, ed. *Välfärd, vård och omsorg*. [Online] SOU 2000: 38. Stockholm: Fritzes offentliga publikationer. pp137–170. Available at: http://www. regeringen.se/contentassets/8cb9e509941e4e289cde557048328636/del-1-kap.-1-4-valfa rd-vard-och-omsorg [Accessed 21 September 2015].

Bartky, S. L., 1990. *Femininity and domination: Studies in the phenomenology of oppression*. London, New York, NY: Routledge.

Bê, A., 2012. Feminism and disability. In N. Watson, A. Roulstone and C. Thomas, eds. *Routledge handbook of disability studies*. New York, NY: Routledge, pp363–375.

Bengtsson, H., 2004. Vägen till personlig assistans. In K. Gynnerstedt, ed. *Personlig assistans och medborgarskap*. Lund: Studentlitteratur, pp39–71.

Berg, S., 2007. *DHR. 80 år av rörelse*. Stockholm: De handikappades riksförbund DHR.

Berg, S., 2008. *Independent Living i Sverige 25 år*. Johanneshov: Stiftarna av Independent Living i Sverige, STIL.

Berger, R. J., 2004. Pushing forward: Disability, basketball, and me. *Qualitative Inquiry*, 10(5), pp794–810.

Blume, S., 2012. What can the study of science and technology tell us about disability? In N. Watson, A. Roulstone and C. Thomas, eds. *Routledge handbook of disability studies*. New York, NY: Routledge, pp348–359.

Bolibompa, 2011. [TV programme] Barnkanalen, SVT, 2011.

Bolling, H., 2008. OS för 'andra'? Paralympics – de parallella spelen. *Idrott, historia och samhälle*, pp31–51.

Bordo, S., 2004. *Unbearable weight: Feminism, Western culture, and the body*. Berkeley, CA: University of California Press.

Bourdieu, P., 1984/1993. *Sociology in question*. London: Sage.

Bourdieu, P., 1987/1990. *In other words: Essays toward a reflexive sociology*. Oxford: Polity Press.

Bourdieu, P., 1994/1998. *Practical reason: On the theory of action*. Stanford, CA: Stanford University Press.

Bourdieu, P., 1998/2001. *Masculine domination*. Cambridge: Polity Press.

Brah, A., 2001. Difference, diversity, differentiation. In K.-K. Bhavnani, ed. *Feminism and 'race'*. Oxford: Oxford University Press, pp456–478.

Briant, E., Watson, N. and Philo, G., 2013. Reporting disability in the age of austerity: The changing face of media representation of disability and disabled people in the United Kingdom and the creation of new 'folk devils'. *Disability and Society*, 28(6), pp874–889.

Brittain, I., 2004. Perceptions of disability and their impact upon involvement in sport for people with disabilities at all levels. *Journal of Sport & Social Issues*, 28(4), pp429–452.

Broberg, G. and Tydén, M., 1996. Eugenics in Sweden: Efficient care. In G. Broberg and N. Roll-Hansen, eds. *Eugenics and the welfare state*. East Lansing: Michigan State University Press, pp77–149.

Bryman, A., 2012. *Social research methods*. 4. ed. Oxford: Oxford University Press.

Bråkenhielm, G., 2008. Ingen gympa för mig! En undersökning av skälen till att elever inte deltar i ämnet idrott och hälsa. *Svensk Idrottsforskning*, 17(2), pp30–33.

Cahill, S. E. and Eggleston, R., 1994. Managing emotions in public: The case of wheelchair users. *Social Psychology Quarterly*. 57(4), pp300–312.

Campbell, F. K., 2008. Refusing able(ness): A preliminary conversation about ableism. *M/C Journal*, 11(3), [online] Available at: http://journal.media-culture.org.au/index.php/mcjournal/article/viewArticle/46 [Accessed 21 September 2015].

Campbell, F. K., 2012. Stalking ableism: Using disability to expose 'abled' narcissism. In: D. Goodley, B. Hughes and L. J. Davis, eds. *Disability and social theory: New developments and directions*. Basingstoke: Palgrave Macmillan, pp212–230.

Collins, P. H., 1997. Comment on Hekman's 'Truth and method: Feminist standpoint theory revisited': Where's the Power? *Signs*, 22(2), pp375–381.

Collmar, L., 2010. Se ut som andra. *Stiletten*, 1, pp14–17.

Combahee River Collective, 1977. *A black feminist statement*. [online] The Feminist eZine. Available at: http://www.lilithgallery.com/feminist/modern/Black-Feminist-Statement.html [Accessed 21 September 2015].

Connell, R., 2002. *Gender*. Cambridge: Polity Press.

Connell, R., 2005. *Masculinities*. Cambridge: Polity Press.

Connell, R., 2014. *Gender and power: Society, the person and sexual politics*. [e-book] Wiley: Hoboken. Available through: Malmö University Library Website http://www.mah.se/bibliotek [Accessed 21 September 2015].

Crow, L., 1996. Including all of our lives: Renewing the social model of disability. In J. Morris, ed. *Encounters with strangers: Feminism and disability*. London: Women's Press. pp206–226.

Deal, M., 2003. Disabled people's attitudes toward other impairment groups: A hierarchy of impairments. *Disability & Society*, 18(7), pp897–910.

de Beauvoir, S., 1949/2011. *The second sex*. New York, NY: Vintage Books.

de los Reyes, P., 2000. Var finns mångfalden? Konstruktionen av mångfald inom svensk forskning och samhällsdebatt. *Working life research in Europe*, 2, Solna: SALTSA.

de los Reyes, P. and Mulinari, D., 2005. *Intersektionalitet: Kritiska reflektioner över (o)jämlikhetens landskap*. Malmö: Liber.

de los Reyes, P., Molina, I. and Mulinari, D., 2003. Introduktion: Maktens (o)lika förklädnader. In P. de los Reyes, I. Molina and D. Mulinari, eds. *Maktens (o)lika förklädnader: Kön, klass & etnicitet i det postkoloniala Sverige*. Stockholm: Atlas, pp11–30.

Dellgren, A., Kloow, M., Westholm, E. and Conner, P., 2008. *Fosterdiagnostik och riskvärdering: Information till gravida*. [pdf] Stockholm: Centrum för fostermedicin CFM, Karolinska Universitetssjukhuset. Available at: http://www.karolinska.se/globalassets/global/kvinnokliniken/centrum-for-fostermedicin/broschyr-webb-att-publicera.pdf [Accessed 21 September 2015].

Du Bois, W. E. B., 1903/2007. *The souls of black folk*. [e-book] New York, NY, Oxford: Oxford University Press. Available through: Malmö University Library Website http://www.mah.se/bibliotek [Accessed 21 September 2015].

Dworkin, S. L., 2001. 'Holding back': Negotiating a glass ceiling on women's muscular strength. *Sociological Perspectives*, 44(3), pp333–350.

Dworkin, S. L. and Messner, M. A., 2002. Just do... what? Sport, bodies, gender. In S. Scraton and A. Flintoff, eds. *Gender and sport: A reader*. London: Routledge, pp17–29.

Eduards, M., 2007. *Kroppspolitik: Om moder Svea och andra kvinnor*. Stockholm: Atlas.

Edwards, C. and Imrie, R., 2003. Disability and bodies as bearers of value. *Sociology*, 37(2), pp239–256.

En andra chans, 2011. [TV programme] SVT, August to October 2011.

Eriksson, C., Gustavsson, K., Johansson, T., Mustell, J., Quennerstedt, M., Rudsberg, K., Sundberg, M. and Svensson, L., 2003. *Skolämnet Idrott och hälsa i Sveriges skolor: En utvärdering av läget hösten 2002*. Örebro: Örebro universitet.

Fagrell, B. 2005. Den handlande kroppen: Flickor, pojkar, idrott och subjektivitet. *Kvinnovetenskaplig tidskrift* 26(1), pp65–80.

Fasting, K., 2005. Research on sexual harassment and abuse in sport. *Idrottsforum. org*, [online] Available at: http://www.idrottsforum.org/articles/fasting/fasting050405. html [Accessed 21 September 2015].

Fellers, J., 2010. På egna ben: En motivanalytisk studie av Svenska handikapp-idrottsförbundets bildande. *Idrottsforum.org*, [online] Available at: http://www. idrottsforum.org/articles/fellers/fellers100512.html [Accessed 21 September 2015].

Finkelstein, V., 1996. *Outside, 'inside out'*. [pdf] Leeds: The Disability Archive UK, Centre for Disability Studies, University of Leeds. Available at: http://www.disability-archive.leeds.ac.uk/authors_list.asp?AuthorID=73&author_name=Finkelstein%2C+Vic [Accessed 21 September 2015].

Folkhälsomyndigheten, 2015. *Delrapportering av regeringsuppdrag inom ramen för 'En strategi för genomförande av funktionshinderspolitiken 2011–2016'*. [pdf] Stockholm: Folkhälsomyndigheten. Available at: http://www.folkhalsomyndigheten.se/docum ents/livsvillkor-levnadsvanor/funktionsnedsattning/delrapportering-regeringsuppdra g-funktionshinderspolitiken-2015.pdf [Accessed 21 September 2015].

Forum Women and Disability in Sweden, 2015. *Forum Kvinnor och Funktionshinder*. [online] Available at: http://www.kvinnor-funktionshinder.se [Accessed 21 September 2015].

Foucault, M., 1975/1991. *Discipline and punish: The birth of the prison*. Harmondsworth: Penguin.

Foucault, M., 1976/1990. *The history of sexuality: Vol. 1, An introduction*. New York, NY: Random House.

Foucault, M., 1982/2000. *The Battle for chastity: Essential works of Foucault. 1954–1984. Vol 1. Ethics: subjectivity and truth*. London: Penguin.

Fundberg, J., 2003. Kom igen, gubbar! Om pojkfotboll och maskuliniteter. PhD. Stockholm: Carlsson.

funktionshinder.se, 2015. *funktionshinder.se*. [online] Available at: http://www.funktion shinder.se [Accessed 21 September 2015].

Förhammar, S., 2004. Svensk handikappolitik: Från separation till integration? In S. Förhammar and M. C. Nelson, eds. *Funktionshinder i ett historiskt perspektiv*. Lund: Studentlitteratur. pp45–65.

Gadamer, H.-G., 1986/2006. Classical and philosophical hermeneutics. *Theory, Culture & Society*, 23(1), pp29–56.

Ganetz, H., 1991. Inledning: Unga kvinnor? In H. Ganetz and K. Lövgren, eds. *Om unga kvinnor: Identitet, kultur och livsvillkor*. Lund: Studentlitteratur, pp7–19.

Garland-Thomson, R., 1997. *Extraordinary bodies: Figuring physical disability in American culture and literature.* New York, NY: Columbia University Press.

Garland-Thomson, R., 2009. *Staring: How we look.* Oxford: Oxford University Press.

Ghai, A., 2012. Engaging with disability with postcolonial theory. In: D. Goodley, B. Hughes and L. J. Davis, eds. *Disability and social theory: New developments and directions.* Basingstoke: Palgrave Macmillan, pp270–286.

Ghersetti, M., 2007. *Bilden av funktionshinder: En studie av nyheter i Sveriges Television.* Göteborg: Göteborgs universitet.

Gibson, B. E., 2005. Co-producing video diaries: The presence of the 'absent' researcher. *International Journal of Qualitative Methods,* 4(4), pp1–10.

Gilje, N. and Grimen, H., 2007. *Samhällsvetenskapernas förutsättningar.* 3. ed., Göteborg: Daidalos.

Goffman, E., 1959/1990. *The presentation of self in everyday life.* London: Penguin.

Goffman, E., 1963/1990. *Stigma: Notes on the management of spoiled identity.* Harmondsworth: Penguin Books.

Goodley, D., Hughes, B. and Davis, L. J., 2012. Introducing disability and social theory. In: D. Goodley, B. Hughes and L. J. Davis, eds. *Disability and social theory: New developments and directions.* Basingstoke: Palgrave Macmillan, pp1–14.

Goodley, D., 2013. Dis/entangling critical disability studies. *Disability & Society,* 28(5), pp631–644.

Grue, L. and Heiberg, A., 2006. Notes on the history of normality: Reflections on the work of Quetelet and Galton. *Scandinavian Journal of Disability Research,* 8(4), pp232–247.

Grönvik, L., 2007. Definitions of disability in social sciences: Methodological perspectives. PhD. Uppsala: Acta Universitatis Upsaliensis.

Grönvik, L. 2008. Sexualitet och funktionshinder. In L. Grönvik and M. Söder, eds. *Bara funktionshindrad? Funktionshinder och intersektionalitet.* Malmö: Gleerup, pp47–63.

Gustavsson Holmström, M., 2002. Föräldrar med funktionshinder: Barn, föräldraskap och familjeliv. PhD. Stockholm: Carlsson.

Guthrie, S. R. and Castelnuovo, S., 2001. Disability management among women with physical impairments: The contribution of physical activity. *Sociology of Sport Journal,* 18(1), pp5–20.

Gynnerstedt, K., 2004. Personlig assistans: En medborgelig rättighet. In K. Gynnerstedt, ed. *Personlig assistans och medborgarskap.* Lund: Studentlitteratur, pp13–38.

Hacking, I., 1999. *The social construction of what?* Cambridge, MA: Harvard University Press.

Hall, E., 2000. 'Blood, brain and bones': Taking the body seriously in the geography of health and impairment. *Area,* 32(1), pp21–29.

Hanisch, C., 1969. *The personal is political.* [online] Carolhanisch.org. Available at: http://carolhanisch.org/CHwritings/PIP.html [Accessed 21 September 2015].

Hansson, K., 2007. I ett andetag: En kulturanalys av astma som begränsning och möjlighet. PhD. Stockholm: Critical Ethnography Press.

Haraway, D., 1988. Situated knowledges: The science question in feminism and the privilege of partial perspective. *Feminist Studies,* 14(3), pp575–599.

Haraway, D., 1991. *Simians, cyborgs, and women: The reinvention of nature.* London: Free Association Books.

Hardin, M. M. and Hardin, B., 2004. The 'supercrip' in sport media: Wheelchair athletes discuss hegemony's disabled hero. *Sociology of Sport Online,* 7(1), [online]

Available at: http://physed.otago.ac.nz/sosol/v7i1/v7i1_1.html [Accessed 21 September 2015].

Harding, S., 1997. Comment on Hekman's 'Truth and method: Feminist standpoint theory revisited': Whose standpoint needs the regimes of truth and reality? *Signs*, 22(2), pp382–391.

Harding, S., 2004. Introduction: Standpoint theory as a site of political, philosophic, and scientific debate. In S. G. Harding, ed. *The feminist standpoint theory reader: Intellectual and political controversies*. New York, NY: Routledge, pp1–15.

Hargreaves, J., 1994. *Sporting females: Critical issues in the history and sociology of women's sports*. London: Routledge.

Hargreaves, J. 2000. *Heroines of sport: The politics of difference and identity*. London: Routledge.

Helmius, G., 2004. Three generations: Looking at physically disabled women's lives. In K. Kristiansen and R. Traustadottir, eds. *Gender and disability research in the Nordic countries*. Lund: Studentlitteratur, pp97–113.

Hochschild, A. R., 2003. *The commercialization of intimate life: Notes from home and work*. Berkeley, CA: University of California Press.

Holme, L., 1995. 'En liten ensam, ofärdig flicka': Om tillkomsten av Föreningen för bistånd åt lytta och vanföra i Stockholm år 1891. In B. E. Eriksson and R. Törnqvist, eds. *Likhet och särart: Handikapphistoria i Norden*. Södertälje: Fingraf, pp231–240.

Holme, L., 2000. Begrepp om handikapp: En essä om det miljörelativa handikappbegreppet. In M. Tideman, ed. *Handikapp: synsätt, principer, perspektiv*. Lund: Studentlitteratur, pp67–78.

Holth, L. and Mellström, U., 2011. Revisiting engineering, masculinity and technology studies: Old structures with new openings. *International Journal of Gender, Science, and Technology*, 3(2), pp313–329.

Hugemark, A. and Roman, C., 2007. Diversity and divisions in the Swedish disability movement: Disability, gender, and social justice. *Scandinavian Journal of Disability Research*, 9(1), pp26–45.

Hughes, B., 1999. The constitution of impairment: Modernity and the aesthetic of oppression. *Disability & Society*, 14(2), pp155–172.

Hughes, B., 2000. Medicine and the aesthetic invalidation of disabled people. *Disability & Society*, 15(4), pp555–568.

Hughes, B., 2009. Wounded/monstrous/abject: A critique of the disabled body in the sociological imaginary. *Disability & Society*, 24(4), pp399–410.

Hughes, B. and Paterson, K., 1997. The social model of disability and the disappearing body: Towards a sociology of impairment. *Disability & Society*, 12(3), pp325–340.

Hughes, B., Russell, R. and Paterson, K., 2005. Nothing to be had 'off the peg': consumption, identity and the immobilization of young disabled people. *Disability & Society*, 20(1), pp3–17.

Huldt, C., 2007. Språket speglar attityder: Kan nya ord påverka vårt sätt att se verkligheten? *Allt om hjälpmedel*, 3, pp10–12.

Hvinden, B., 2004. Nordic disability policies in a changing Europe: Is there still a distinct Nordic model? *Social Policy and Administration*, 38(2), pp170–189.

Jönsson, K., 2003. Idrott och kön. *Idrottsforum.org*, [online] Available at: http://www.idrottsforum.org/features/gendersports/gender%26sports.html [Accessed 21 September 2015].

Koivula, N., 1999. Gender in sport. PhD. Stockholms universitet.

Kristén, L., 2003. Possibilities offered by interventional sports programmes to children and adolescents with physical disabilities: An explorative and evaluative study. PhD. Luleå: Luleå tekniska universitet.

Kristeva, J., 1982. *Powers of horror: An essay on abjection*. New York, NY: Columbia University Press.

Kvale, S., 2007. *Doing interviews*. Thousand Oaks, CA: Sage Publications.

Köping Hillbillies, 2010. [TV programme] SVT, April to June 2010.

Lapper, A. and Feldman, G., 2006. *My life in my hands*. London: Pocket Books.

Larsson, H., 2004. Idrott och genus: Kroppens materialisering. *Dansk sociologi*, 15(2), pp55–72.

Larsson, H., 2005. Queer idrott: Annika Sörenstam, kvinnligheten och den jämställda idrotten. In D. Kulick, ed. *Queersverige*. Stockholm: Natur och Kultur, pp110–135.

Larsson, H., 2006. A history of the present on the 'sportsman' and the 'sportswoman'. *Historical Social Research/Historische Sozialforschung*, 31(1), pp209–229.

Larsson, H., Fagrell, B., Johansson, S., Lundvall, S., Meckbach, J. and Redelius, K., 2010. *Jämställda villkor i idrott och hälsa med fokus på flickors och pojkars måluppfyllelse: På pojkarnas planhalva*. Stockholm: Skolverket.

Lindqvist, R., 2000. Swedish disability policy: From universal welfare to civil rights? *European Journal of Social Security*, 2(4), pp399–418.

Ljuslinder, K., 2002. På nära håll är ingen normal: Handikappdiskurser i Sveriges television 1956–2000. PhD. Umeå: Umeå Universitet.

Longhurst, R., 2003. *Bodies: Exploring fluid boundaries*. [e-book] London: Routledge. Malmö University Library Website http://www.mah.se/bibliotek [Accessed 21 September 2015].

Loseke, D. R., 2001. Lived realities and formula stories of 'battered women'. In J. F. Gubrium and J. A. Holstein eds. *Institutional selves. Troubled identities in a postmodern world*. Oxford: Oxford University Press, pp107–126.

Lundgren, E., Heimer, G., Westerstrand, J. and Kalliokoski, A.-M., 2001. *Slagen dam: Mäns våld mot kvinnor i jämställda Sverige: en omfångsundersökning*. Umeå: Brottsoffermyndigheten.

Malmberg, D., 1996. Höga klackar och rullstol: En könsteoretisk studie av kvinnor med livslångt funktionshinder. *Kvinnovetenskaplig tidskrift*, 3–4, pp19–30.

Malmberg, D., 2002. Kvinna, kropp och sexualitet: Könsteoretiska perspektiv på handikapp och funktionshinder. *HumaNetten*, (10), [pdf] Available at: http://lnu.se/polopoly_fs/1.105244!Nr_10.pdf [Accessed 21 September 2015].

Malmö Open, 2015. *Rullstolsbasket*. [online] Available at: http://www.malmo-open.com/index.php/idrotter/rullstolsbasket [Accessed 21 September 2015].

Marston, C. and Atkins, D., 1999. Pushing the limits: An interview with Shelley Tremain. *International Journal of Sexuality and Gender Studies*, 4(1), pp87–95.

Martinsson, A., 2011. Kritiserad bedömning av assistans klar att använda. *Svensk Handikapptidskrift*, 31 August.

McNay, L., 2004. Agency and experience: Gender as a lived relation. *Sociological Review*, 52(2), pp173–190.

McRobbie, A., 2007. Top girls? Young women and the post-feminist sexual contract. *Cultural Studies*, 21(4/5), pp718–737.

McRuer, R., 2006. *Crip theory: Cultural signs of queerness and disability*. New York, NY: New York University Press.

Meekosha, H. and Dowse, L., 1997. Enabling citizenship: Gender, disability and citizenship in Australia. *Feminist Review*, 57(1), pp49–72.

Meekosha, H. and Shuttleworth, R., 2009. What's so 'critical' about critical disability studies? *Australian Journal of Human Rights*, 15(1), pp47–76.

Mellström, U., 2004. Machines and masculine subjectivity: Technology as an integral part of men's life experiences. *Men and Masculinities*, 6(4), pp349–367.

Merleau-Ponty, M., 1945/2012. *Phenomenology of perception*. London: Routledge.

Michailakis, D., 2005. Systemteoretisk handikappforskning: En mångfald av perspektiv. In M. Söder, ed. *Forskning om funktionshinder: Problem, utmaningar, möjligheter*. Lund: Studentlitteratur, pp125–152.

Mitchell, D. T. and Snyder, S. L., 1998. Talking about 'Talking back': Afterthoughts on the making of the disability documentary 'Vital signs, crip culture talks back'. *Michigan Quarterly Review*, 37(2), pp316–336.

Mitchell, J., 1971. *Woman's estate*. New York, NY; Toronto: Pantheon Books.

Mohanty, C. T., 1984. Under Western eyes: Feminist scholarship and colonial discourses. *Boundary 2*, 12/13(3), pp333–358.

Moi, T., 1999. *What is a woman?* Oxford: Oxford University Press.

Moi, T., 2008. *Simone de Beauvoir: The making of an intellectual woman*. 2. ed., Oxford: Oxford University Press.

Morris, J., 1995. Creating a space for absent voices: Disabled women's experience of receiving assistance with daily living activities. *Feminist Review*, 51(51), pp68–93.

Morris, J., 1996. Introduction. In J. Morris, ed. *Encounters with strangers: Feminism and disability*. London: Women's Press.

Moser, I., 1998. Kyborgens rehabilitering. In K. Asdal, ed. *Betatt av viten: Bruksanvisninger til Donna Haraway*. Oslo: Spartacus, pp39–76.

Moser, I., 2000. Against normalisation: Subverting norms of ability and disability. *Science as Culture*, 9(2), pp201–240.

Moser, I., 2006. Disability and the promises of technology: Technology, subjectivity and embodiment within an order of the normal. *Information, Communication & Society*, 9(3), pp373–396.

Mot alla odds, 2012. [TV programme] SVT, January to March 2012.

Mulinari, D. and Neergaard, A., 2005. 'Black skull' consciousness: The new Swedish working class. *Race & Class*, 46(3), pp55–72.

Mulinari, D. and Sandell, K., 1999. Exploring the notion of experience in feminist thought. *Acta Sociologica*, 42(4), pp287–297.

Mulvey, L., (2000). Visual pleasure and narrative cinema. In T. Miller and R. Stam, eds. *Film and theory: an anthology*. Malden, MA: Blackwell, pp483–494.

Narayan, U., 2004. The project of feminist epistemology: Perspectives from a nonwestern feminist. In S. G. Harding, ed. *The feminist standpoint theory reader: Intellectual and political controversies*. New York, NY: Routledge, pp211–224.

New, C., 1998. Realism, deconstruction and the feminist standpoint. *Journal for the Theory of Social Behaviour*, 28(4), pp349–372.

Odenbring, Y., 2010. Kramar, kategoriseringar och hjälpfröknar: Könskonstruktioner i interaktion i förskola, förskoleklass och skolår ett. PhD. Göteborg: Acta Universitatis Gothoburgensis.

Olenik, L. M., Matthews, J. M. and Steadward, R. D., 1995. Women, disability and sport: Unheard voices. *Canadian Woman Studies/Les cahiers de la femme*, 15(4), pp54–57.

Oliver, M., 1996. *Understanding disability: From theory to practice*. London: Macmillan.

Oliver, M., 2004. The social model in action: If I had a hammer. In C. Barnes and G. Mercer, eds. *Implementing the social model of disability. Theory and research*. Leeds: Disability Press, pp18–31.

Olofsson, E., 1989. Har kvinnorna en sportslig chans? Den svenska idrottsrörelsen och kvinnorna under 1900-talet. PhD. Umeå universitet.

Östnäs, A., 1997. Handikappidrott mellan tävling och rehabilitering: En studie av handikappidrotten mellan idrottsrörelse och handikapprörelse med utgångspunkt från fallstudien rullstolstennis. PhLic. Lund: Socialhögskolan.

Östnäs, A., 2003. Handikappidrott som socialt fenomen. *Idrottsforum.org*, [online] Available at: http://www.idrottsforum.org/articles/ostnas/ostnas.html [Accessed 21 September 2015].

Paterson, K. and Hughes, B., 1999. Disability studies and phenomenology: The carnal politics of everyday life. *Disability & Society*, 14(5), pp597–610.

Patriksson, G. and Wagnsson, S., 2004. *Föräldraengagemang i barns idrottsföreningar.* FoU-rapport, 2004: 8. Stockholm: Riksidrottsförbundet.

Pauwels, L., 2010. Visual sociology reframed: An analytical synthesis and discussion of visual methods in social and cultural research. *Sociological Methods & Research*, 38(4), pp545–581.

Peers, D., 2009. (Dis)empowering Paralympic histories: Absent athletes and disabling discourses. *Disability & Society*, 24(5), pp653–665.

Peterson, T., 2000. Idrotten som integrationsarena? In G. Rystad and S. Lundberg, eds. *Att möta främlingar.* Lund: Arkiv, pp141–166.

Peterson, T., 2008. The professionalization of sport in the Scandinavian countries. *Idrottsforum.org*, [online] Available at: http://www.idrottsforum.org/articles/peter son/peterson080220.html [Accessed 21 September 2015].

Pratt, M. B., 1991. *Rebellion: Essays 1980–1991.* Ithaca, NY: Firebrand Books.

Redstockings, 1969. *Redstockings manifesto.* [online] Redstockings. Available at: http:// www.redstockings.org/index.php?option=com_content&view=article&id=76&Item id=59 [Accessed 21 September 2015].

Reeve, D., 2012. Cyborgs, cripples and iCrip: Reflections on the contribution of Haraway to disability studies. In: D. Goodley, B. Hughes and L. J. Davis, eds. *Disability and social theory: New developments and directions.* Basingstoke: Palgrave Macmillan, pp91–111.

Reinikainen, M.-R., 2004. Gendered subject positions for the disabled woman and man. In K. Kristiansen and R. Traustadottir, eds. *Gender and disability research in the Nordic countries.* Lund: Studentlitteratur, pp257–274.

RF, 2002. *Sports in Sweden.* [pdf] Riksidrottsförbundet: Stockholm. Available at: http://www.rf.se/imagevaultfiles/id_32905/cf_394/sports_in_sweden.pdf [Accessed 21 September 2015].

RF, 2009. *Idrotten vill: En sammanfattning av idrottsrörelsens idéprogram.* [pdf] Riksidrottsförbundet: Stockholm. Available at: http://www.rf.se/imagevaultfiles/id_ 29061/cf_394/idrotten_vill_09_kort_webbvers_singlep.pdf [Accessed 21 September 2015].

Riksförsäkringsverket, 2002. *Frihet och beroende: Personer med funktionshinder beskriver samhällets stödsystem.* Stockholm: Riksförsäkringsverket.

RG Active Rehabilitation, n.d. *About RG international.* [online] Available at: http:// www.rgaktivrehab.se/?page_id=1565 [Accessed 21 September 2015].

Rich, A., 1980. Compulsory heterosexuality and lesbian existence. *Signs*, 5(4), pp631–660.

Riessman, C. K., 2007. *Narrative methods for the human sciences.* London: Sage.

Robertson, S., 2003. 'If I let a goal in, I'll get beat up': Contradictions in masculinity, sport and health. *Health Education Research*, 18(6), pp706–716.

Rousso, H., 2013. *Don't call me inspirational.* Philadelphia, PA: Temple University Press.

Rydström, J., 2012. Introduction: Crip theory in Scandinavia. *Lambda Nordica*, 17(1–2), pp9–20.

Rönnberg, J., Classon, E., Danermark, B. and Karlsson, T., 2012. *Forskning om funktionsnedsättning och funktionshinder 2002–2010: Kartläggning, analys och förslag.* Forskningsrådet för arbetsliv och socialvetenskap.

Sandahl, C., 2003. Queering the crip or cripping the queer? Intersections of queer and crip identities in solo autobiographical performance. *GLQ: A Journal of Lesbian & Gay Studies*, 9(1–2), pp25–56.

Sandell, K., 2001. *Att återskapa 'det normala': Bröstoperationer och brännskador i plastikkirurgisk praktik.* Lund: Arkiv.

Sandell, K., 2003. Att operera kroppen för att bli 'riktig' kvinna?! Feministiska tolkningar av kosmetisk kirurgi. In D. Mulinari, K. Sandell and E. Schömer, eds. *Mer än bara kvinnor och män: Feministiska perspektiv på genus.* Lund: Studentlitteratur, pp189–216.

Sandvin, J. T., 2008. Ålder och funktionshinder. In: L. Grönvik and M. Söder, eds. *Bara funktionshindrad? Funktionshinder och intersektionalitet.* Malmö: Gleerup, pp64–88.

Statistiska centralbyrån, 2014. Situationen på arbetsmarknaden för personer med funktionsnedsättning 2013. *Information om utbildning och arbetsmarknad 2014*: 1; Örebro: Statistiska centralbyrån.

Sellerberg, A.-M., 1999. Reviews: Karin Barron. Disability and gender: Autonomy as an indication of adulthood. *Young*, 7(1), pp66–67.

SHIF, 2006. *Handikappidrottspolitiskt program.* [pdf] Svenska Parasportförbundet. Available at: http://www.shif.se/ImageVaultFiles/id_44271/cf_78/Handikappidrottsp olitiskt_program.PDF [Accessed 21 September 2015].

Shildrick, M., 2012. Critical disability studies: Rethinking the conventions for the age of postmodernity. In N. Watson, A. Roulstone and C. Thomas, eds. *Routledge handbook of disability studies.* New York, NY: Routledge, pp30–41.

Shildrick, M. and Price, J., 1996. Breaking the boundaries of the broken body. *Body & Society*, 2(4), pp93–113.

Siebers, T., 2012. A sexual culture for disabled people. In R. McRuer and A. Mollow, eds. *Sex and disability.* [e-book] Durham, NC: Duke University Press. Available through: Malmö University Library Website http://www.mah.se/bibliotek [Accessed 21 September 2015].

Sjöberg, M., 1998. *Kvinnor, män och funktionshinder: Rapport om bemötandet av personer med funktionshinder.* [Online] SOU 1998:138. Stockholm: Fritzes offentliga publikationer. Available at: http://www.regeringen.se/sb/d/403/a/23244 [Accessed 21 September 2015].

Skeggs, B., 1997. *Formations of class and gender: Becoming respectable.* London: Sage.

Skolinspektionen, 2010. *Mycket idrott och lite hälsa: Skolinspektionens rapport från den flygande tillsynen i idrott och hälsa.* [pdf] Stockholm: Skolinspektionen. Available at: http://www.skolinspektionen.se/Documents/Regelbunden-tillsyn/flygande% 20tillsyn/slutrapport-flygande-tillsyn-idott.pdf [Accessed 21 September 2015].

Slater, J., 2012. Youth for sale: Using critical disability perspectives to examine the embodiment of 'youth'. *Societies*, 2(4), pp195–209.

Smith, B. and Sparks, A. C., 2012. Disability, sport and physical activity: A critical review. In N. Watson, A. Roulstone and C. Thomas, eds. *Routledge handbook of disability studies.* New York, NY: Routledge, pp336–347.

Smith, D. E., 1997. Comment on Hekman's 'Truth and method: Feminist standpoint theory revisited'. *Signs*, 22(2), pp392–398.

Socialstyrelsen, 2010. *Bedömning av behov av personlig assistans.* [online] Stockholm: Socialstyrelsen. Available at: http://www.socialstyrelsen.se/nyheter/2010januaritillsep tember/assistans [Accessed 21 September 2015].

Sunderland, N., Catalano, T. and Kendall, E., 2009. Missing discourses: Concepts of joy and happiness in disability. *Disability & Society*, 24(6), pp703–714.

Svenska Parasportförbundet, 2015. *Idrotter.* [online] Available at: http://www.shif.se/ Idrotter/ [Accessed 21 September 2015].

Svenskidrott.se, 2015. *LOK-stöd.* [online] Available at: http://www.svenskidrott.se/ Ekonomisktstod/LOK-stod/ [Accessed 21 September 2015].

Sveriges Paralympiska Kommitté, 2014. *Tidigare Paralympics.* [online] Available at: http://www.paralympics.se/TidigareParalympics/ [Accessed 21 September 2015].

Swartz, L. and Watermeyer, B., 2008. Cyborg anxiety: Oscar Pistorius and the boundaries of what it means to be human. *Disability & Society*, 23(2), pp187–190.

Söder, M., 2005. Hur det är eller hur det bör vara? Om normativa inslag i social forskning om funktionshinder. In M. Söder, ed. *Forskning om funktionshinder: Problem, utmaningar, möjligheter.* Lund: Studentlitteratur, pp85–102.

Söder, M., 2009. Tensions, perspectives and themes in disability studies. *Scandinavian Journal of Disability Research*, 11(2), pp67–81.

Söder, M., 2013. Swedish social disability research: A short version of a long story. *Scandinavian Journal of Disability Research*, 15(1), pp90–107.

Söder, M. and Grönvik, L., 2008. Intersektionalitet och funktionshinder. In L. Grönvik and M. Söder, eds. *Bara funktionshindrad? Funktionshinder och intersektionalitet* Malmö: Gleerup, pp9–24.

Taub, D. E. and Greer, K. R., 2000. Physical activity as a normalizing experience for school-age children with physical disabilities. *Journal of Sport & Social Issues*, 24(4), pp395–414.

Taub, D. E., Blinde, E. M. and Greer, K. R., 1999. Stigma management through participation in sport and physical activity: Experiences of male college students with physical disabilities. *Human Relations*, 52(11), pp1469–1484.

Thomas, C., 2007. *Sociologies of disability and illness: Contested ideas in disability studies and medical sociology.* Basingstoke: Palgrave Macmillan.

Traustadottir, R. and Kristiansen, K., 2004. Introducing gender and disability. In K. Kristiansen and R. Traustadottir, eds. *Gender and disability research in the Nordic countries.* Lund: Studentlitteratur, pp31–48.

Trinh, T. M., 1989. *Woman, native, other: Writing postcoloniality and feminism.* Bloomington: Indiana University Press.

Trondman, M., 2005. *Unga och föreningsidrotten: En studie om föreningsidrottens plats, betydelser och konsekvenser i ungas liv.* Stockholm: Ungdomsstyrelsen.

Turner, B. S., 2001. Disability and the sociology of the body. In K. D. Seelman, M. Bury and G. L. Albrecht, eds. *Handbook of disability studies.* Thousand Oaks, CA: Sage, pp252–266.

Turner, B. S., 2008. *The Body & Society: Explorations in social theory.* 3. ed., Los Angeles, CA: Sage.

Tøssebro, J., 2004. Introduction to the special issue: Understanding disability. *Scandinavian Journal of Disability Research*, 6(1), pp3–7.

United Nations, 1993. *Standard rules on the equalization of opportunities for persons with disabilities.* [online] United Nations Enable. Available at: http://www.un.org/disabilities/default.asp?id=26 [Accessed 21 September 2015].

Wegerup, J., 2005. Damelvan: Pionjärerna, dramatiken och guldåren. Ett porträtt av svensk damfotboll. Stockholm: Forum.

Wendell, S., 1997. Toward a feminist theory of disability. In L. J. Davis, ed. *The Disability Studies Reader.* London: Routledge, pp260–278.

West, C. and Zimmerman, D. H., 1987. Doing Gender. *Gender and Society,* 1(2), pp125–151.

WHO, 2001. *International classification of functioning, disabilities and health.* [online] World Health Organization. Available at: http://www.who.int/classifications/icf/en/ [Accessed 21 September 2015].

Wickman, K., 2004. 'I try and be as athletic like, forget the other side of me': Constructions of elite female wheelchair athletes' identities. *Kvinder, køn & forskning,* 13 (2–3), pp22–33.

Wickman, K., 2007a. The discourse of able-ism: Meanings and representations of gendered wheelchair racers in sports media texts. The 4th EASS Conference, Local Sport in Europe, Münster.

Wickman, K., 2007b. 'I do not compete in disability': How wheelchair athletes challenge the discourse of able-ism through action and resistance. *European Journal for Sport and Society,* 4(2), pp151–167.

Wickman, K., 2008. Bending mainstream definitions of sport, gender and ability: Representations of wheelchair racers. PhD. Umeå Universitet.

Young, I. M., 1980. Throwing like a girl: A phenomenology of feminine body comportment motility and spatiality. *Human Studies,* 3(2), pp137–156.

Young, I. M., 1990/2011. *Justice and the politics of difference.* Paperback reissue, Princeton, NJ: Princeton University Press.

Young, I. M., 2002. Lived body vs gender: Reflections on social structure and subjectivity. *Ratio,* 15(4), pp410–428.

Index